Praise for *Kids These Days*

Kids These Days is a must-read book and protest against harmful mental health treatments for children and youth. Dobud and Harper truly understand youth and care about their safety.

—Paris Hilton, global advocate for institutional reform, founder of 11:11 Media

Kids These Days challenges the over-analytic, pathologizing, self-absorbed focus on children and youth in today's world. Relationships are key to healthy development, yet the nature of the relationship makes all the difference: present, attentive, attuned, and appropriately responsive. With a combination of quality scholarship, insights from a range of experts, and effective storytelling, the authors make a strong case to "back away from the developing child!" The power of healthy (i.e., non-intrusive) adult presence balanced with unstructured play, exploratory opportunities, and the tolerance of discomfort can build confidence, create resilience, and promote health and wellness. This is a crucial read for anyone living or working with children and youth. Highly recommended.

–Bruce D. Perry, M.D., Ph.D., Principal of The Neurosequential Network, and co-author with Oprah Winfrey of the *New York Times* #1 Bestseller, *What Happened to You?*

Problem–solution–celebration. Alas, it is deeper and more complex than that—as is whatever seems to be raining sorrow and dysfunction on a whole lot of "kids these days." Here's hoping this book's light shines into every corner of the problem and helps us toward a real and practical solution.

–Lenore Skenazy, author, *Free-Range Kids*, and president, Let Grow

Kids These Days is a fresh, provocative look at the challenges facing our kids in today's world. Instead of simple answers and tired clichés, Dobud and Harper take a broad and nuanced approach, zeroing in on the ways in which our attempts to shelter and protect kids from risk may be backfiring.

–Alex Hutchinson, *New York Times* bestselling author, *Endure* and *The Explorer's Gene*

In an era where discussions about child and adolescent psychology often call for greater nuance and contextual understanding, this book stands out by delivering precisely that. It masterfully weaves rigorous science, compelling narratives, and unconventional insights, offering a fresh perspective that challenges traditional thinking. A timely and essential read for anyone seeking a deeper understanding of young minds.

–Dr. Todd B. Kashdan, Professor of Psychology, and author, *The Upside of Your Dark Side* and *The Art of Insubordination*

A powerful and revolutionary book about what's really going on with kids today. *Kids These Days* doesn't just blame phones or schools or parents—it looks at the bigger picture and asks hard questions about the deeper reasons kids are in crisis, and what we can do to turn this around. Clear-eyed, thoughtful, and full of compassion; a book with the potential to help heal a generation.

–James Davies, Associate Professor in Psychology, University of Roehampton, London, and author, *Sedated*

This is the book about kids I have been waiting for! With too many books that propose single causes and single solutions, Dobud and Harper go broader and deeper. With their extensive experience, wisdom, and knowledge, they show us how to understand youth problems in a way that will be helpful to all kids in the long run. It is not a quick fix. *Kids These Days* is groundbreaking and fundamentally important for our kids' future. Read this book and step up.

–Birgit Valla, clinical psychologist and author, *Beyond Best Practice*

Kids These Days cautions the "adults in the room" to avoid the trap of blaming the next generation, and instead calls upon all of us to support young people growing up in an increasingly complex world. The authors avoid simple solutions that are bound to fail. Instead, this book offers deep insights into the opportunities and risks that youth and adults need to face *together* to build healthier brains, bodies, and relationships.

—Candice L. Odgers, Chancellor's Professor, Associate Dean, and Professor of Psychology and Informatics at the University of California Irvine, and co-director, Child & Brain Develoment Program, Canadian Institute for Advanced Research

Grounded in expert interviews, researched arguments, compelling anecdotes, and compassion for young people, *Kids These Days* reminds us of the wisdom of emotion. Dobud and Harper pierce through the knee-jerk conceptual habits and trending theories that trick us into ignoring social, cultural, and environmental factors. Instead of blaming smartphones, they invite us into a multifaceted approach grounded in simple interventions. Maybe we need to spend a bit less time signing up for every program that claims to fix every little tendency we notice in our children, and spend a bit more time simply being with them.

-Jay Vidyarthi, bestselling author,
Reclaim Your Mind, and founder, Still Ape

Moral panics about "kids these days" are everywhere, but Dobud and Harper cut through the hysteria with real science and clear thinking. They show how well-intentioned interventions often backfire—and what actually helps. A must-read for anyone who cares about kids.

—Kurt Gray, Professor, Ohio State University, and author, *Outraged*

KIDS THESE DAYS

Understanding and Supporting Youth Mental Health

Will Dobud, PhD | **Nevin Harper, PhD**

new society
PUBLISHERS

Cover design by Diane McIntosh.

Cover title font: ©iStock ("Kids")

Printed in Canada. First printing September, 2025.

This book is intended to be educational and informative.
It is not intended to serve as a guide. The author and publisher disclaim
all responsibility for any liability, loss, or risk that may be associated with
the application of any of the contents of this book.

Inquiries regarding requests to reprint all or part of
Kids These Days should be addressed to New Society Publishers
at the address below. To order directly from the publishers, please
call 250-247-9737 or order online at www.newsociety.com.

Any other inquiries can be directed by mail to:

New Society Publishers
P.O. Box 189, Gabriola Island, BC V0R 1X0, Canada
(250) 247-9737

New Society Publishers is EU Compliant. See newsociety.com for more information.

LIBRARY AND ARCHIVES CANADA CATALOGUING IN PUBLICATION

Title: Kids these days : understanding and supporting youth mental health / Will
Dobud, Phd, Nevin Harper, Phd.

Names: Dobud, Will W., author | Harper, Nevin, 1970- author

Description: Includes bibliographical references and index.

Identifiers: Canadiana (print) 20250214415 | Canadiana (ebook) 2025021444X |
ISBN 9781774060223

(softcover) | ISBN 9781550928150 (PDF) | ISBN 9781771424110 (EPUB)

Subjects: LCSH: Youth—Mental health. | LCSH: Youth—Mental health services.

Classification: LCC RJ503 .D63 2025 | DDC 616.8900835—dc23

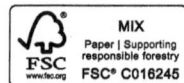

Funded by the Government of Canada | Financé par le gouvernement du Canada | **Canadä**

New Society Publishers' mission is to publish books that contribute in fundamental
ways to building an ecologically sustainable and just society, and to do so with the
least possible impact on the environment, in a manner that models this vision.

EU COMPLIANCE PARTNER✓   new society PUBLISHERS   Certified Ⓑ Corporation   FSC www.fsc.org   MIX Paper | Supporting responsible forestry FSC® C016245

CONTENTS

ACKNOWLEDGMENTS

This book started with a single, pressing question: *What's really going on with youth mental health?* As therapists, researchers, and educators, we had our hunches. But we knew the conversation had to expand beyond that. We turned to experts who have spent their lives listening, questioning, and bucking the mainstream. These conversations became the heart of this book, and we remain grateful for their contributions.

Martin Brokenleg, renowned for bridging Indigenous wisdom with modern psychology, reminded us that culture and tradition aren't just relevant, they're essential to belonging. Mari Swingle, who earned her degree at 18 before heading to Paris to become a model, brings a rebel's clarity to the impacts of technology on childhood. Bruce Lanphear, a passionate advocate for children's environmental health, pushed us to notice the invisible predators out there and question what we take for granted.

Psychiatrist Simon Davidson, a lifelong champion of the underdog, challenged us to be honest and not pull punches when discussing the experiences of youth today. Gordon Neufeld, known for his groundbreaking work on attachment-based parenting, spoke with urgency about the need for critical thinking in a world full of noise. The late Sue Johnson, a fierce advocate for connection and belonging, left a legacy of courage and compassion that we hope echoes through these pages.

Scott Miller, whose prolific career in psychotherapy continues to transform mental health care, reminded us that while people crave safety, it can sometimes keep them silent. The interplay between freedom and safety is a recurring theme throughout this book. From Norway, Ellen Beate Hansen Sandseter—an authority on outdoor risky play—taught us that the word "thrill-seeker" doesn't need to come with a warning label.

Resilience expert Michael Ungar made a compelling case that in trying to make everything safe, we may actually be harming our kids. We're too safe for our own good.

And finally, Ryan Rhodes showed us how meaningful change doesn't always need to be dramatic. Sometimes, the most powerful solutions are the simplest. And simple can be elegant.

To each of these thinkers, thank you for lending your voice and vision. You helped us shape not just a book, but a broader, braver conversation about kids these days.

INTRODUCTION

WICKED PROBLEMS

*Sometimes the first duty of intelligent men is the
restatement of the obvious.*
—George Orwell

During the years compiling the research for this book, we
shopped our project to numerous outlets. We heard time and
time again of a "saturated market" of parenting books that
examined how cell phones and social media are hurting our
kids. Many of these books were written by mental health professionals like us and offer solutions to the wicked problems we are
facing. We insisted we offered a different approach, but still, we
faced multiple rejections. Like Orwell's quote above, we wanted
to state the shockingly obvious—to say what so many of us
know but can't quite face. We also allowed space in our research
for narratives hidden behind mainstream headlines to provide
a fuller picture of what's going on with kids these days. We felt
a book that stated the obvious would be, in a very literal sense,
refreshing. In this book, we consider the complexity adults are
faced with when trying to protect kids or families, and we question how we can best help in the face of uncooperative systems.

Crisis in Plain Sight

In 2021, the eight-episode miniseries *Dopesick* premiered on
streaming services across the world. Inspired by Beth Macy's
bestseller *Dopesick: Dealers, Doctors, and the Drug Company
that Addicted America*, the series, starring Michael Keaton
and Kaitlyn Dever, focused on America's opioid crisis and the
conflicts of interest among Purdue Pharma, the Food and Drug
Administration (FDA), the US Department of Justice, and professionals associated with the medical industry. Millions streamed
the show about how the very people presumed to care about
our health broke our trust. Many paid the price with the death
of loved ones.

Purdue Pharma was a privately owned pharmaceutical
company primarily producing medications for pain management. Owned by the Sackler family, Purdue's most notable
contribution to medicine was the development of the painkiller
OxyContin, made up of the semisynthetic opioid called oxy-
codone, a derivative of opium. The highly addictive and dangerous pain medication, initially designed for cancer patients,
was rebranded and pushed for chronic pain management. The
Sacklers, described publicly as the worst drug dealers and most
evil family in American history,[1] provided "incentive trips" for
doctors to attend pain-management seminars, which were basically expenses-paid, all-inclusive vacations for those prescribing opioids to their patients.

Swayed by evidence from Purdue Pharma-funded studies
and ignoring the absence of long-term research into potential
side effects, the FDA approved the use of OxyContin in 1995. The
addictive qualities of the opioid were not investigated. OxyContin was marketed as not only more effective, but safer than its
competition. At about the same time, the American Pain Society
also campaigned for pain to be understood as the *fifth vital sign*,[2]
along with body temperature, pulse rates, breathing rates, and
blood pressure. Their campaign produced those cute pain scales

with smiling faces doctors use when they ask you to rate your pain from 1 to 10.

Lobbying efforts effectively conflated chronic pain with post-operative pain, and the checklist and treatment protocols they advocated for led many doctors to prescribe even more potent opiates—those produced with fentanyl.[3] To put the strength of this chemical in perspective, fentanyl is about fifty times stronger than heroin, and one hundred times stronger than morphine.

To get their product on the market, Purdue organized a team of one thousand representatives for a three-week training session.[4] The plan was to create a workforce of salespeople to broaden the use of OxyContin for all types of pain, not only for post-surgery or those living with chronic pain. Purdue Pharma's goal was antithetical to just about every public health initiative—to prescribe the least amount of any drug to the least amount of people. However, the Sackler family's team of sales reps easily convinced doctors that their pharmaceutical was safe for broad use and not addictive. The evidence showed otherwise.

From 1999, opioid deaths rose from fewer than 3,500 per year to more than 17,000 in 2017.[5] Sadly, most of those overdoses began with the prescription pad. In 2007, Purdue Pharma was sued for the largest sum in pharmaceutical history. They were accused of misleading the public about the addictive qualities of OxyContin. While some senior leaders at Purdue took the fall, no Sacklers were implicated in the one-hundred-plus pages of court documents.

Two years later, in 2009, Pfizer paid out an even higher settlement, $2.3 billion, for fraudulent marketing and promotion of their pain medication, making them the largest healthcare felons of the day.[6] Purdue, however, continued to sell opioids until they ultimately filed for Chapter 11 bankruptcy in 2019. The American Pain Society closed that same year when faced with allegations of colluding with opioid producers. Many knew about the damage, but not enough people spoke out against the harmful overprescription of the drug. In January 2025, the Sackler family agreed to pay up to 6.5 billion dollars and give up ownership of Purdue Pharma in order to settle the lawsuits from numerous local, state, and tribal governments.[7]

Shows similar to *Dopesick* were soon seen on other channels. The limited drama series *Painkiller* became one of Netflix's most streamed shows, providing yet another exposé on the Sacklers and America's opioid crisis that displaced pain with addiction. This was a regrettable substitution.

The opioid epidemic in North America and other nations is well-known. (Though it is worth noting that in the media it is now often linked with problems with fentanyl and other synthetic opioids laced into more common prescription and street drugs). Overdose and fatality are not uncommon.

Judging by the success of Macy's *Dopesick* and the popularity of the related television shows, most of you will be familiar with this story. But our book isn't about OxyContin or Big Pharma. It's about youth—teenagers and young adults—and the adults in their lives. From youth suicide to the overprescription of psychiatric medications to the poorer outcomes from the education system to, yes, the phones and social media, we want to examine what's going on with kids (and adults) these days. We see how bad it is, and we know how shockingly obvious it is to most of you.

OxyContin is a case study. It's just one example of the ways adults impact our health and well-being. There are many more. Here, we give just a few examples.

One of the most popular questionnaires used in the medical industry to "detect" depression is the Patient-Health Questionnaire-9 (PHQ-9). (It is found easily online; you can rate yourself and see how your doctor would be instructed to respond to your total score.) The PHQ-9 was created by *marketers* for the antidepressant Zoloft (Sertraline),[8] which was produced by Pfizer, who funded the development of the questionnaire. Even though it was commercially backed, the PHQ-9 has been cited in over 11,000 scientific papers.[9] The PHQ-9 lowered the bar for doctors to prescribe antidepressant medications[10] with one large study finding 79.1% of people assessed by the PHQ-9 were given a prescription for an antidepressant.[11]

The stimulant Ritalin (methylphenidate hydrochloride, by Novartis) was not originally developed for treating attention-related issues in youth. Chemist Leandro Panizzon developed the drug to test his discovery of synthesized methylphenidate on his wife Marguerite in 1944. He wanted his wife, nicknamed Rita, to have more energy and focus—and to slim her waistline. He named his success after her: *Ritalin.*[12]

It wasn't until the so-called godfather of medication for ADHD (attention-deficit hyperactivity disorder), Dr. Keith Conners, tested the drugs in the late 1960s and early 1970s that stimulants became everyday treatments for youth described as distracted, troubled, or unable to sit still at school.[13]

In the 1990s, Roger Griggs purchased a small pharmaceutical company known for producing Obetrol, a weight-loss pill he suspected might help children diagnosed with ADD. The drug would require a rebrand, however, and Griggs started putting words together. ADD. For all. *Adderall.* Griggs said, "It was meant to be kind of an inclusive thing." Adderall and Ritalin were now competing for the market share.[14]

Griggs strongly opposed the direct-to-consumer pharmaceutical marketing after introducing Adderall, and Conners is said to have regretted the overuse of stimulant medications. But they aren't solely to blame. Overuse was driven by decades of aggressive marketing by manufacturers, including industry-funded campaigns like the one just mentioned for depression.[15]

And, of course, there's more. Cell phones and social media have been correlated with drastic effects on youth mental health and education outcomes. They interfere with child and youth development in several ways, yet it is challenging to protect children from digital interference or put them down ourselves.[16] Despite having more therapists, counselors, educators, experts, and medications than ever, today appears to be a really difficult time for young people. "Why?" is what we are asking.

Wicked Problems

A term first coined by design and urban planning professors Horst Rittel and Melvin Webber[17] at the University of California, Berkeley in 1973, *wicked problems* are those with no definitive solution. There is no way to know if a particular solution will be decisive, and it is almost impossible to say when or if wicked problems are properly solved. Sounds complex? It is.

Consider a cracked foundation in your home or a math equation; both have a solution or even an ideal resolution. Wicked problems do not. The experience of today's youth is dynamic and multifaceted. Problems may require several interventions, with many consequences and numerous possible outcomes over time. What may at first appear to be a good solution may turn out to be the next phase of the problem. Maybe without end. There is no quick fix for these problems.

Rittel and Webber suggested, "There is no rule or procedure to determine the correct explanation or combination of them." We assess situations, make choices, and take actions we believe will alleviate the negative consequences of a problem. We know there is no one correct solution to increased concerns about youth mental health, so let's apply this idea of wicked problems to understand kids these days.

Best-selling books have tried to propose a single cause for the youth mental health crisis. Abigail Shrier's *Bad Therapy* blamed mental health experts. Jonathan Haidt's *The Anxious Generation* took on phones. Lenore Skenazy's *Free-Range Kids* focused on overprotective parenting, while Leonard Sax's *The Collapse of Parenting* suggested a lack of parental authority was responsible. And we agree with all of them, to some extent, but we do not believe any single facet is causal. Solving just one of these problems is not an antidote to this wicked problem.

Addressing wicked problems requires innovative app-roaches that acknowledge and embrace complexity because they lack clear boundaries and are often deeply ingrained in societal structures and behaviors. Unlike simple (or even complicated) problems, wicked problems cannot be successfully addressed using straightforward analysis or expertise. Attempts to solve one aspect of a wicked problem may inadvertently exacerbate other problems or create unintended consequences.

One classic example of a wicked problem being addressed as easily solvable was the introduction of the cane toad to Australia to control cane beetles, which were wreaking havoc on sugarcane crops. It backfired royally.

The cane toad, native to Hawaii and Puerto Rico, was brought to Australia in the 1930s. They ran amok.[18] With no predators to control their proliferation, the giant toad population skyrocketed, initiating numerous unintended consequences, with environmental disruption being the foremost issue. The toads decimated other species of frogs, lizards, small mammals, and even livestock, which upset the balance of natural predators and competitors. These other species had no adaptation to counter the toad's toxins. Each species affected had a knock-on effect, causing further disruptions to the ecosystem. Biodiversity was compromised.

Some species were driven to extinction. Others faced significant declines in their numbers. The fallout from attempting this simple solution to a wicked problem also had significant economic impacts for many years as humans attempted to restore nature's balance. So, in this case, the desire to control pests led to widespread ecological imbalances, which led to new problems to deal with. As is too often the case, intervention caused even more significant complications. This example underscores the importance of carefully considering the potential consequences of interfering and intervening in complex systems *before* implementation.

While we agree with Jonathan Haidt about the effects of smartphones on mental health, with Abigail Shrier about diagnoses, medication, and social-emotional training, and with Lenore Skenazy about the need for more outdoor, unstructured, independent, and unsupervised play, these factors are only parts of a complex story. Decline in youth mental health is a wicked problem, and we know of numerous aspects that need to be addressed from multiple angles. We also know there is no one solution or panacea. Remove the phones? OK. And then what?

This is why we approach this problem with breadth, even knowing that we, too, will miss parts of the story. No one can see all of it. But, putting our thoughts and research to paper, we realized the importance of zooming out and observing kids these days from forty thousand feet. What we sought was an approach that could prepare readers to decide for themselves how to preserve and protect the spirit of youth based on the best available evidence we could find.

In doing so, we found ourselves getting fired up, as we hope you do too. We found ourselves asking how the research literature and mainstream depictions of harm (such as *Dopesick*) are so visible, yet the harm still persists. This book is about standing up for a pragmatic approach to protesting harmful fads and ideologies harming young people today.

The longer adults stay complacent in waiting for *someone* (governments, corporations, politicians, etc.) to make it all better, the easier it becomes for those addicted to power (such as governments or corporations) to grab it, hold onto it, and never let it go.

The Adventure Ahead

> *Until the lion learns how to write, every story will glorify the hunter.*
> —CHINUA ACHEBE (THINGS FALL APART, 1958)

The critical reader will ask who we are to write this book, and they may question the absence of a youth voice. Fair questions. Youth voice makes for an important follow-up, but this book is for adults. We want to show how adults can advocate—even protest—for youth's health and well-being in the face of uncooperative systems, the attention economy, and simply bad ideas. Sometimes this requires deviating from dominant narratives and cultural norms and bucking the mainstream. We hope our readers will become *positive deviants* who will attempt to find what works when it comes to supporting youth mental health.

The two of us have worked with youth in many circumstances: some in corrections, some eager to abandon school or run away from home, and some were teens referred for self-harm, drug use, abuse, and family conflict. We've spent our careers as youth-serving educators, therapists, and academics, and we've talked with thousands of adolescents over the years. We've learned from working in underprivileged communities, including rural, remote, vulnerable, refugee, and Indigenous populations, as well as in our therapeutic work with the more affluent. Our experiences and interventions with families and the environments they inhabit eventually led us to research and study what helps young people thrive. Alongside our clinical work, we collectively teach social work, counseling, recreation, health, and leadership, and yet we still ask ourselves: *Why aren't we doing better for kids these days?* We keep coming back to questions about whether our careers as researchers and therapists are helping, especially now, when so many youth are suffering.

We originally connected over a shared interest in outdoor therapies. We are good friends and maintain a productive academic working relationship. We are fierce advocates for practicing therapy outside of the counseling room and do not shy away from difficult conversations, even in our own professional circles.

Our research on improving youth experience is often met with resistance. We've fielded accusations from industry-funded researchers of misrepresenting data and have had to endure slanderous comments from our colleagues. Outdoor therapy is a small field of practice, so when we speak out, trouble ensues. We are speaking particularly about our efforts to fight an industry that has sprung up in the last forty years: America's *troubled teen industry*, and *wilderness therapy programs* in particular. Often using the guise of "healing in nature," these mostly for-profit organizations provide involuntary, residential treatment to struggling adolescents. Under the supervision of qualified mental health professionals, these particular wilderness therapy programs operate in ways that are contradictory to just about everything we know about psychotherapy and child care. Additionally, their research claims are misleading and seldom disclose unethical practices and experiences of harm.

We've interviewed many youth who have been harmed—in various ways—by practitioners of outdoor therapy in these settings, and we've written extensively on the trauma, danger, harm, and infringements on human rights caused by these residential treatments. We've begged our professional communities to stand up against harmful practices associated with this industry. Unsurprisingly, we've found that earning the respect of youth and young adults who were harmed by these programs was much easier than influencing the academics and licensed professionals endorsing (and/or accepting funding from) an industry saddled with a laundry list of unethical principles and harmful practices.

You may have seen recent Netflix documentaries such as *Hell Camp*[19] or *The Program*,[20] or Paris Hilton's YouTube 2020 documentary about her horrifying experience in one of these residential treatment programs.[21] After we published a paper in 2022 that questioned the ethics of licensed and certified mental health professionals advocating for the legalized kidnapping of troubled youth in the name of therapy,[22] industry researchers asked that we retract our article. The journal editor scoffed at their request, denied the plea, and commended our work in protecting kids from adults promoting harmful and traumatic interventions.

Advocating for adolescents requires adults who will listen and act on the research evidence. In this sense, we are comfortable with the approach we took. Much of our book is about adults who stand up for kids in the face of uncooperative systems impacting the environments youth grow up in.

Throughout, we deal with contentious topics. We take an analytical swing at the rising use of medications, psychotherapy's effectiveness and shortcomings, the changing educational system, overprotection, and sociopolitical debates impacting youth today. We don't approach these issues to gain rank in the popularity contest of controversy. We focus on *what works* and *who it works for*. To do so, we wanted to find the voices of those who are on the frontlines and working to make change. As you'll read, we talked to many experts to hear what they have to say about kids these days.

Some may find our approach overly critical. We assure you as researchers, therapists, husbands, and parents, that we wrote this book because so much is at stake for today's youth.

We try not to *should* on people. We know most parents, educators, doctors, and therapists are trying their best. After all, we agree with our colleague, psychotherapist Dr. Daryl Chow, who wrote, "Parenting is an amateur sport. The moment you think you've turned pro, the rules change."[23] But today, youth need more adults in the room. Not for overprotection, but to create environments for them to thrive. As you will read herein, overprotection has become one of the problems. An ideology of safety interfered with and transformed a reasonable path to walk onto a precipitous cliff with loose footing. Like the impact of the PHQ-9, overprotection and ideologies of safety have interfered with youth development and inspired an increased medicalization of childhood.

To be clear, we aren't saying our careers as clinicians have not been a thrilling and rewarding journey, or that people should not seek professional help. Of course, when all else fails, professional or medical help is important—and mostly effective. Some people *do* benefit from psychiatric medications; many people do *not* become addicted or overdose on OxyContin. But many experience irreversible harm. We care most about how people are impacted by these interventions, and we want all involved to know that universal applications of these somewhat extreme interventions are not solutions to wicked problems.

We live in a time where words such as *evidenced, scientific,* and *research-based* are used to market certain approaches to improving one's health, and one's *mental health.* Of course, reading any book is not a substitute for expert opinion because one expert might be totally unhelpful in a particular context and another might be incredibly helpful. People who think they have the answers can topple from the mantle of expert and descend to imposter quickly; we've been there—with the youth and families we failed to help.

Regarding the evidence, we know not every casual reader can access research articles (often stored behind preposterous peer-review journal paywalls), let alone interpret what is being published beyond mainstream headlines. While we all hope that the medical, political, and professional helpers we lean on are using the most up-to-date evidence about *what works,* keep in mind that there is a 15-to 20-year gap between the publication of research and when it actually becomes everyday practice.[24]

Our task was to make sense of and share the research in an engaging way. We remain surprised by some of the evidence we found, and we wonder why it is not more mainstream and in the public's consciousness. There is solid evidence of harm, yet it is often left in the dark. We are shining light into those dark corners and illuminating issues that could make for safer and healthier environments for our kids to grow up in.

We encourage readers to become the adults in the room that young people need, yet we remain humble in stating that even though we have explored a range of factors, there is always more to learn.

As you read on, you will see we are nonconformists; we continue to ask unscripted questions, interrogate our own work, and hold our professions and colleagues to a high standard. We always look for the trail of evidence that will help us improve as we move forward. In the Notes section at the book's end, you will find the sources informing our discussion. (After all, one cannot write a book such as this without showing one's receipts!) Additionally, you can visit www.kidsthesedaysbook.com to find links to the research we cite and additional resources for parents, educators, and therapists.

Many of the questions we raise do not condense. They often simply generate more questions. We encourage the curious reader to make their own decisions about the value of our exploration and its pragmatic meaning for themselves. In the end, our goal was to understand why so many young people are hurting, starved for connection, and lacking the autonomy to adventurously explore adolescence.

The book is organized by three types of harm needing to be addressed to promote healthy, positive child and youth development: *Interference*, *Intervention*, and *Ideology*.

Part I: Interference explores increased loneliness, loss of connection, digital interference, and the impact of environmental toxins on youth development. *Part II: Intervention* takes a critical look at the labeling of mental disorders, psychotherapy, the overprescription of psychiatric medications, and universal school-based programs teaching social-emotional learning. *Part III: Ideology* shows how the dogma of safety has led to an *extinction of experience* and how this impacts youth. We aim to show how adults can, at first, at least notice these shockingly obvious concerns, and more importantly, be courageous in addressing them. We shouldn't be blaming kids these days. We should be listening, learning, and leading.

This book is about stepping up and assuming responsibility, especially when others are not. It's about becoming a stabilizing force and setting an example. It's doing or saying what others are unwilling and/or unprepared to do. This book is about being the "adult in the room"—an idiom used figuratively to encourage us to demonstrate maturity, responsibility, and leadership in the face of unhelpful and uncooperative systems or where others are acting irresponsibly, unethically, or immaturely. In the end, it's about giving today's youth something to imitate.

PART I

INTERFERENCE

1

THE KIDS THESE DAYS EFFECT

The children now love luxury; they have bad manners,
contempt for authority; they show disrespect for elders
and love chatter in place of exercise.
—K. J. FREEMAN

Often attributed to Socrates, the above quote is from an Oxford dissertation written in 1907.[1] Kenneth Freeman paraphrased lines from a caricatured version of Socrates in a play, *The Clouds*, written in 423 BC by Aristophanes. The play mocked prominent Greek intellectuals and is still considered one of the finest comedies of its time. Like many adults today, the famous Greek philosopher complained roughly 2,500 years ago about *"kids these days."*

So, it's not a new phenomenon. For millennia, young people have been labeled by adults as apathetic, arrogant, disrespectful, and self-absorbed. Each generation obtains a new label and stereotype. Millennials are the so-called *entitled generation*, assessed as lazy, self-obsessed, and uninspired. Baby boomers in their youth were viewed as pampered and neglectful of religious conventions—hippie kids pushing back on war and capitalism.

Although, those boomers are now old enough to be referred to as hardworking and innovative.

The youth of today consist of Generation Z (aka Zoomers) and Generation Alpha, the oldest members of which are 15 in 2025. These two are sometimes called *mini-millennials*. We don't yet know what the objections will be to the behavior of these new generations, though social psychologist Jonathan Haidt recently labeled today's youth the *Anxious Generation*. Inevitably, every young person survives twenty or so years as a member of the world's most criticized generation, until the next one arises. This is the *kids these days effect*. The first child born in 2026 will be the start of a new generation: Generation Beta. The jury is still out on how they will be categorized.

American psychologists John Protzko and Jonathan Schooler found prejudice against "kids these days" dates back even earlier than Socrates, to around 624 BC.[2] They put this bias against teens to the test in a series of studies involving 3,458 adults. First, they measured adults' levels of authoritarianism, such as how much they believe in the need for "old-fashioned values" and the honoring of their elders. The higher people ranked in authoritarianism, the more likely they were to believe youth of the day held less respect for older generations. The second study tested for intelligence, and smarter adults perceived kids today as less intelligent. The third study found well-read adults more likely to believe today's youth read less than generations before.

As it has through the centuries, the kids these days effect seems to say much more about us adults. The current state of this persistent tendency is impacting our approach to flattening the curve of what has been called a *youth mental health crisis*.[3] What follows in this book is our exploration of the impact of well-educated adults (those among the most likely to bemoan kids these days) and the troubling youth mental health trends we could no longer ignore in our work as clinicians, researchers, and parents. If anything, we propose that what is happening with kids these days has more to do with the "adults these days" than the kids themselves.

In 2023, psychologist Dr. Jean M. Twenge published the book *Generations*, an illustration of how generations differ and what this means for the future of America.[4] Dr. Twenge showed that we often oversimplify how one generation differs from the next—pathologizing an entire generation as anxious, for example.

Adolescents and young adults today are diagnosed with mental disorders at rates higher than any other generation and are subject to the overprescription of psychiatric medications—meant to be quick fixes for a person's distress or challenging behavior. This approach comes with real risks, and overdiagnosing and overprescribing are becoming more and more widespread, despite the armies of psychiatrists, physicians, researchers, social workers, etc. offering expert opinions. What we've found is a shift away from what works in positive youth development toward increased interference, intervention, and ideology.

We argue that placing mental health *within* youth while ignoring social and environmental factors truly misses the mark. We are led to believe we can "fix" kids, when the truth is that kids develop in relationship to their surrounding environment. If youth *are* more anxious today than ever, what does this really say about the world and environments we are all living in?

Smells Like Teen Spirit

While we do speak about protecting childhood in the chapters that follow, our focus is on teenagers and young adults—those often referred to as *adolescents*. What do we mean when we say *adolescents* or *adolescence*?

Images of teen culture probably spring to mind, and, depending on your experience, may include particular fashion trends, attitudes, behaviors, and language. Yes, yes, and yes. Still, definitions are important. As researchers, we are taught to define our terms clearly to avoid any distortion of language so readers can know exactly what we're talking about. We cannot tackle wicked problems with different understandings of the words we are using.

Take *climate change*, for example, another wicked problem. Many scientific studies use the term to refer specifically to changes in average global temperatures, while others use the term as a "catch-all" for all things environmentally related, be it erratic weather, rising tides, CO_2 levels, species adaptations, wildfires, extinctions, etc.

The climate change example provides an illustration of misunderstanding words. You can see how a debate among numerous people, each adopting distinct uses of a term, could become frustrating, or worse, futile. We experience this in our work with youth; terms such as *trauma*, *depression*, and *anxiety* often carry different meanings. Defining words is key to any successful communication of ideas. Without clear definitions, we can't move forward to develop and apply responses to wicked problems.

The origin of the word *adolescent* comes from the Latin *adolescere*, simply meaning *to mature*. Adolescence is the transition from childhood to adulthood. Of course, it's not a point in time where a person magically drops childish things and takes out a mortgage on their first house. (Actually, in terms of today's economy, we are sad to report that many youth, including our young university students, may struggle to *ever* get a mortgage on a house![5])

Adolescence is also considered a stage of development, but this is a pretty rough delineation. Is adolescence an age, the onset of puberty, or reaching a certain grade in school? This time of life can be so dramatically different for different people that it's hard to imagine defining adolescence beyond an abstract concept. There are, however, patterns of behavior and measurable variables that provide enough rigidity for us to work with the concept of adolescence. We explore these briefly to ensure you know what we're talking about.

Giving Childhood Back

In the 1700s–1800s, factory owners preferred to hire children because they were cheaper, easier to manage, and too disorganized to go on strike. Children could work 12–18-hour days, with one day off, and come away with a single dollar after the week's work. According to an 1890 US Census report, more than 1.5 million children aged 10–15 were employed, which was about 20% of all children that age. Only 6% of 14–17-year-olds were in school. A decade later, the number of child laborers had risen to 1.75 million.

Teachers, pastors, labor groups, and social workers, including one of our superheroes, Jane Addams, were outraged. (We'll return to Addams's work and her influential contribution to the field of social work in chapter 8 in our discussion about youth and their spirit of adventure.) Addams was concerned about how adults, the juvenile courts, and the education system interfered with youth development. By 1920, collective efforts from Addams and other advocates helped 30% of 14–17-year-olds to be educated in schools. Child labor laws were revised, drastically changing the landscape for kids. Not everyone was thrilled by the shift.

Critics protested the removal of adult demands from teenage years. The first American to earn a PhD in psychology and cofounder of the American Psychological Association, G. Stanley Hall, described pre-adolescents as "savages" who needed adults to lead them to be God-fearing and country-loving and to develop strong working bodies. He believed adolescence was the time for children to overcome their animalistic and beastlike impulses. Corporal punishment and authoritarian discipline were necessary to burn the evil out of them. Hall saw adolescence as a time for "storm and stress." Society needed to break youth from their moodiness, conflict with parents, and risk-taking behaviors.[6] He encouraged high school educators to lead youth to love discipline and authority and entice them toward military service.

In those days, children were still being beaten at school for noncompliance with rules. While times have changed, Nevin recalls getting the strap in his northern Alberta school in the 1980s. The school principal, Mr. Teed, applied the first of three strikes of the leather strap on Nevin's outreached hand. When it didn't have the intended effect, Mr. Teed asked the much-feared vice-principal, Mr. Watson, a large and jovial Englishman, to apply the next two strikes to encourage a more desirable outcome.

G. Stanley Hall's ideas about adolescence went relatively uncontested until the 1950s, when the psychology, counseling, and social work professions grew in popularity. One of the new voices was Erik Erikson, the German-American analyst who became famous for his theories of psychological development, arguing that adolescents struggled between forming their identity and finding their place in society. He called this *role confusion*, and for him, the sole purpose of adolescence was to shape an identity—to discover where one fits in the world. This sounded like the field was on the right track. But an influential contemporary of Erikson, Sigmund Freud's youngest child, the British psychoanalyst Anna Freud, believed the problems associated with youth were universal across cultures and biologically based. She described adolescence as a *developmental disturbance* difficult to distinguish from psychopathology or neurosis. Based on her criteria, just about every adolescent could be called mentally ill.

While this sounds like a practical joke, it seems to have been adopted as the prevailing guideline. In 2024, The US National Institute of Health estimated the lifetime prevalence of mental illness for adolescents is an astonishing 49.5%.[7] That is, in their estimation, around half of today's youth will experience what could be labeled a diagnosable mental disorder. Over the past century, we've continued to play along with medicalizing and labeling youth's journey of finding themselves, all while constantly shifting the social, political, and emotional environments they navigate.

Changes in child labor laws had surprisingly big consequences beyond the protection of children. These laws delayed young people's entry into the workforce, and teenagers in urban settings became people of leisure. They had free time and money to spend. Corporations paid attention. So much so, that the term "teenager" became popularized in the 1940s as advertisers targeted marketing to the spending power of this specific, and very visible, consumer age group. By the end of World War II, *teenager* had become an established international buzzword. In fact, American teens came to epitomize all things "cool."

Not surprisingly, the new, outsized influence of teenagers frustrated and even frightened adults (more of the kids these days effect). In 1953, the director of the FBI, J. Edgar Hoover, warned citizens to expect an "appalling increase in the number of crimes that will be committed by teenagers in the years ahead."[8] Despite their contributions to the global economy, teenagers were labeled an issue of concern, primarily due to fear of crime and disorderliness.[9] President Eisenhower used his 1955 State of the Union address to ask for legislation to "assist the states in dealing with this nationwide problem." We find ourselves today agreeing there is a worrying trend among teens, not related to crime specifically, though youth crime in some metropolitan areas is currently on the rise.[10]

What emerged over the last century are movements to either *fix* the teenager or *aid in positive development*. If a youth's propensity was toward crime, correctional approaches were applied; if a youth's conduct and motivations were seen as outside of the norm of regular "teen" behavior, mental health treatments were recommended. At the same time, if teens stayed within the boundaries of normative behavior (whatever that is for a teenager) they were ignored by interventionists, even if there were signs of undue stress or struggle.

How we perceive adolescents, their behavior, and their emotional lives comes with consequences. If we label them as "savages" as G. Stanley Hall did, we are likely to think of them as such. When anxiety and depression are focused on, the likelihood of the youth being placed on the pharmaceutical treadmill increases. Understanding the kids these days effect can help us do more of what matters in helping youth, especially when they are struggling.

Recognizing Humanity Amongst Symptom Checklists

Medical professionals conduct biopsies and imaging tests for heart issues and cancers. We don't routinely do the same for emotional distress and well-being. Most so-called mental illnesses are identified by subjective groupings of symptoms, some of which are contradictory or vague (such as with the PHQ-9). For major depressive disorder, symptoms are loss of interest or pleasure, weight loss or gain, and insomnia or fatigue. For attention-deficit disorder, symptoms are persistent inattention lasting longer than six months or simply not listening when spoken to—something we know all teenagers will do at some point or another. Symptoms may be useful to a medical professional, but common symptoms such as headaches, fevers, muscle tightness, fatigue, or dizziness tell us little. Are they the result of the body's natural reaction to a virus? Or something more sinister? We are skeptical of diagnoses based solely on a list of symptoms. Search your own symptoms on WebMD, and you'll fear you have a host of possible illnesses.

Most clinicians diagnosing mental illnesses rely on the American Psychiatric Association's (APA) *Diagnostic and Statistical Manual of Mental Disorders* (DSM). This book is often described as psychiatry's bible.[11] Before they will reimburse for therapeutic services, insurance companies in the US require the assignment of a code associated with a diagnosed mental disorder. The codes are assigned based on lists of symptoms that are often quite general, like those found on WebMD. Researchers use the lists of mental disorders in the DSM to study whether psychotherapy and medications attack the symptoms of said disorder, as antibiotics do with infections. As the DSM evolved into its fifth edition, we were left asking how this book—so central to many Western countries' healthcare systems—reflects the realities of the current state of youth mental health.

The history of psychiatry's bible is rife with uncertainty, political conflict, and economic motivations. One study found that 90% of psychologists reported actively using the DSM despite having serious concerns about its effectiveness and ethics.[12] The culturally bound nature of the classification of mental disorders is often shockingly obvious, and at times troubling.

For example, in the DSM's first edition in 1952, homosexuality was described as "sexual deviation." Worse, the classification remained under the umbrella of "sociopathic personality disturbance," along with sexual sadism, pedophilia, transvestism, and fetishism. In the 1968 edition, the APA expanded sexual deviation to include voyeurism and masochism, and homosexuality was labeled a "mental disorder." In the 1970s, gay rights activists organized to get homosexuality reclassified. The next edition of the DSM did rebrand homosexuality as a "sexual orientation disturbance," and it included a short line of descriptive text stating that homosexuality "by itself does not constitute a psychiatric disorder." Activists considered this a major victory. Still, the term *homosexuality* wasn't removed from psychiatry's bible until 1987.

This history of psychiatry and homosexuality reveals a troubling tale about how we view mental health, our culture, and people in general. Cancer, diabetes, and arthritis objectively exist whether your doctor finds it or not, and our understanding of these diseases evolves as we investigate and research them. But a mental disorder can be seen as a culturally informed con-

struct—one that can disappear when culture shifts and/or if definition changes are demanded when those impacted the most by
the label push back and speak out about what is affecting them.
These kinds of changes are an uphill battle.

Like the lion to the hunter, it is not the underdog who usually gets to control mental health narratives. In this case, it is
controlled by what could be called the *mental health industrial complex*, which perpetuates biomedical explanations for
human suffering. In essence, the prevailing attitude toward
mental health is that problems lie within the person and are
independent of environment. We question that attitude. And
we question what the youth mental health crisis really is. How
much of it is a subjective myth, and how much of it is really
about something going on inside the minds of kids these days?[13]
Who benefits the most from these declines in mental health?
Looking at one "new" mental disorder is particularly telling.

The revision of the fifth edition, the 2022 *DSM-5-TR*, introduced a new mental disorder: *prolonged grief disorder*. While
the American Psychiatric Association acknowledges grief
is a natural response to losing a loved one, according to them,
the "symptoms" of grief should decrease over time. When we
stepped back and asked ourselves why grief—one of the most
natural and ancient human emotions—was included in the DSM
as a disorder, we found ourselves also asking who might be
behind its inclusion. Who would want grief to be documented
as a disorder? Is it something the general public was campaigning for? No. Were therapists and social workers demanding
something more be done about a grief epidemic? No. We think
the answer is capitalism. Digging deeper, we found that there
were nine "expert" psychiatrists tasked with creating the mood
disorder guidelines in this DSM revision. Six of them had financial interests tied to pharmaceutical companies (a 21% increase
since the DSM-4), and three had been paid to conduct clinical
trials on the antidepressant use for grief.[14] A recent study found
60% of the doctors serving on the DSM-5-TR "received more

than $14 million in publicly undisclosed industry funding."[15] Because of these conflicts of interest, we feel healthcare providers should be questioning the faith they put in the ubiquitous DSM. Are the labels and codes helpful in improving well-being? Or are they the result of capitalist intervention in the healthcare system and society as a whole?

Spikes in mental health diagnoses and prescriptions may suggest something is plaguing our youth. However, by medicalizing adolescent distress—which might be misinterpreted as adolescent exploration—we place the responsibility of change on the neurological, the biological, the so-called chemical imbalance all while the adolescent brain undergoes drastic developmental changes. We make the problem something *within* the child (aligning with Anna Freud's theories about the biological basis of adolescence). This keeps the *kids these days* fiction alive and well.

What if it is something else? What if it is simply that humans cannot adequately cope with the amount of information we now have access to today? What if we are reacting to the lack of community and cultural cohesion? Currently, most environmental and social factors are not taken into account; often, they are even off-limits in discourses about mental health. This results in a skewed sense of societal improvement. Medical interventions, clean drinking water, and better sewage systems improve life expectancy, yes, but the identification (or label) of a mental health condition has no correlation to improved quality of life. Continuing down this path of labeling youth distress and nonconforming behavior—the very hallmark of adolescence—has one certain outcome. Our responsibility as adults is removed. We blame biology, genes, chemical imbalances, and neurochemical deficiencies for the suffering of kids these days.

Again, our concern is not about what works in each specific context. If medication helps, fantastic. We care most about what works for each youth and their families, and know we can't provide an across-the-board answer of what is right for whom. At a macro level, observing the current trends and evidence from forty thousand feet tells us something is not quite right. Homogenizing people into the best-marketed and most easily administered intervention falls short nearly every time. What works for one does not work for all, but labeling and medicating are efficient and profitable.

Across the Western world, there are more psychologists, social workers, and counselors than ever, though positive psychotherapy outcomes for youth and adults have remained flatlined for fifty years.[16] That's right, not one percentage of improvement. In 1993, psychologist James Hillman and journalist Michael Ventura took a critical swing at the field of psychotherapy—the talking cure—illustrated well by their book's title alone, *We've Had a Hundred Years of Psychotherapy—and the World's Getting Worse.*[17] For the authors, therapy had become overly focused on the individual, contending that mental illness resided *within* the patient. Of course, some people going to therapy have real and legitimate histories of trauma, attachment issues, and neuroticism. But the authors accurately predicted a tragic vision of the future if we continue to ignore societal and environmental factors. Tracking another thirty years of trends and outcomes confirms their prediction.

One of our concerns in discussing the rising rates of mental disorders are the proposed consequences that often follow. Our current theories of pathology—that is, what is wrong with kids these days—glorify *interference* from an ideology that mental health is most effectively treated by medicine and behavioral intervention. The statistics portrayed below do suggest youth mental health is a growing concern, especially as it relates to the tragic rates of youth suicide. However, if we respond with more of the same, we are likely to continue labeling youth and inspiring further disconnection.

The US Centers for Disease Control and Prevention (CDC) began exploring the leading causes of morbidity and mortality in youth in the late 1980s.[18] Nearly 70% of all child and young adult deaths were attributed to four causes. Car accidents, unintentional injury, and homicides made up the majority, but 10% of deaths at the time were caused by suicide. (Drug use was associated with many deaths, and alcohol factored in roughly 50% of vehicle-related deaths, murders, and suicides.) In an attempt to bring these numbers down, the CDC established the *Youth Risk Behavior Surveillance System*, a survey designed to monitor 9th- and 12th-grade students across the US.

In 2023, the American Psychological Association reviewed the CDC's data.[19] The results were less than encouraging. The number of youth reporting hopelessness, persistent sadness, suicidal thoughts, and suicidal behaviors increased by about 40% in the decade leading up to the pandemic.

The COVID-19 pandemic ushered in a further 20% increase. Social isolation, uncertainty, and unpredictability are not recommended for improving one's well-being, no matter the context, but the trend of worsening mental health existed well before mandates, house arrests, social isolation, and lockdowns exacerbated the fear and unpredictability of 2020. While it is tempting to discuss youth well-being and mental health in the context of how detrimental some COVID-19 mitigation strategies were, this is not our focus. Blaming the pandemic for our current state is only part of the story. If anything, the pandemic threw gasoline on a fire already growing out of control. Let's take a deeper look at data from across the globe. (The reader will notice, though, that the way data is collected can lead to differences in what is reported.)

According to *Statistics Canada*, in 2023 intentional self-harm (suicide) was the second leading cause of death for adolescents and young adults in Canada—behind accidents, but ahead of cancer.[20] The World Health Organization's (WHO) 2019 report, using slightly different metrics, showed self-harm as the leading cause of death for 10–19-year-old Canadians. The order they gave was as follows: (1) self-harm, (2) road injury, (3) drug use disorders, (4) interpersonal violence, and (5) cancer. The

WHO's reporting on fatalities in the US found self-harm was second only to car accidents. Interpersonal violence and drug use were third and fourth.

In Australia, Russia, Japan, Germany, Ireland, Norway, Finland, Sweden, Belarus, and Iceland, self-harm is the leading cause of death for adolescents; in dozens of other countries, it came in second to car accidents as of 2023.[21]

In a 2020 study of 1.5 million 11-to-17-year-olds, more than 50% described thinking about suicide or self-harm "nearly every day."[22] The US CDC reported that 2022 saw the highest peak of suicide since 1941.[23] As therapists, educators, and parents, we find these numbers alarming, to say the least. As researchers, we have questions.

Teens should be excited for the adventure of life ahead, instead of living in the emotional states evidenced by these statistics. We asked ourselves, and the experts, why kids, who should be getting ready to take on the world, would instead want to turn their world off.

High rates of suicide tell of a wicked problem. According to the WHO, depression and anxiety diagnoses—the two most common mental health labels—increased by nearly 50% from 1990 to 2013, contributing a one-trillion-US-dollar dent in the global economy.[24] According to the National Institute of Health, depression and anxiety, along with pain, are the most common causes of disability. Mental and substance abuse disorders are more than 20–35% higher for 15–25 year-olds than any other condition.[25] Meanwhile, the average government spends less than 2% of their health expenditure on mental health.[26] Hardly the response we'd expect to a so-called crisis.

In 2020, the WHO reported only 51% of their 194 Member States had policies or plans for mental health in line with treaties and legal standards set out to protect human rights, falling well short of the WHO's target of 80%.[27] The WHO reported reaching only one of their 2013 targets of reducing suicide by 10% by 2020, though only thirty-five member countries maintained any stand-alone prevention strategy, policy, or plan to prevent these tragic deaths. Of the limited financial resources available for mental health, 70% of government expenditure in middle-income countries went to mental hospitals, and in countries identified as high-income, 35% went to hospitals. Institutional inpatient care and the mental hospital are centralized; this type of service is often only used for the most difficult of situations. Prevention and community-based care are second to the medicalization of our well-being and mental health, all of which is evidenced by the stopgap approaches of disorder labeling, prescription medication, and institutionalization.

In 2021, 8.5% of all children in the US were taking medication to address difficulties with concentration, behavior, and emotion.[28] 1.2% of them were preschool-aged, and one in eight young people aged 12–17 were medicated. Antidepressant use from 2015 to 2021 had a 10% annual growth. Prescriptions for antipsychotics and drugs used for ADHD saw the most yearly increase in this time (7.9 and 12.7%, respectively)—*for preschoolers!* In the UK, antidepressant use increased 26% for children younger than 17 from 2015 to 2020. Again, this started happening before the pandemic. Every country is experiencing a steady increase in the use of medication for youth. But the biggest and fastest increases are in the US, the UK, and Australia.

These trends continue despite numerous large-scale studies, such as one published in the *Cochrane Review* in 2021.[29] Cochrane is a global, independent network of researchers and healthcare professionals. They use explicit, rigorous methods to minimize bias and improve decision-making, which produces more reliable findings. Cochrane is recognized globally as the highest standard of evidence-based health care.[30] In a systematic analysis of the available evidence, researchers found that although antidepressants may, indeed, reduce depressive symptoms, their impacts are statistically small, and, to quote the researchers, "unimportant" when compared directly to placebos—pills inherently designed to be ineffective.

How did we get here? Is the rate of prescription of psychiatric medications warranted? Did we move the goalposts? Are preschoolers, elementary-aged, and high-school-attending kids actually sicker than those from twenty years ago? Is there something "more wrong" with the kids of today than with previous generations, or do we just have better testing to sanction the use of chemical interventions? Could it simply be genetics? Environmental conditions? The pandemic? The changing climate— including our political and social climate? Is the school system failing our children? Or is it simply the mobile phone and social media, as some experts have argued? Is there something wrong with *us*—the adults? These are the questions we interrogated for this book. If it is about the adults, what are they doing, what do they need to know, and how can they help?

Beyond mental health, things seem to be improving in many aspects of human health and safety. Following are a few examples.

Already flying at a high standard, airline safety improved by 95% over the last twenty years.[31] Cars are safer than ever with the introduction of three-point seat belts, airbags, electronic stability controls, blind spot detections, automatic driver systems, and even backup cameras. Despite more and more vehicles on the road, the average vehicle today is estimated to be nearly 60% safer than those from the 1950s.[32] The worldwide life expectancy in 1900 was 32, and by the 1950s, 46.5 years. In 2020, the average person on planet Earth made it to 72.[33] With the internet and our tiny phones, people have access to a lifetime of information at the press of a button. So, many safety and quality of life indicators seem to be improving, while we simultaneously find study results suggesting we are more unhappy, lonely, frustrated, and anxious. Something doesn't add up.

Moving the needle as we have with life expectancy, airplanes, and cars required persistence and ruthless collective efforts from engineers, researchers, medical professionals, and even patients. The better we get at anything, the harder it gets to improve.

Swimmer Michael Phelps, the decorated Olympian with twenty-eight medals, broke the world record for the 400-meter men's medley at the 2004 Summer Olympics in Athens. He swam the 1,312 feet in 4 minutes, 8 seconds, and 26 milliseconds. Four years later, he broke the record again. He was nearly five seconds faster. Four years of extraordinary dedication, with many small changes shaving milliseconds from his time, made Phelps the fastest ever to race in a pool (until Léon Marchand from France broke the record in 2024!). This same effort is needed to save lives and improve medical and health outcomes. Milliseconds become seconds. Seconds become minutes. We ask if diagnosing and labeling youth distress and behavior is the right approach to make the incremental progress required to improve the well-being and mental health of adolescents. Is this about kids *these* days, or has something been transpiring in the previous decades?

Dr. Jean M. Twenge, the above-mentioned American psychologist and author of multiple books, including *iGen*,[34] examined youth anxiety data from 1952 to 1993.[35] Dr. Twenge found the *average* child in the 1980s reported levels of anxiety on par with child psychiatric patients in the 1950s. The benchmark level of anxiety for a 1950 psychiatric patient had become the new normal for every child! Imagine if the most unsafe car in 1950 became the average in the 1990s. It's hard to even imagine. These stats make us question whether or not we adults—guided by the mental health industry—have created a subjective myth called the "youth mental health crisis." Not that teens are not hurting, but rather that we've manufactured the conditions, criteria, and complex for it to exist.

Let's put Twenge's number into perspective. Her research showed that rises in anxiety correlated to social conditions, in particular to low social connectedness and environmental threats, like the fear of a nuclear strike during the Cold War. If societal and environmental factors play into the worsening trends of mental health, we adults must explore these aspects, despite the enduring medicalization of human suffering and distress that basically ignores these external influences. We've endured—and played along with—a century-long tradition of placing mental illness within the person, not taking into consideration the environments in which we live. Take, for example, the two recent criminal investigations against Character.Ai and its founder Google. The first related to a teen suicide, and the second involved a chatbot companion that suggested a teen murder his parents for imposing screen-time limits.[36] Talk about a conflict of interest! Are these really *kids'* problems, or are kids trying their best to navigate today's social and environmental conditions created by adults?

We conclude it's really all about us, the adults, the so-called experts. Ignoring the sociocultural and environmental contexts is how we became more therapized and medicated than ever. Pathologizing youth development, as we are doing with grief today, contributes to the inflation of mental illness diagnoses, and this labeling pandemic is not reducing youth suicide. We do not believe there is anything biologically, genetically, or medically wrong with this generation of kids today, nor the ones to follow. We do agree with social psychologist Jonathan Haidt that levels of anxiety have increased; it's a wicked problem, yes, but one with numerous contributing factors. It's not just the phones. We found some troubling aspects of the environments and systems in which kids develop and the interference, or lack of action taken, by adults around them. As pronounced by one of Australia's favorite parenting authors and queen of common sense, Maggie Dent, we are stealing childhood and adolescence from our young people in the name of education—and worse, mental health.[37]

Youth: Crew or Passengers?

What we need is for the adults in the room to step up. Historically, some have. One of them is Kurt Hahn, the influential educator who informed much of our work in the outdoors.

During the rise of Hitler's National Socialism (Nazism), Jewish progressive educator Kurt Hahn founded Salem, a rural German boarding school focused on the character development of youth.[38] A strong-willed and outspoken man, Hahn was jailed and then exiled from Germany for his truth-telling and public contempt for Hitler's ideologies—and for the future he envisioned if they were left unchallenged. Hahn described what he saw as another version of the kids these days effect—*the declines of modern youth*—and the connection between societal change and youth being taken in by dangerous ideas and false promises of a better future. It was Kurt Hahn's educational principles (along with significant influence from others, such as Marina Ewald) that led to the founding of Outward Bound, the outdoor leadership programs for youth and adults.[39]

These declines, Hahn suggested, would leave youth either listless or lawless and vulnerable to negative influence. The recruitment of kids (ages 10–18) into the Nazi Party's Hitler Youth organization dates back to 1922, and Hahn was astute in his observations and predictions in the decade before Hitler came to power.

Here are the elements Hahn identified as being responsible for the failing of kids in his day:[40]

- The decline in fitness and physical health due to the modern methods of locomotion.
- The decline in initiative and the spirit of adventure, due to the widespread disease of *spectatoritis*.
- The decline of memory and imagination due to the confused restlessness of modern life.
- The decline in care and skill, due to the weakened tradition of craftsmanship.
- The decline in self-discipline, due to the ever-present availability of tranquilizers and stimulants.
- The decline of compassion, which William Temple (the Archbishop of Canterbury) called "spiritual death."

Remember, this was youth pre-World War II. The methods of locomotion Hahn blamed for making kids lazy and out of shape were trains and cars with an average top speed of 45 miles per hour. He blamed the lack of youth engagement on the distractions of new media—radio, film, and eventually television. Media allowed kids to remain on the sidelines, spectating as the world flew by in front of them. Stimulants and tranquilizers made them lack self-discipline, and they didn't work with their hands enough to gain important life skills and craftsmanship. Possibly the most damning thing on his list was how youth of his day held little compassion, demonstrated by diminished community life and the growth of individualism and egoism.

What Kurt Hahn described as the decline of modern youth parallels Socrates's complaints about their bad manners. But Hahn set out to do something about it. He embodied the adult in the room we call for in this book. He was brave in the face of adversity, speaking out against strong sociopolitical forces, at risk of imprisonment or worse. Further, Hahn's proposed solutions define much of our own professional work, which is dedicated to bringing outdoor education and psychotherapy together. Not fixing kids, but giving them what they need to develop.

Hahn's proposed solution was school based on *experience therapy* (*Erlebnistherapie* in German), which had four main elements:

1. **Fitness Training:** to compete with oneself in physical fitness; in so doing, train for discipline and determination of the mind through the body.
2. **Expeditions:** to engage in long, challenging endurance tasks over land or sea.
3. **Projects:** involving crafts and manual skills.
4. **Rescue Service:** e.g., mountain rescue, marine lifesaving, firefighting, or first aid.

Hahn's schools offered what he believed was a more complete *education*, something extending beyond learning mathematics, language, and science. Students read philosophy and worked in the gardens, studied classic literature and cared for farm animals, learned trade skills and how to sail well enough to negotiate open waters. Students ran rescue services and came to believe they were needed and contributed meaningfully to the community. One of Hahn's adages was "Students are all crew, not passengers!"

These principles have informed our own decades of work outdoors with young people. But we don't see them as a panacea for rising rates of mental illness. We know not every young person will have access to these types of experiences, and many wouldn't want to go on a long adventurous expedition. And, of course, we are not trying to publish a self-serving book about outdoor therapy, but we couldn't resist sharing this story of this educator who, after making the same complaints about youth we've heard throughout history, actually attempted to do something about it! We remain focused, however, on how an understanding of youth development may lead to *less* adult interference and *fewer* interventions, ultimately leading to the development of more resilient youth. And more-recent research backs up this approach.

One study conducted in 1999 at Search Institute,[41] a child and youth development research organization in Minneapolis, Minnesota, revealed a need to identify both risk and protective factors in kids' lives. Years of data collection and the review of hundreds of studies informed the researchers' construction of a framework they called *developmental assets*. The lists were categorized into *internal assets*, such as support, empowerment, boundaries and expectations, and constructive use of time, and *external assets*, such as positive values, commitment to learning, social competencies, and positive identity. Imagine a +/- scorecard showing where investments should be made in a child's life to aid in growth and development, rather than a diagnosis of a problem within the individual. This approach just makes sense when thinking about how to help raise healthy and happy kids. So why is it, that twenty-five years on from this seminal youth development research, society continues to intervene and "treat" youth, problematize adolescence, and limit creativity, risk-taking, and exploratory behaviors of teens?

Learning to Walk

What we found in our explorations and our discussions with the experts was rewarding, illuminating, and at times deeply frustrating. Our book would probably do much better if we found a few norms, 10 Fool-Proof Steps, 12 Simple Rules, or 7 Principles for Raising the Perfect Child. We didn't do that. We feel that would be an impossible (and potentially dangerous) endeavor. What we discovered was the importance of principles and guardrails. We feel that it is imperative that children are provided safe-enough environments where they can make the big mistakes from which they can bounce back and become stronger than before. These are the settings where teenagers get to know themselves, find out who they are, and learn about their bodies and their place in the world—places where they feel safe enough to feel what they feel. The adults in their lives need to be able to sit with them in uncertainty and normalize the tough times as well as the good. We adults must also be prepared to sit with our own anxiety, recognizing we can only do our best. We also need to deal with the invisible predators of our time: toxins in the environment. We'll discuss this in chapter 4.

Remember: This is *not* a parenting book! This is a book about modern youth written for adults.

When observing neighborhood libraries, bookstores, and airport bookshops, senior editor of *The New York Times*, Melonyce McAfee, saw what many of us see: lots of *parenting books*. McAfee named the 2010s the *Decade of the Parenting Manual.*[42]

Parents read they should do more, be more proactive—or do less and allow more freedom. A good example of the divide is the comparison between Amy Chua's *Battle Hymn of the Tiger Mother* and Lenore Skenazy's *Free-Range Kids* (which came to fame when her 9-year-old was spotted alone on the New York City subway). Though the authors were on opposite ends of the parenting spectrum, both were widely criticized—though both books sold extensively. Chua's approach appeared cruel to many; Skenazy's neglectful. As these (and many other) books landed in the hands of millions, parents had to decide whether to keep with their natural parenting style or conform to one of the varying approaches across the spectrum of caregiving. As McAfee wrote, "No parenting style escaped scrutiny." And Hillary Frank, author of *Weird Parenting Wins*, addressed the elephant in the parenting book room when she said: "Parenting looks nothing like what the experts say."[43]

The swarm of written protocols for parents is a multi-million-dollar industry, though the impact remains unclear. For example, when researchers from Swansea University's Department of Public Health, Policy, and Social Sciences in Wales attempted to examine the impact of the parenting book mania, they found no clear indications any of them had moved the dial. Lots of parenting books recommended strict routines around infant sleep and feeding and offered interesting ideas for combating postnatal depression.[44] Most mothers did not find the books useful. Instead, parents told the researchers, these books increased depressive symptoms and stress. We feel that what parenting books often miss is the spirit of youth and the nature of childhood. They often treat children and adolescents as passengers in need of expert opinions, interference, and techniques, not as crew who contribute, take courageous action, and become confident in what they have to offer.

For example, no matter what the most respected expert's opinion is on the matter, no one can make an infant crawl or walk. We have to wait and remain patient for the combination of growth, development, stimulation, and the appropriate environmental conditions. Crawling and walking, to a baby, are massive experiential adventures, an *individual* test of functional movement skills, even if they are in the company of a loving adult. If you're ever feeling nervous about an upcoming obstacle or challenging circumstance, be reminded that few things are more difficult than learning to walk.

When a child pulls themselves up to take their first steps, adults provide encouragement and elements of safety. We ensure sharp-edged furniture and other obstacles are removed. Stairs are blocked off. When the toddler inevitably falls, they look up for reassurance. Our facial expression communicates that despite the shock of the fall, the child is in safe hands. We extend a hand for support and help the child stand up again so they can keep going. And keep falling.

For parents or guardians, this is a short-lived yet precious and memorable time in their child's development. It is also one where understanding "ages and stages" can help make sense of it. On average, babies crawl between 6 and 12 months and toddlers begin walking between 10 and 18 months. Of course, a range of skills and circumstances exist, and no child can be fairly measured against these imaginary developmental timelines. Some generalizations can be made, but raising every child is a unique adventure in and of itself. Most children, in the absence of infirmity or trauma, will move on to running, climbing, and jumping only shortly after learning to walk. Riding a bicycle might be next. Progress is rapid, and to new parents, surprisingly eventful, as they rush to make the home a safe place for the burgeoning activities of their young child.

Once language is developed, even at a basic level, parents and other adults influence the child's behavior related to mobility; however, getting to that point was primarily the result of the infant's experience of exploration, play, and repetition—learning unencumbered by an adult's interests or motivations. Without intervention. This is not to say parents and caregivers did not have influence. But the child operated on their own volition far more than following the directions of an adult.

Parents do not provide verbal instruction or feedback to control a newborn's process when they begin to roll from back to front, or in developing their first crawling technique. The excitable parent may encourage, challenge, rush, and quite likely desire their child to crawl or walk. These developmental markers are, however, on the schedule of the child rather than that of the adult.

Imagine an infant crawling in the "wounded soldier" style. One active leg with the other dragging behind. The parent may instruct the child that they need to use both legs equally for maximum efficiency. Not going to happen. The infant is absorbed by the environment and their ability to maneuver themselves and manipulate the objects within it.

Likewise, adolescence is full of exploratory events requiring the same experimentation, reflection, and risk-taking as the infant's rolling over, learning to crawl, and then walk. As the adolescent brain undergoes its drastic development, the ability to process listening and speak clearly eventually improves, yet if you want to talk an adolescent into dropping adolescent behaviors, good luck.

Much like when the infant is learning to walk, adults need to provide some safeguards during adolescence. We remove or control the metaphorical and real sharp-edged objects as best we can and offer a hand for support and a sense of safety when needed. But when an ideology of overprotection comes into play, interference can be overly intrusive. Healthy growth and development would be more successful if adults could withhold giving instruction when the child's self-exploration and reflection would suffice.

What we see and hear from adolescent clients—and their parents—is that youth have a bit too much programming, coaching, and management in their lives. Too much interference is preventing youth from learning the skills and gaining the self-efficacy to successfully crawl through adolescence and walk into adulthood.

Anyone reading this will likely remember how awkward, uncomfortable, and weird it felt to be a teenager. As your caregivers' influence waned, you explored new ways to seek connection and express yourself. Maybe you pierced a metal rod through your eyebrow or rocked a new fashion trend. Then you dabbled with some illicit substance some Saturday night in the spirit of experimentation. All of this occurred while you were trying to navigate relationships, sexual exploration, and your changing body.

Adolescence is the time all of us figure out where we fit in, what being an adult might mean, and how and where we could challenge the status quo. All the while, the adults, experts, and policymakers carry on making new rules and mandates for adolescents. Not with bad intentions per se; they might be trying to be progressive. However, decisions regarding adolescents are sometimes regressive and antithetical to the evidence. We need to be more careful about interrupting the maturing brain as it undergoes drastic changes. This may be at odds with what we have come to learn is evolutionarily vital to youth development. But when we impose labels of identity (e.g., attention-deficit, anxious, neurodivergent) and pathologize youth behavior (e.g., oppositional, hyperactive, depressed) and then medicate or therapize in response, we disrupt important, naturally occurring identity-forming years. Interference and intervention are too often used to "manage" kids these days. We don't have to do that.

As we've already pointed out, *for millennia,* adults have held that the youth *they* live with were the weakest, most selfish, and least respectful ever to exist. Ironically, for all those same millennia, the youths so reviled by the previous generation have been going on to raise children of their own, who *they* go on to describe as even more lazy, rude, self-absorbed, and lost to the luxuries of modern living than they were accused of before!

Every generation has likely been responsible for a moral panic among the adults. In the 1930s, the older generation blamed the radio for the degradation of adolescents. By the

1960s, it was the television. Elvis Presley and The Beatles, with their tight pants and shaking hips, brought chaos, just as jazz and big band swing did during prohibition. In 2007, the iPhone became the leading scapegoat. (We examine the highly problematic arena of social media and the internet in chapter 3.) It is easy to scapegoat single factors that are responsible for the "downfall" of teenagers, but our understanding of humans as a social species should evolve our approach to youth—and to understanding and supporting their mental health. The mirror should be turned toward ourselves.

Our *kids these days* concerns are very different from those of Socrates, Kurt Hahn, President Eisenhower, or even the parents of teens dancing to Elvis. We recognize the critical state youth are in today, quite likely driven by social and environmental factors, and the need to be responsible adults that help young people feel safe and secure to explore the world. Calling youth chemically imbalanced, attention-deficit, insular, fragile, anxious, and more mentally ill than ever is only part of the story.

What if all of us together observe the context we describe and bring all this to a grinding halt? Everyday heroes fought for decades against the giant American Psychiatric Association to convince doctors that homosexuality never belonged in a book alongside pedophilia or masochism. Everyday parents, teachers, therapists, coaches, mentors, aunties, and uncles—more heroes—know the importance of small gestures that communicate to teenagers that they matter. They let them know teens are allowed to be sad, to fail, to take risks, and to think freely because the world should be a safe-enough space for opinion and bravery. This is how we build *assets* and let young people know they have something to offer.

What follows from here is an exposé of where we may all have failed to be the proverbial "adults in the room" and, hopefully, it provides encouragement for all of us to step up, protect our kids, and do what we know is right.

2

STARVING

We are like islands in the sea, separate on the surface but
connected in the deep.
—WILLIAM JAMES

In the early 1990s, many people working with youth were presented with a new resource which affectionately became known
as "The Little Green Book." This 150-page paperback, often seen
with earmarked corners and chock-full of Post-it Notes, remains
comfortably positioned on bookshelves in schools, treatment
centers, and many youth-serving organizations. It still resonates
today as a straightforward recipe for meaningful and healthy
child development. The book's real title is *Reclaiming Youth
at Risk.*[1] It became an international training manual for youth
workers, including those in South Africa under Nelson Mandela's leadership, who himself paid tribute "to the endless heroism of youth."

Guided by Native American teachings and visualized
through the yellow, red, black, and white quadrants of the Medicine Wheel, the book centered on a model for youth development, and it challenged families and communities to engage
with, protect, and "reclaim" youth at the margins. The concept

of reclaiming youth put forward in the little green book intends to initiate change that will meet the needs of youth "at risk" in society. Authored by three friends who are professional colleagues working in South Dakota—Larry Brendtro, Martin Brokenleg, and Steve Van Bockern—the book (with a foreword by South African bishop and Nobel Peace Prize winner Desmond Tutu) launched the authors into careers providing training programs and doing speaking engagements internationally, which they continue to do to this day. The book is now in its third edition.

We asked Dr. Martin Brokenleg, a psychologist and Rosebud Sioux Tribe member, to discuss what's going on with kids these days. Martin has traveled several distinct yet integrated paths. He was a professor, now retired, of Native American Studies at Augustana University in Sioux Falls and First Nations Ministry and Theology at the Vancouver School of Theology. He is also an ordained Anglican minister and an Indigenous knowledge keeper. Martin was educated in an Episcopalian boy's grammar school called *Shattuck*, now Shattuck-St. Mary's School. (Ice hockey fans may recognize the school's name as the place where future hall-of-famer Sydney Crosby attended their exceptionally strong hockey academy.)

Dr. Brokenleg's most impactful contribution to helping youth comes through the *Circle of Courage* model which was first popularized in the little green book. The model is informed by Indigenous child-rearing traditions and is based on four developmental needs of children, each of which is deeply relational. The Circle of Courage is illustrated as a Medicine Wheel. For Indigenous cultures in North America, its four colored quadrants represent various things: the four cardinal directions (East, South, West, North), seasons, stages of life—many interpretations are offered by various tribes and Indigenous knowledge keepers. The Circle of Courage model places *belonging, mastery, generosity,* and *independence* into the four quadrants, showing their order and relationship to each other.

For youth, a sense of *belonging* involves a relationship of trust and the experience of feeling loved. When provided appropriate opportunities for learning, young people feel they can succeed, that is, have a sense of *mastery*. *Independence* occurs through increased responsibility and awareness of control in one's life. *Generosity* is based in meaningful contributions—having a purpose in life and wanting to help others. Being crew and not a passenger.

These categories were proposed to prioritize four essential ingredients for human well-being: *significance, competence, power,* and *virtue*. In the Circle of Courage model, significance is described as belonging, and competence as mastery. Virtue is understood as generosity, power as independence. When one or more of these basic needs are compromised, one's spirit risks becoming unhealthy. To belong, for example, is a basic primary need, which, when not met, leads to ill health. Our kinships with others, bonding and belonging with the human and more-than-human communities, are foundational; it's where the development of the self begins.

We are mammals—herd animals—and we need to know we have a tribe. It's no accident that we readily use the proverb "*It takes a village*" to describe raising children in a community. Cofounder of the APA (and doctoral advisor to G. Stanley Hall who was introduced in the previous chapter), William James offered the analogy of islands in the ocean being connected underwater. Just as islands don't appear to be connected from above, we don't always recognize where and when connection occurs. Belonging occurs in many aspects of one's life, from immediate family to school environments, to the community, and beyond. One's spirit of belonging should ideally be defined by trust, inclusion, warmth, friendship, and cooperation.

The Circle of Courage model also recognizes Four Ecological Hazards: *destructive relationships, climates of futility, learned irresponsibility,* and *loss of purpose*. Note that these hazards are described as *ecological*, speaking to the environment in which youth engage, instead of pathologizing adolescent behavior as if there is something wrong within the child. Destructive relationships leave children rejected and hungry for love. They lose trust in adults and become increasingly anxious that adults will hurt them again. It's a climate of futility that evokes feelings of inadequacy and a fear of failure that will prevent the youth from recognizing what they have to contribute. In response, they may become increasingly rebellious and defiant. Learned irresponsibility invites further powerlessness. A loss of purpose materializes in what many call "self-centered" youth. These kids, however, are embarked on a journey. They're paddling a turbulent river—hiking a dark wilderness with no map, no compass. It's a tiresome search for meaning in a world full of confusing and contradicting values and expectations.

From his Vancouver Island home, Dr. Brokenleg shared this idea with us: "I think essentially what I'm seeing is young people who are just on the brink of starving spiritually to death because of the absence of human relationship." Despite all the technological advances and possibilities for being connected via the internet and social media, relational disconnection is impacting adolescents now more than ever.

"It seems so odd to me," he said, "that in a culture in society in which we think we are so intelligent. And we are. But we're somehow missing the importance of that human connection. Yet, we're claiming to be so..." he paused and raised his hands to make air quotes with his fingers: "...connected."

Martin and his colleagues worked with youth and Indigenous elders for decades before the Circle of Courage model was tested, albeit not directly or knowingly, by the Search Institute we introduced in chapter 1. When the Search Institute ran a large-scale study of 5 million youth across the US and Canada, they identified developmental *assets* and *deficits* in young people's lives. Their findings were essentially the same as Dr. Brokenleg's, which didn't surprise him. He told us: "The consilience of research from very different sources convinces me, over and over again, that this model is accurate." What he sees at the heart of it, and as the problem for youth everywhere, is the absence of quality human connection—and it starts in the home. "Well-meaning parents are oblivious to it because they're so stressed themselves with their duties for work, managing the home, and other responsibilities and distractions."

Before advanced methods of communication fit into our pockets, many adults were more able to leave work at the workplace. Over the past two decades, parents are increasingly greeted by their excited children when walking in the front door only to think, "Maybe I have time for one more email..." Going to a restaurant, you may see a family whose young children are occupied with a tablet or a parent's phone. Of course, we all need space to pacify the energy of kids, but overuse of these techniques fosters further social disconnection.

The disconnection brought on by digital distraction is not just a *kids these days* phenomenon. Many adults, parents among them, are highly susceptible to digital interference, an impact we will discuss more fully in the next chapter. Educational psychologists Cory Kildare and Wendy Middlemiss looked at the literature in 2017 on the impacts of mobile devices on parent-child interactions and found the obvious: Persistent connection (device use), along with the unwritten demand to respond quickly to calls or messages, led to less responsive parent-child interactions.[2] The researchers outlined what they saw as the negative impacts of this parent-child disconnection due to device use, such as not responding to child behaviors for attention, reduced attachment, and the sense that parents are emotionally unavailable. In the eight years since the study was conducted, we've seen nothing to contradict their findings.

We've talked to many experts in their respective fields, and we found a common thread in their conclusions. Youth are *starving for connection.* Dr. Martin Brokenleg, who, as we've seen, has had an impactful career and possesses a unique cross-cultural understanding of what is going on with kids these days, agrees. For him, belonging is the most important factor for a person.

Imagine a baby playing with a stuffed animal in a room full of unfamiliar faces.[3] What will the baby do? Look around, find their mother or another familiar face, and crawl in that direction. There is no need to educate or place arrows on the ground as to where belonging is. Belonging is experienced, never taught. And a sense of belonging is absolutely fundamental to well-being.

While belonging, spirituality, and human connection may feel like obscure or vague concepts, the work of Martin Brokenleg and his colleagues is supported in a 2022 study commissioned by the United Nations and published in the *British Medical Journal*.[4] The researchers, from the United Nations International Children's Emergency Fund (UNICEF) and Johns Hopkins, described *social connectedness* as the cornerstone of health and well-being.

Connectedness is measured by a sense of belonging and closeness with others, feeling cared for, and being supported in protective relationships with adults, such as family members, educators, and other members of the community. Studies such as this one, as well as our discussions with Martin Brokenleg, left us asking if social and spiritual connectedness are keys to a healthy upbringing. If connectedness is the foundation for effective interventions for improving youth mental health and what it means to live a so-called healthy life, then why is it becoming more incidental than ever? We feel social connection has become a trivial aspect in public health policy; it is being ignored, but it is a fundamental and evolutionary need.

During the COVID-19 pandemic, US Surgeon General Vivek Murthy reported the following:

"1 in 3 high school students reported persistent feelings of sadness or hopelessness. That's a 40% increase from 2009 to 2019. In a similar timeframe, suicide rates went up 57% among youth 10 to 24. And we've also seen that during the pandemic, the rates of anxiety and depression have gone up. So, I believe that this is a critical issue that we have to do something about now."[5]

As mentioned in chapter 1, governmental approaches to mitigating COVID-19 transmission remain a scapegoat for the decade's increase in mental illness and decreased social connectedness. The increases described in the previous chapter, and those echoed by Dr. Murthy, show the acceleration of disconnection and distress was well underway before the pandemic grabbed everyone's attention. The silent pandemic, the one hurting kids these days, is one of social disconnection. And the numbers are stacking up.

UNICEF reported that of the 4.4 million deaths globally attributed to COVID-19 from spring 2020 to spring 2023, 17,400 were children under the age of 20.[6] About half were between 10 and 19 years old; the rest were younger than 9. In comparison, there are approximately 5,000 completed youth suicides *per year* in the US alone. That is one death around every two hours for people 25 years and younger. (And keep in mind that with every completed suicide, there are an estimated more than 100 to 200 attempts.)

In Australia, 322 young people took their lives in 2021. In perspective, across all age groups, 1,122 deaths were attributed to COVID-19 in Australia that same year, though just 8% of those deaths (approximately 90 people) were those under the age of 55.[7] Divide that number even further to enter the realm of adolescents. The decline in youth well-being and social connectedness is leading to the loss of our youngsters at a far greater rate than the coronavirus that stopped the world. Protective factors, such as community, education, and human contact, were the first to be compromised as governments quickly tried to *protect* everyone. The approaches taken to flatten the curve and stop the spread illustrated a sincere lack of understanding about mental health, social connection, and well-being—all of which are protective of human health. Consider the use of the term *social distancing* when *physical distancing* was the real intention. Research evidence clearly supports how critical human-to-human physical contact and social connectedness are for our health and well-being.[8] The research supports this. Somehow, policy does not.

A long-running "Happiness Study" is being conducted by researchers at the Harvard Medical School.[9] Begun in the 1940s, the study continues to this day. The research team initially followed 268 Harvard-educated men (among them, President John F. Kennedy), and 456 disadvantaged youth from inner-city Boston. Every two years, the researchers give questionnaires to physicians who conduct personal interviews with the participants. Their goal? To isolate factors predictive of healthy aging.

Psychiatrist George Vaillant, a professor at Harvard Medical School, directed the study for more than 30 years; his findings point to the desperate problems examined throughout our book. For example, contrary to popular belief, financial success was not tied to intelligence, but rather to the warmth of relationships youth experienced with caring adults. By their mid-fifties, adults who scored the highest in the realm of "warm relationships" earned more each year than those who scored lower. People who experienced more "relationship satisfaction" were also healthier in their older years.

As Dr. Vaillant put it, "Happiness is love. Full stop."

Harvard graduate and professor at UCLA's Semel Institute for Neuroscience and Human Behavior, Matthew Lieberman, described how the human brain's lifelong passion is to be socially connected. In his book, Lieberman explains how social connection is evolutionarily hardwired into our neurological operating system.[10] Connection is essential to survival, and Lieberman argues that our everyday institutions, from schools to workplaces to healthcare settings—and even the military— would experience increased performance if we structured these environments based on our evolutionary understanding of humans' social nature. It is this type of research that supports Dr. Martin Brokenleg's work. He just didn't need neuroscience, randomized clinical trials, or academic research to make his conclusions. The research clearly supports what people across populations and cultural contexts have known for millennia. The drive to live in connection with others and knowing you belong are parts of being human.

"In Indigenous cultures, when a person's life is not going well, we find a way to connect," he shared with us.

Indigenous Ways and Sound Biology

When the buffalo are under threat, they organize themselves into a protective formation that is the most likely to guarantee the survival of the herd. The buffalo bulls form the outside perimeter of the protecting circle. They are the strongest ones in the herd and, as the males, they are not the most necessary for herd survival. Inside that perimeter is the circle of the buffalo cows. They are the next-strongest members of the herd. As adult females, they are second in importance for herd survival, so they are protected by the bulls. Should the danger get past the males, the females are there to protect that which is the most necessary for the survival of the herd—the young— the buffalo calves.

—LAKOTA TEACHING STORY

Dr. Martin Brokenleg included this parable in an article he wrote for the *Reclaiming Youth Journal* in 2015 about Indigenous ways of child-rearing and the protection of children.[11] He shared how the Lakota, the Indigenous nations in north central US and across the Canadian Prairies (colonial boundaries that meant little to the Lakota and the buffalo) followed the wisdom of Mother Buffalo. Teaching stories from nature are rife with metaphors and provide, at times, a clear mirror for us as humans to gain wisdom through simple but practical examples, often grounded in biology.

The expression of care and concern in this story shows the natural order of a species intent on survival. The cows and calves are not expected to defend themselves from predators or to be independent of the rest of the herd, and individual families within the herd are not expected to fend for themselves. It is in community, in protection by numbers, and in prioritizing importance that buffalo preserve their herd. This may sound a bit traditionalist to some, but there is a powerful metaphor for childcare inherent in the story. Fathers, with their evolutionary drive to provide and protect, and mothers, with an equally strong drive to protect and nurture, tuck the calves—the future of the herd—in the center, where they are as safe as can be, out of harm's way. The calves are shown that they matter the most. Further, the lessons inherent in development are represented in the story. Our roles in life are seen and felt. We can model a future for our kids, giving them something to imitate, and making their future roles and responsibilities in the community less uncertain.

This metaphor also exemplifies the Circle of Courage model: *belonging* (recognizing your place in the herd), *mastery* (bulls and cows with size and skills to protect), *generosity* (order of protection caring for those more vulnerable and valuable), and *independence* (in that calves know where they will be in these circles as they grow, eventually moving to the middle or outside circles). The order needs to be honored for the herd's sake. This is not a tradition in the human sense, but rather an ecological and evolutionary reality for biology's sake. Instincts and evolution, over time, have preserved this child protective practice. The lesson here is that uncertainty is reduced for kids who see defined roles for adults in family and community. Instead of a *kids these days* effect, this becomes about *all of us* these days. We need to avoid trying to fix the youth or blame the generation and instead look at what works and how we can simply do more of that. There's a reason why certain parenting and cultural practices stick across generations and don't fall prey to new trends, innovations, or ideologies. Sometimes things work, and a return to the old ways often comes with gratitude and a sense of "it just feels right."

A good example of this is the now rather outdated norm of children being raised by extended family and communities. The pressure today for a couple or even a single adult to raise one or more kids, to work, to manage home life, and to pay the bills is, on reflection, an almost outlandish model, and yet it is a common one. The lack of extended family in Western child-rearing has increased the amount of uncertainty in family life. Like William James' quote above, islands do not appear connected from this perspective. Old ways don't have to be viewed as dated. Maintaining old ways, developed over millennia, is sometimes worthwhile. Some may call that being conservative. Well, that's exactly right. It is what the word means, to *conserve*, to *protect something valuable*.

A Bad Connection

The irony of today's technological climate is the possibility of remaining *connected* with people through smartphones and the internet. Despite Facebook's mission statement of "Giving people the power to build community and bring the world closer together,"[12] research suggests those who use social media excessively are more likely to experience loneliness. Loneliness isn't just a bad feeling; it increases a person's odds of early death by as much as 45 percent. Youth suicides are most often connected to conditions described as pain and loneliness—the sense of disconnection. Of course, the smartphone can be used for connection, though psychology professor Dr. Ethan Kross from the University of Michigan, argues that "When people use Facebook passively, they feel worse from one moment to the next."[13] Nothing can replace human contact and social connectedness.

What solutions look like varies in every home and cultural context, but they don't have to be complicated or difficult. A 2011 report from the National Center on Addiction and Substance Abuse at Columbia University focused simply on families eating together.[14] Teenagers of families who had dinner together fewer than three times per week were four times more likely to smoke cigarettes, twice as likely to drink alcohol, and more than two times more likely to use marijuana. The study also found parents of families infrequently eating together may fail to routinely check in on their children's well-being. Does it sound odd to be suggesting families have meals at the table together, free from digital distractions and in conversation? This seems to be a simple remedy, backed by research—and centuries of evidence.

Dr. Martin Brokenleg knew social connection and human contact were central to the healthy development. His daughter built on this work when she began working with second graders in a federally funded school for low-income families in deprived neighborhoods in the US (often referred to as *Title 1 schools*). The children in these schools come from families with serious difficulties, such as substance abuse and domestic violence. On Fridays, some children were welcomed to the school gymnasium to fill a backpack with food they could take home to share with their siblings.

"Their parents were dysfunctional enough that they wouldn't feed their kids," Dr. Brokenleg said. Providing food to get the children through the weekend allowed the kids to come back to school on Monday morning enabled to engage with other kids and a range of caring adults.

For this food project, the children and teachers used the themes from the *Circle of Courage* model; the language is easy enough for children at a kindergarten level to understand. The children coming together represented *belonging*. While selecting which food to bring home for themselves and their family, they would problem-solve and exhibit *mastery*. Then, providing food for their families led to some level of *independence*. The students thanked the organizers for the food, so they witnessed and displayed *generosity*. To bring sustenance home for the weekend, youth were the crew. Not passengers.

Of course, there are many other methods that are used by researchers, educators, and clinicians that can be used to elicit similar outcomes. When the Search Institute supported the Circle of Courage model with their list of forty assets and deficits for youth development, they told Dr. Brokenleg and his colleagues (although it was not surprising to them) that central to all this youth development work is *human connection.* Nothing works without it. Dr. Brokenleg simply sees this as a modern interpretation of the ancestral teachings that have guided Indigenous child-rearing practices for centuries.

Dr. Martin Brokenleg's work provided us with a fascinating "theme" for this book. What if the factors he and his colleagues established decades ago were not only *preventative* of the problems we see impacting adolescents today? What if these conditions were also remedial? What if prevention *and* intervention need to look the same when it comes to adolescent well-being and mental health? To put this to the test, we have to recognize what happens when youth are starved of belonging and social connection. We actually know one of the main things that happens: They'll seek other means to fill the void.

Connectivity

When kids are starving, they'll gorge. Be it the phone, alcohol, drugs—anything to fill the void. Removing the phone or banning the drugs might provide immediate and superficial relief, but nothing will provide an impact like a human-to-human, heart-to-heart connection. According to the 2022 United Nations-commissioned study mentioned earlier, meaningful approaches to helping youth must enhance connection. The study found that most government programs aimed at reducing adolescent problems fail. Worse, those aimed at suppressing adolescent behavior risked furthering the very problems the programs aimed to alleviate. Successful initiatives should help youth to strengthen connections with their parents, peers, teachers, and adults in the community. As the authors of the UN study concluded, any youth program should "view young people as resources rather than problems." Crew, not passengers. We need to harness the spirit and inherent heroism of youth.

In many ways, the heroism of youth is about partnering with the natural evolutionary traits of adolescents, getting out of the way when necessary, and communicating to young people they have something to contribute. We need to build connections based on their resources, strengths, desires, motivations, and passions.

As therapists, we have choices. One option is to navel-gaze at how sick, traumatized, and demoralized some of our teenage clients are. We may view them as annoying, frustrating, and oppositional. Kids these days. This path will lead us to not liking them—not a good look for a therapist. That said, we may also consider how wonderful they are. The choice is ours ... the person with the power in the room. The same is true for any adults connecting with teenagers. If we look for it, adolescents are brave, heroic, curious, and resilient. We're not encouraging coddling here, but rather an emphasis on the youth's strengths and capabilities. Cultivate and develop what makes them wonderful and brave already. But, like partners in a struggling marriage, we can sometimes wait around for someone to prove our negative assumptions correct. In the process, we can miss how wonderful the mundane moments are by simply not noticing them. What do you choose to notice? Just the negative? This is how youth prove to be kids these days; lazy, selfish, unmotivated. One approach fosters connection, the other division. *The kids these days effect* is a trap. It's like a therapist calling a young person resistant, unmotivated, in denial, and not ready for the therapist's expertise. The client is to blame. The therapist's hands are clean. We know this is not the truth of the matter. Resistance is not a human characteristic; it's a response *to* or opposition to something. It can only exist within a relationship of some kind. Adults blaming youth for resisting—those damn kids these days—prevents the adults from connecting.

We must identify and address the reasons that kids are starving emotionally and spiritually. This all begins with *positive parenting*, which includes emotional availability, responsiveness, connectedness, behavioral monitoring, and educational expectations. In school settings, the most effective environments are physically and emotionally safe enough for students to take risks and make mistakes. In such environments, teachers are caring and supportive, not controlling or imposing their values and ideas on their captive audience. Students in these schools are pushed toward academic achievements, but ideally, the environment is enriched with resources and support. When boundaries, rules, and discipline must be enforced, students know and accept them as fair. In community, our local neighborhoods foster belonging, safety, and group membership. Adolescents in these communities can engage with not only their friendship group but, more importantly, with nurturing adults who are not their own parents. This is the *emotional playground*, which we will explore in chapter 6. When positive parenting and its parallel in schools and communities are not met, kids may starve. We know, in response, they may also gorge.

3

GORGING

It has become appallingly obvious that our technology has exceeded our humanity.
—ALBERT EINSTEIN

As a child in the 1970s, Mari wasn't allowed to watch television, yet she feels absolutely blessed for her childhood experiences, growing up partly on a wilderness property with no electricity or running water and partly in the city. She had to find things to do for her own entertainment, and that often meant playing outside. Now, in her fifties, she can reflect on those early experiences and she knows what they afforded her in terms of knowledge and abilities.

Filled with the challenges of self-directed play to avoid boredom, and some loneliness due to isolation because of where she lived, Mari knows her childhood and adolescence left her with a greater capacity for independent study than her peers in high school or at university. She had an increased ability to focus.

She did, however, experience some disconnection because she wasn't watching the same television programs as others her age. She missed some of the relatedness that came with media consumption. Now recognized as a blessing, it wasn't great at the time. She recalls the sense of being different from teens her own age.

Comparing her upbringing to the average child in her community today, Mari grew concerned. She believes things started going sideways in the 1970s, with the passive brain response to television. In 1950, only 10% of American homes had a TV; by 1960, only 10% *didn't*. The mass explosion of television programming occurred in the seventies.

"I don't think the kids now stand a chance with the extreme hyper-arousal, the near-to-zero emotional resilience, fear, and the anxiety we are seeing in children," she told us. The bottom line for her is that children just don't have enough physical interaction with others, in real-time—face-to-face and heart-to-heart—to learn the social and emotional skills necessary to successfully negotiate adolescence.

This reality informs Dr. Mari Swingle's clinical work;[1] she sees clients who are struggling with attention issues, emotional dysregulation, and other ailments. She mentioned the lack of belonging and social connection as a drastic part of what is happening today. When Nevin shared that Dr. Martin Brokenleg raised the concern of youth starving for connection, Dr. Swingle responded abruptly: "That's why they're gorging."

Dr. Swingle is a registered psychologist, clinical counselor, and board certified neurotherapist. She is well-recognized as an expert on the effects of screen-based devices on our brains and behavior. Her views on technology, societal shifts, and mental health are the result of more than twenty years of observation and clinical testing of brain function in her clinic, which uses electroencephalography (EEG) as the principal modality.

EEG, or brain mapping, is a noninvasive, yet comprehensive neurological measurement tool. Dr. Swingle uses EEG scans to identify numerous brain functions related to learning difficulties, attention, nervous system regulation, and patterns associated with drive, intelligence, creativity, and emotional and cognitive states. These readings show whether a person's brain is over-stimulated, under-stimulated, or excessively challenged relative to their social and emotional lives. She concluded that many of her young clients are either addicted or at least negatively affected by recent technologies (iPhones, tablets, etc.). A neurological scan, along with an initial consultation, can give her more than enough information to design a family-based intervention.

This blend of modern technology, along with her clinical training, provides significant insights into a client's condition, and helps with tailoring the treatment because she can also usually see the severity and degree of symptoms requiring intervention. While Dr. Swingle's reporting of the mechanisms of addiction to screen-based devices is scary to us, she also brings plenty of optimism for recovery and balanced suggestions for living with the powerful technology few of us can manage safely. We wonder if this hopeful perspective is why her approach was overlooked in recent discussions about the impact of phones and social media in childhood. Sensationalism sells.

The claim that social media and i-tech *caused* a youth mental health crisis has gained media attention over the last year. This is mostly spurred by recent best-sellers, such as Jonathan Haidt's *The Anxious Generation*. The four "norms" proposed in Haidt's book—(1) no phones before high school, (2) no social media before age 16, (3) phone-free schools, and 4) more independence, free play, and responsibility in the real world—feel more like demands than norms. The first three recommend increased adult interference and the fourth suggests the opposite. Leave the kids alone. But policymakers are listening to Haidt. These recommendations have spurred local, state, and federal government legislation to control social media access and ban cell phone use during the school day. Sure, that feels right. But in this chapter, we look at the evidence. We explore how social media impacts all of our day-to-day lives. We avoid the sensationalism that comes with this topic. Social media is only part of the story about what is impacting kids today.

Much of our disconnection appears to be caused by what Dr. Swingle termed *digital interference* (e.g., gaming, pornography, social media, online sports betting, and overworking). Digital interference describes what goes wrong with i-media and technology (addiction, for example). Opposed to this is *digital integration*, which can be thought of as a healthy and functional use of those same technologies. Problems with technology are not an issue for just young people, all ages are afflicted. This is easily explained when you come to understand the addictive design and development strategies built into the technologies. More on that to come.

Drive is usually considered an admirable feature, an internal state of motivation that energizes a person toward a specific goal or action, yet some people's use of technology is more akin to *addiction*. Professional gamers or game testers access rational thinking parts of their brains to problem-solve, while the brain of a game-fixated youth will be emotion driven and lack self-regulation control. To confuse matters more, we can find ourselves engaged both as an addicted gamer (digital interference) and as an active user of the same technology for positive, pragmatic outcomes (digital integration). While she is positive about treatment outcomes and repairing brain changes through abstinence and regulated, restrictive, and routinized behaviors, Dr. Swingle's biggest concern is that many of these screen-based activities are displacing real-time human experiences related to the developmental needs of young people. This is when it becomes a problem.

Swingle stressed in our conversations that she is not anti-technology and that even if you are more at-risk neurologically, media consumption itself isn't harmful. While any substance overconsumed can become problematic, be it alcohol, drugs, or i-media, there is a mix of predisposition (genetic inheritance) and exposure. As we discuss in the following chapter, our genes interact with our surrounding environment, making it hard to pinpoint whether *nature* or *nurture* is responsible for what is going on. We agree it is nature *and* nurture.

As we heard more about how Dr. Swingle's work relates to kids these days, we learned that much of the response—the interventions and practices that support recovering from screen-based addictions—is in the context of relationships, primarily the family. It is no surprise that much of the addiction witnessed is closely linked to filling the void of connection— the absence of quality human relationships. So, youth who are hungry eat, and youth who are hungry and unhappy eat more. Hence, the gorging.

The Attention Economy

When we asked Dr. Swingle to expand on the differences between what we grew up with as kids in the seventies to nineties and what kids these days experience, she said the key difference is in the brain's response to the technology of the day. Television, she clarified, is completely *passive*. Screen-based devices today are *interactive*.

"We sort of became brain-dead watching TV," Mari shared with us. "Late at night you're exhausted, and there is some stupid infomercial on or whatnot. You couldn't care less about what's on, and you can't find the energy to get up, turn it off, and get yourself to bed."

Nevin's mother used to say the television would rot his brain. Well, it turns out that excessive TV watching *can* reduce gray matter in the brain. Researchers from Johns Hopkins Bloomberg School of Public Health and the National Institute on Aging followed 599 people's television viewing habits from 1990 to 2011.[2] They found, even after controlling for variables such as levels of physical activity, that those who watched an above-average amount showed reduced volume in their frontal cortex and entorhinal cortex, both responsible for information processing, judgment, creativity, and social appropriateness—not something anyone wants to compromise by choice.

That's the effect of the passive technology of old. Our current technologies are exactly the opposite: They hyper-arouse and stimulate us. They keep us awake. Advertising agencies understand this as *the attention economy,* where your attention is a scarce commodity and companies try to maximize the time you give to certain products.

"I call it a *vestibular lock-in,*" Dr. Swingle said. "A syndrome, where you can't even break the arousal pattern, and you click, and you click, and you click, and you are locked in, and you stay over-engaged." Anyone with a mobile device probably understands this phenomenon.

Our vestibular system is what keeps track of where our head is in time and space, and it organizes eye movement, posture, and balance (from the inner ear). In fact, it is responsible for organizing and responding to most sensory input. This is the "captain" of the central nervous system. Mobile devices actively capture the vestibular system, as opposed to being in passive captivity with the television.

This interactive captivity, of *like buttons* and the *infinite scroll,* according to Dr. Swingle, "shows very different brain states in our scans and something very important to be aware of, especially regarding child development."

While any excessive use of screen-based media can be detrimental, she said gaming may be the one to really be worried about, primarily due to disturbances of the frontal lobes and messing with alpha brain waves. Alpha waves are associated with being calm and creative and being able to take in and process new information. It's not hard to understand why teachers and other adults in a young person's life would like them to be in an alpha wave state.

This is one explanation for why we have witnessed the proliferation of mindfulness and social-emotional learning training in the classrooms of our children. Although we have some questions about the need to teach Zen to five-year-olds (which we address further in chapter 6) to induce alpha wave states, we understand the reasoning behind it. When our brain waves are functioning well, we can move from rest to action and back again efficiently. Top athletes, pilots, and other technical professionals focus on alpha wave training to increase safety and performance outcomes. Swingle said that robust alpha brainwaves can bloom in creativity or be hijacked by i-tech. The hijacking is not innocent either; the technology has been purposefully developed to take advantage of how our brains work. Few of us can claim to be unaffected.

The *infinite scroll*, for example, was invented by Aza Raskin in 2006. The infinite scroll occurs on apps like Facebook where new content automatically loads no matter how long you scroll without having to click to another page. Most social media apps eventually incorporated this interactive, highly addictive, and dopamine-inducing feature. Dopamine is a neurotransmitter often referred to as our brain's *reward center*. Dopamine makes us feel good.

It is interesting to know that Raskin now reportedly hardly uses social media, knowing its effective hook-and-grab techniques. Similarly, coinventor of Facebook's *like button*, Leah Pearlman, recognized her self-worth was being reflected in the number of likes she was getting, and she tried to stop using Facebook after leaving the company. Both designers realized the addictive nature of tools they created, and how they capture the brain's reward center, and they felt guilt over how damaging these products have become for so many. Entering 2024, Facebook had over 3 billion active users—with predictions for continued growth.[3] Obviously, these designers' features continue to grab the attention of their users.

In October of 2023, more than forty US states were taking legal action against Meta Platforms, Inc., the parent company of Facebook and Instagram.[4] The allegations to be settled in federal court included Meta collecting user data, including on minors, and using addictive design features to manipulate and exploit vulnerable children and youth. State Attorneys General and lawyers involved in filing the lawsuits attempted to show the connection between corporate interests and the burgeoning child and youth mental health crisis. In mid-summer of 2024, the *Financial Times* reported seeing documents that implicated Google and Meta for bypassing their own rules for protecting minors.[5] Their secret plan was to target 13–17-year-olds on You-Tube (Google) with ads to promote Instagram (Meta).

A third feature of social media worth demonizing here is the algorithms that hide behind the veil of the apps we use. Many platforms and developers don't share how their algorithms work. In essence, they are filtering and collating systems that attempt to direct material to the user for either the user's benefit or that of a commercial interest. User behavior is but one guide for an algorithm. What one follows, likes, shares, purchases, or visits, along with scrolling patterns, followers' and connections' preferences, the popularity of content, and other factors are all analyzed. While primarily an AI process, algorithms are rule-based, and often platforms are moderated, including forms of censorship that elevate or diminish content to increase or decrease its likelihood of being consumed. The result is content that you probably want to be exposed to, and, quite likely, a reinforcement of your own biases, views, and beliefs—and reduced exposure to alternate or conflicting content. Because of this, what these algorithms produce are *echo chambers*.

With controversial or provocative content getting more attention—as it always has (e.g., "if it bleeds, it leads" from the TV news desk era), echo chambers are very effective at inhibiting the exchange of diverse viewpoints, increasing polarity and inciting conflict, and furthering disconnection. Not only are our teens missing out on learning through dialogue and debate, but they are also compelled to take sides, and in many cases don't feel they can speak out for fear of being called out, canceled, or shunned by their peers. Though many of us are aware of the harms of this technology, we are still witnessing the stranglehold of i-tech across societal contexts and age groups. When we continually hear of corporate players intentionally targeting youth and government regulators unable to hold them accountable, we (again) have to be the adults in the room and take action to protect our kids from harm.

The American Academy of Pediatrics recommends children under 2 should not experience any screen-based technologies, and 2- to 5-year-olds should be restricted to no more than 2 hours daily.[6] Limits are not as concretely recommended for older children because screens are so integrated into day-to-day activities, getting schoolwork done, communications, and yes, entertainment. Electronic technologies are a ubiquitous part of life for billions of people. Technologies are now part of everyday child-rearing. The convenience of a screen to "mind the kids" while cleaning the house, commuting, and having "adult" conversations is hard to resist.

Average daily screen time of 13- to 18-year-olds in 2019 was commonly cited at about 7.5 hours each day[7] with an average increase across all but the youngest age groups of one hour in 2022, suggesting a pandemic influence.[8] The most significant increases were in the use of mobile or handheld devices, which showed a 30% bump from 2019 to 2021, and the trends suggest continued growth in this type of screen use.[9] While no screen interaction is recommended for our youngest children, current global surveys show that 49% of children under 2 are interacting with smartphones and 74% with TV.[10] Television viewing, as a passive technology, appears to plateau around 3–4 years of age, and the more addictive interactive technologies of mobile devices and gaming increase at a steady rate with age, at least until age 11.

Teens in the US have shown significantly increased mobile device use and social media platform engagement. In 2022, 95% of youth 13–17 years old were using YouTube; TikTok (67%),

Instagram (62%), and Snapchat (59%) clustered behind. The US and global stats are quite similar in that most of the daily usage is split equally between mobile devices and computer screens, and about an hour and a half is spent gaming, and nearly three hours on social media. These are averages, taken across large populations around the world. While it's hard to be specific about population studies, when we started looking at the increasing rates of screen time, specifically for children and youth, we found troubling evidence of detrimental effects.

Device use is pervasive; very few teens are without daily access to the internet. We also learned that 54% of youth 13–17 said it would be hard to give up social media.[11] A similar percentage of parents and other adults said the same. Many of them expressed feeling guilty about their own use and about letting their children use screens as much as they do. They also saw their own loss of productive time in work and life, and how too much screen time was affecting their own health.

Reviews of the available research found links between excessive screen time and negative effects on the physical, cognitive, and socio-emotional development of children, as well as on the overall mental health of adolescents. For example, a 2015 study of more than 240 Canadian students in grades 7 through 12 found the duration of screen time was correlated with the severity of symptoms of depression and anxiety.[12] Gaming and other computer use were more damaging to youth mental health than television. It is interesting to note that studies conducted in the mid-2010s such as this one would not have fully captured the role of social media relative to the ramping up of screen use year after year. Today, kids in the US are reported by the CDC to be on some type of screen for up to 7.5 hours per day for entertainment purposes alone.[13] Add in any educational screen use, and you've surpassed the length of a standard workday!

Recent reviews of the evidence are plentiful and show specific ailments associated with increased screen time. One systematic review in the BMJ (British Medical Journal) from the

Institute of Child Health at the University College of London identified associations between screen time and childhood health issues.[14] Increases in screen time are associated with higher levels of obesity, depressive symptoms, increased food intake, a less-healthy diet, and an overall lower quality of life. There are also indications that excessive screen time increases behavior problems, anxiety, hyperactivity, inattention, poorer self-esteem, lowered well-being and psychosocial health, lower levels of fitness, poorer cognitive development and educational attainment, and decreased quality of sleep. These effects are obvious, and we exhibit a conscious avoidance if we continue to ignore these realities. Willful blindness.

"We're consumers in the attention economy," Dr. Mari Swingle stated prophetically. "The longer our attention is captured, the more we consume, and we need to be present to what it is we're consuming."

Problems really arise when technology displaces human interaction and experiences that require full mental and emotional engagement if they are to learn and grow from these interactions. The child without "friends"—which don't include those they play online games with—misses the real trials and tribulations of human friendship and the learning that comes from negotiating those relationships. The extinction of experience.

"Technology is a beautiful tool and, I emphasize 'tool' in that it was designed to be there for our benefit, and there is nothing wrong with that," Dr. Swingle shared with us. However, she is critical of many of the producers of these technologies, who include addictive features that put profit over the health of their users. It's a capitalistic tale as old as time. More on that in the following chapter.

This is not just a child development phenomenon. Most adults can likely identify a scenario in their own lives regarding technology when they have felt captive by the infinite scroll, the click, or the speed of information or images fed to their brains.

Screens and Sex

Our coverage of technology and screen-based addiction would be incomplete without addressing pornography and the sexualization of young people online via social media. We found in our research that youth are engaging much less in physical relationships these days, let alone having sex. Comparing rates of sexual activity between 2009 and 2018, researchers from The Center for Sexual Health Promotion at Indiana University found that 89% of 14- to 17-year-olds had not had intercourse in the previous year, a full 10% less than reported in 2009.[15]

Further, they found decreases in all forms of sexual activity, including solo masturbation. Youth seem to be replacing intimate human connections with artificial and virtual versions online. This phenomenon, coupled with significant global declines in sperm count, has major population implications.[16] Dr. Swingle shared with us that she sees young males interpreting porn as some resemblance of what sex is supposed to look like, often expecting females in real life to perform in degrading, misogynistic power dynamics and the unhealthy (and often abusive) manner seen online.

"When a young male cannot find his place," she said, "he's being sucked into gaming and pornography. Young males should learn from their older brothers, their fathers, their uncles, and maybe even an elder auntie here or there."

And for females, Dr. Swingle believes many have "opted out" because they, too, have seen pornography and want nothing to do with sex if that's what it looks like!

We also heard from our experts that in an age of "call-out" and "cancel" culture, some youths are so concerned about consent that they won't even venture into experimenting with sexual relationships. Immediate access to pornographic materials has also been detrimental to youth development because it permits and even encourages gorging. Starving in the real world, but gorging online—Dr. Swingle's chief concern for kids these days.

Pathologizing Disconnection

Dr. Swingle, like several of the other experts we chose to consult, is a rebel. We think she will relish hearing the application of this label. Her backstory supports the moniker.

Dr. Swingle raced through school and had finished an undergraduate university degree by the age of 19. Bored with school, she took off to Europe to model before returning to graduate school at an age-appropriate time and eventually joined her father at the Swingle Clinic as a neurotherapist.

Early in her career, Mari rejected medicalized labeling of the young people she worked with. She recognized that elements of their learning had been missed or disrupted by technologies. (We refer to these missed developmental stages throughout this book as *fractures*.) If a child seems to be having difficulties in a learning environment, Swingle's clinical work with EEG brain scans can be used to point to the type of learning deficits involved. Once identified, some deficits can be remediated by returning to a neglected learning phase and/or by training the brain for increased focus. If this training became more of our concentration, instead of diagnostic labels, Dr. Swingle argues, we could help kids develop the skills and abilities they need to carry on with childhood without being saddled with a diagnosis of ADHD or another set of letters plucked from the DSM.

Dr. Swingle provides a strong viewpoint on education today—one we strongly agree with. She fears that our modern school system too frequently *manufactures* disability while ignoring the greater problem of youth starving for connection, human interaction, and belonging. Diagnosis and medications are used to correct behavior that doesn't fit perfectly with school processes.[17] And we know more recent types of assessments, such as the PHQ-9, have lowered the bar of what it means to be mentally ill. (We discuss this in chapter 7, where we address more fully the mental health "industry.") When a learning difficulty exists with writing or spelling skills, today's youth are often provided more *technology*, such as voice-responsive eLearning applications. Dr. Swingle strongly believes we need to address missed learning opportunities and/or writing and reading skills *before* providing a technological solution.

On the school front, Dr. Swingle also said, "We used to hit kids for not behaving, but now we medicate them."

This statement resonated with us. We ourselves lived through the shift from hitting to medication. As described in chapter 1, Nevin was strapped at school for misbehaving; Will was medicated for being the class clown who created chaos for his teachers. The fear of pain has simply been replaced with sedation! Based on our discussion in the following chapter, we would refer to this development as a *regrettable substitution*, where one harmful practice is discontinued and replaced by a different but equally harmful one.

Recent calls for a "bell-to-bell" ban on phones and devices in schools have us concerned about the top-down, prohibitionist approach being adopted. As of January 2025, eight US states have pushed through legislation to ban cell phones during the school day.[18] In November 2024, the Australian federal government proposed "world-leading" measures to ban all kids under 16 years of age from social media use.[19] The irony here (or cognitive dissonance) is that the criminal age of responsibility for children across the vast majority of Australia is 10! A 10-year-old is perceived as mature enough to know right from wrong when it comes to the law but too irresponsible to navigate the digital world.

To us, these initiatives feel eerily similar to the solutions proposed for the *kids these days effect* described in chapter 1. Obviously, there are problems to be solved. One in 5 youth are being diagnosed with a mental disorder. This sounds like a lot, and it is. We know another 1 in 5 youth is likely subthreshold of a diagnosis. But this also means 60% of youth, while maybe negatively affected by social media, are *not* struggling with a mental disorder. Legislating a ban on phones for those who may have successfully integrated the phone into their lives appears to be reactionary—and likely to lead to our next regrettable substitution. Our "be the adult in the room" plea is about building and preserving relationships with youth, not to lord over them. The challenge to "stand up for kids" is intended to take up the fight against the source of the problem (in this case, Big Tech), and not those affected by it.

Oxford University researcher and adolescent expert Lucy Foulkes wrote that this ban-the-phone movement is taking off so quickly because banning phones "just sort of *feels* right—look at all those teenagers glued to their phones, listen to the accounts of self-harm images, cyberbullying and sexting gone wrong. They're suffering, and of course, it's their phones ... Except that psychological science (and life) is rarely this neat."[20]

Reviewing data from forty studies in 2020, psychology professor Candice Odgers found no evidence of a causal relationship to indicate social media *caused* an epidemic of adolescent mental illness.[21] Odgers has argued the correlation is backward. Yes, social media impacts the lives of all of us. But if youth are already struggling, and adults are struggling, maybe we gorge on social media due to a lack of social connectedness. Maybe anxiety and the deterioration of well-being leads to increased social media use, similar to how trauma and learning differences can lead to increased drug use. It's not the technology itself, it's the connection.

Odgers and her colleagues wrote: "Finally, we need to move past the fear-based dialogue around social media and adolescent development and toward frameworks that can weigh potential risks and benefits of online spaces for young people. The future is increasingly digital, and rigorous and developmentally informed science is required to ensure that all adolescents are supported and protected as they navigate the online world."[22]

Some teachers use phones for surveying their classrooms for feedback on curriculum, and others employ phones for game-based learning. Many outdoor therapists we know use phones for geocaching and nature interpretation with young clients to build a sense of adventure in a person's immediate environment and to introduce them to nearby nature. The call to regulate phone use is, of course, timely and in many ways well-reasoned. It's easy for everyone to see that rising rates of youth mental illness link very well to cell phone use and social media. That is, however, only part of the wicked problem. Rising rates of interference, intervention, and ideology have persisted for more than half a century. Overprotection and the safety trap were becoming a problem years before the first iPhone. This cell-phone-ban movement feels, to us, like adults starting a kids-these-days movement without talking to the youth. Steps taken by Australia and many US states are quickly becoming a "universal" program for everyone.

But we know interventions like these have historically been ineffective at best, and at worst, harmful. Much more on that in chapter 6.

While we're concerned about the impact of the phones, banning them may limit independence and mastery, two of the four quadrants of the *Circle of Courage* model. Remember the United Nations 2022 study mentioned in the previous chapter; it found that trying to fix adolescent behavior through universal intervention is likely to fail. We must view kids these days as resources, crew with something to contribute. Recent bestsellers about social media and adolescent mental health ignored experts like Dr. Mari Swingle who called out digital *interference* yet wholeheartedly believe in digital *integration*. It's a wicked problem. Dr. Swingle suggested to us that she sees the cell phone ban in schools as a possible stopgap measure, but it needs to be followed rapidly by solutions to work toward integration. If we treat youth as passengers, empty vessels who require this level of adult protection, we may further reduce their autonomy, disempower those who had integration, and overall, enable the *kids these days effect* to continue. As you'll find in the following chapter, if we're going to ban anything, let's start with the toxins.

4

LIONS, TIGERS, AND BEARS

Monsters exist, but they are too few in number to be truly dangerous. More dangerous are the common men, the functionaries ready to believe and to act without asking questions.
—Primo Levi

Fred remembered being carried out of the garage by his older brother in waist-high, oil-stained water during the Great New England Hurricane of 1938. He was only three, living upstairs in the family-owned Lanphear's Garage, a mechanic's shop and chauffeur service in Watch Hill Bay, Rhode Island, a small community on the estuary of the Pawcatuck River. At the time, the garage served the wealthy taking their holidays at the picturesque beachfront.

The garage was a large three-story building with room on the ground floor to service, repair, house, and clean dozens of vehicles; many of their drivers boarded upstairs in the Lanphear family home. The building had served a similar purpose in generations past, but instead with horse-drawn carriages. Fred's first five years of life were intricately enmeshed in the family business, providing wonderful and lasting memories, like his brother heroically rescuing him.

Fred's childhood adventures included clambering over, under, and through the garage—a space occupied with fuel, oil, cleaning solvents, and other products used in the running of an active service and repair shop. Fred spent the remainder of his early years on Broadview Farm, downwind from the Misquamicut Golf Course (a regular user of pesticides).

Fred ultimately became a professor of horticulture at Purdue University, where some of his early career projects, funded by the US Department of Agriculture, involved investigating common weedkillers. In the 1960s, herbicides were often used as convenient weed controllers in nurseries, along roadsides, and for residential landscaping. After not too many years, Fred began to feel that his work was contributing to environmental hazards affecting human health. By the late 1960s, partly in response to Rachel Carsen's *Silent Spring*, which exposed the detrimental health effects of pesticides,[1] Fred had joined the movement addressing the use of these harmful poisons. He saw how well supported these products were by research, driven by the industry for the convenience of their application and increased yields, no matter the environmental cost. Human health was an afterthought. A shifting consciousness put Fred on the side of protecting the public from herbicides and pesticides by working with plants in a more natural way—and calling out the chemical manufacturers causing environmental harm.

The etymology (the origin of a term), for the suffix -*cide* translates to *slayer, cutter,* or *killer* in Latin. To put it simply, it means dangerous, harmful, destructive. Hence, herbicides and pesticides, and sadly, suicides.

Fred was diagnosed with Amyotrophic Lateral Sclerosis (ALS) in 2007, commonly known as Lou Gehrig's disease. This degenerative nervous system disease is terminal and, from the time of diagnosis, it often carries a life expectancy of just 2–5 years. Here, we introduce our next expert, Bruce Lanphear, Fred's son.

We do not have to wonder why Bruce took on a similar line of research in his own career. He witnessed his father publishing research on the ill effects of toxic chemicals. He then experienced it all firsthand, as he watched his father's illness progress and Fred's eventual passing. Wanting more specific answers, Bruce looked to the literature and found three contributing environmental factors to ALS: pesticides, lead, and head injuries.

Fred's life easily included the first two—spending years surrounded by leaded gasoline and pesticides—and Fred's adventures in life also included a head injury in a 1945 scooter accident in Kenya. There were the three causal factors, and yet, there was no family history of ALS. Bruce also found genetic contributions to ALS were only around 10%.[2] The disease had not previously been seen in his family, so he looked outward toward the environment.

So, there was Fred, a potential victim of environmental toxicity, and by extension, corporate greed. A sad fact considering he spent most of his adulthood in scholarly activism fighting against the very things that eventually ended his life.

Bruce Lanphear, MD, is now a clinician scientist and professor in the Faculty of Health Sciences at Simon Fraser University and an investigator at British Columbia's Children's Hospital. Dr. Lanphear studies the toxicity of everyday chemicals in prenatal children, with a focus on early exposures as they relate to neurotoxicity and brain development. He has grown increasingly troubled by what he calls the "pandemic of consumption"—those largely preventable chronic diseases and disabilities caused by widespread exposure to toxic chemicals and industrial pollutants. Dr. Lanphear is heavily involved in educating the public about the links between human health and the environment. His efforts are dedicated to preventing disease, primarily by identifying and removing the causes. When we spoke to him, he shared more than once that research and evidence don't always translate to better policy or changes to improve human health—a fitting narrative given the same trends are true regarding mental health.

We caught up with Dr. Lanphear during his sabbatical; he was spending his days writing a book, *Plagues, Pollution, and Poverty*, aimed at a broad audience. Bruce also maintains an informative substack of the same title. Although he was busy with research of his own, he was gracious with his time, engaging, and supportive. He offered us his thoughts on our question of addressing adolescent mental health and *kids these days*.

Dr. Lanphear reminded us that "most of us living in cities and towns no longer worry about the lions, tigers, and bears. When we send our kids out into the world, it's the media, environmental chemicals ... We are not looking out for dangerous predatory animals, but we need to remain equally vigilant as we were in the past, because these environmental hazards are no less dangerous." Minimizing exposure is Dr. Lanphear's best advice: "You've got to figure out how to help prepare your children to confront all these possible hazards in the environment today."

Bruce shared with us the tragic reality that billions of people do not know of their low-level chronic exposure to toxic chemicals. These chemicals may have a latency period, which means negative effects don't appear until many years later. The exposure can eventually manifest as a disease, such as cancer, or neurological disorders, such as dementia or ALS. The exposure may also materialize as a range of symptoms related to mental health and behavioral issues. This caught our full attention.

When certain toxic chemicals, such as flame retardants (routinely applied to household items such as electronics, furniture, beds, and pillows) are found in blood and urine samples of pregnant mothers, behavioral and neurodevelopmental issues of children have been associated with the levels of toxicity.[3] Studies examining pregnant mothers' exposure to flame retardants (PBDEs) over a longer period of time found exposure may be a risk factor for anxiety symptoms when their child reaches adolescence.[4]

The toxicity of some common chemicals, such as alcohol and tobacco is well-known. Many other toxins are invisible and insidious, such as air pollution, lead in paint and gasoline, mercury in the fish we eat, and even mercury emitted during volcanic activity. The chemicals in our food have also been linked to childhood and lifelong behavioral or neurological issues resulting in a calculable and growing burden of disease.[5] The developing child, either in utero or in the early years of life, is most vulnerable to toxic chemicals and their subsequent negative health effects.

Lead, for example, has been banned from many products, yet the harmful legacy of lead exposure lives on in soil, paints, aviation gasoline … and the bodies of those exposed—most of us in North America today. UNICEF reports that globally, one in three children is lead poisoned, which is defined as having a blood lead concentration of more than 50 parts per billion.[6]

Toxicity research revealed lead's connection to deaths in the 1960s and how exposure contributes to brain and nervous system damage, delayed growth and learning, decreased cognitive ability, attention-related issues, and weakened academic performance.[7] Lead is often ignored today but remains worthy of exploration regarding the mental health and development of kids these days. During our research, we found environmental toxins absent from just about every book and discussion on the topic of youth mental health. Or, they are mentioned briefly and disregarded as a worry of the past.

The impact of toxic chemicals is often relative to the amount of toxin in the blood of pregnant mothers or the children themselves, which affects the severity of certain disorders or lost developmental capacity. Lead poisoning at higher levels has more obvious symptoms: abdominal pain, joint pain, severe headaches, intracranial pressure, neurotoxic effects, anemia, and kidney dysfunction. However, cumulative effects of long-term, low-level exposure often go unrecognized. This is, at least in part, the result of limitations to our safety testing systems. Industry-funded studies conducted with animals in controlled laboratories often rely on the protocol of administering low levels of exposure over short periods of time—and they often find no to minimal harm.[8] These studies have been interpreted as providing support for the notion that low levels of exposure to humans is safe. In response, policymakers have approved products containing lead. The products get to market. We are told these products are safe. Bruce isn't convinced.

Allowable Limits and Regrettable Substitutions

These research and regulatory practices, which Dr. Lanphear described as commonplace since the 1970s, leads us to the concept of *allowable limits*.

"They are all poisons. Nobody questions that," he shared with us. "The only question is at what level do we find evidence of toxicity. The industry says these 'allowable limits' are safe, and our regulatory agencies have accepted this flawed argument."

We have heard about allowable limits on many fronts, from chlorine in pools and drinking water, to fluoride in dentistry, many current medications, and in foods made with fluoridated drinking water. "Allowable limits" are supposed to be trusted information. Regulators are there to keep us safe.

Dr. Lanphear published a 2017 paper entitled *No Acceptable Levels*[9] and has been trying for years to get his point across to regulatory agencies—and the public as well. He served as an expert witness on behalf of the California Attorney General's office on the effects of childhood lead poisoning and has been a consultant for the US Environmental Protection Agency (EPA) and the National Institute of Health. He reiterated that *allowable* never actually meant *safe*. This became, however, the general public's interpretation, trusting our governments and regulatory agencies to test and report honestly any concerns for human health and safety. As these toxins enter our environment, and their detrimental effects emerge, our systems and society have decided to focus on how to heal people harmed by the toxins, rather than removing the toxins themselves. Intervention instead of prevention.

Lead, for example, still has allowable limits in new products today. According to the CDC's website, lead is still used in the production of plastic toys.[10] Lead softens plastic, making it flexible so toys can bounce back to their original shape. When exposed to sunlight, other chemicals, or simply the air, the bond between the plastic and the lead can break down, forming a dust. Children can touch a toy and ingest this lead-riddled dust when they put their fingers in their mouths. Yet the evidence is clear that lead is a poison to the body. (More on lead, below in "Lead's Legacy.")

Allowable does not mean safe. While researching this book, and after speaking to Bruce, we noticed more often when products and interventions were being promoted as "safe and effective." Lifting the veil further, we have grown more concerned with the human drive to find technological and mechanical solutions to wicked problems, instead of preventing the harm or the cause.

Dr. Lanphear says society is "entranced by technology and the never-ending, ever-elusive search for cures." He speaks with conviction that this "fixation on technology fails to recognize or acknowledge that the pandemic of consumption, the worldwide epidemic of death and disability from chronic disease, is largely due to innovative technologies of the past, and yet somehow we are arrogant enough to think that we are going to solve these with new innovative technologies!"[11]

Flame retardants were originally engineered to reduce the number of fires and fatalities caused by people falling asleep while smoking. The innovation is associated with harm to human health. Studies have shown a clear link between exposure to flame retardants and lowered infant IQ. The technology designed to solve one problem created another. This is the difficulty with wicked problems, and it's what Dr. Lanphear and his colleagues refer to as a *regrettable substitution*. Upon learning this term, we began to identify numerous examples of regrettable substitutions. We discuss them throughout this book.

We found Bruce's work intimately tied to our concerns about youth mental health, yet most of us are only now waking up to the depth and complexity of how kids these days are impacted by environmental toxins. Dr. Lanphear and his colleagues point to root causes—the interference—yet we seem to live in a world trying to address symptoms—the intervention. We positioned this chapter early in this book to emphasize how capitalism, ignorance, and bad, misleading, or dated information have infiltrated and interfered with our everyday lives. We encourage any reader left with questions—or disbelief—to follow the trail of the studies we cite and come to their own conclusions. There are many examples of societal emphasis on curing what has been produced versus eliminating the destructive force that produced it. Here, we revisit an age-old debate about nature and nurture and reexamine how genes, our upbringing, and the environment create a complex interaction impacting child and youth development.

Nature and/or Nurture

Autism spectrum disorder (autism) is a neurodevelopmental condition that affects how a person interacts, communicates, learns, and behaves. Often, social relations are compromised by reduced eye contact, lack of facial expression, and a limited ability to sense one's own or perceive others' feelings. Manifesting in myriad combinations of behaviors, skills, and abilities, autism also has a neurological aspect to it which may include repetitive or restrictive bodily movements and behaviors (referred to as *stimming*), such as rocking back and forth while seated or standing.

Rates of people diagnosed with autism have risen dramatically over the years, from 1 in 5,000 in 1975, to 1 in 68 in 2012. Today, while differing numbers can be found in the literature, rates published by the CDC[12] for the US and the WHO[13] globally are now 1 in 38, and 1 in 100, respectively! There is no debate that this condition constitutes a significant concern as prevalence continues to rise.

Of course, there are theories for this rapid upswing.

Could it be improved screening and assessment? Maybe. Early childhood trauma also might be a factor; some experts have argued autism may present like complex trauma stemming from childhood exposure to multiple, invasive, and wide-ranging traumatic or adverse experiences.[14] Plausible. One question seemingly left off the table, though, is the environment. For Bruce Lanphear and his colleagues, however, the rate has risen far too fast to be accounted for by genetics.

"Strangely," said Bruce, "in the first ten years of this century, we spent over a billion dollars on genetics to research the cause of autism, and only 40 million—or 4%—looking at environmental factors."[15]

Bruce expressed his frustration with research that puts genetics and environmental factors in separate boxes. He said researchers looking at genes alone often conclude that genetic contributions to autism are 40-80%; mostly, they ignore environmental factors. In a brief review, we found similar claims in research surrounding twin siblings and the heritability of autism. It's not hard to see the benefit of studying similar genetically composed humans, such as fraternal and identical twins, when exposed to different environments.

A 2016 meta-analysis of twin studies in the *Journal of Child Psychology and Psychiatry* suggested the genetic contribution to autism was 64-93%,[16] and a 2021 review published in *Psychological Medicine* found similar figures (63-93%) but suggested environmental factors contributed 9-36%.[17] But, when considering the environment specifically, and looking at a range of toxins, Bruce Lanphear found the genetic attribution to autism alone is only about 15%. According to him, researchers should conduct their work with the belief that "genes and the environment contribute to complex problems, such as common public health diseases like autism, attention-deficit hyperactivity disorder (ADHD), depression, cardiovascular disease, diabetes, and are due to the *interplay between genes and environment*, probably as high as 90% of the time."[18]

The constant and complex interactions between genes and environment are well explained by the award-winning, best-selling author David Shenk in *The Genius in All of Us*.[19] His well-researched thesis suggested giving up on the nature-versus-nurture debate, adopting instead the concept of *dynamic development*. In sum, Shenk describes development as happening in the interplay between genes and outside stimuli. And, for anyone believing you are limited by your genes, take heart. As Shenk states: "Everything you've been told about genetics, talent, and IQ is wrong!"

Imagine, for example, identical twins separated at birth, but growing up in similar households relative to social, emotional, and cognitive factors. One house, built in 1965, had lead-framed windows with walls covered in lead-based paint. The other house, built in 1990, was free of this environmental toxin. One twin, experiencing low-level lead exposure for eighteen years, may develop behavioral problems or have more difficulty with academic achievement. Later in life, they may suffer from dementia, which seemingly appears out of nowhere. Nothing would be obvious or visible to the parents raising these two children. Their genetic potentials are bound by matched DNA, yet their home environment, and in this case a nasty toxic predator, is a possible link to the difference. It's not that one of the children was more genetically susceptible to illness, but rather their development was dynamic due to the interplay between genes and environment. Not nature versus nurture. Nature *and* nurture.

Dr. Lanphear echoed the words of eminent epidemiologist Geoffrey Rose who famously stated, "If causes can be removed, susceptibility ceases to matter." In simpler terms, if a lion is biting children in your neighborhood, remove the cause, and stop trying to figure out which child will get bitten next, or who has the genetics to reduce the effects of the bite! Even worse, don't spend money researching which child's genes will best respond to an innovative treatment after being bit. Deal with the damn lion!

Prevention

After our own review of the overwhelming amount of research, we were sure that the preventative nature of Dr. Lanphear and his colleagues' work to protect youth and pregnant mothers would lead to significant policy change and reductions in human suffering. We also expected these clinician-scholars to receive international recognition and prestigious awards. They didn't. Dr. Bruce Lanphear has been removed, and resigned from, several prominent committees and working groups formed to provide oversight and transparency for environmental toxins and human health. Corporate influence and interference in government regulatory bodies became very apparent to us as we learned more from Bruce and the available evidence.

Seeking cures through genetic research is based on the premise that the answers to illness are within the bodies of the ill and that medicine and technologies can be developed—and sold—to treat them. Where there is profit potential, corporations will find the product. Preventative approaches have little capitalistic value. Plus, they're hard to measure.

Take crime prevention, for example. If most humans do not live a life of crime, it becomes difficult to argue the effectiveness of crime prevention programs. Hence, prevention often fails to receive the recognition it deserves, and thus, it is inadequately funded. We see this in the realm of youth therapy and the role pharmaceuticals play in the lives of many of our clients. Would prevention, or removing the cause of harm, have sufficed?

Consider one comprehensive study Bruce references that found shocking levels of the following common, and fun-to-pronounce, toxins in the blood of pregnant American women:

lead, mercury, organophosphates, polychlorinated biphenyl (PCBs), bisphenol A (BPA), and polybrominated diphenyl ethers (PBDEs).[20] Biomonitoring data was analyzed from the CDC's National Health and Nutritional Examination survey done in the early 2000s that looked at 12 classes of chemicals across a sample of 268 women. The levels of toxicity found were at or above levels already found to show associations with adverse reproductive and developmental outcomes. Further, most women had been exposed to a cocktail of poisons during this vulnerable fetal developmental period. Consider the findings below and their links to mental and behavioral health.

Lead, found in the paint and dust of older (built pre-1980) homes and contaminated soil, was found in 94% of the women. Lead poisoning leads to brain and central nervous system damage and can show up in youth as intellectual and behavioral disorders.

Mercury was found in 89% of the women, primarily due to exposure from eating fish. Mercury poisoning can lead to neurological and behavioral disorders from damage to the brain and central nervous system.

Over 80% had been exposed to organophosphates, primarily through consuming food sprayed with agricultural pesticides. Exposure to organophosphates can lead to respiratory and behavioral issues, as well as disruptions to the nervous system and cognitive functions.

The entire sample of pregnant women had been exposed to polychlorinated biphenyl (PCBs). Although banned in the 1970s, these persistent organic pollutants, previously used in the electronics industries, persist in the environment today.

Found in 96% of children, BPA received public attention a few years back due to health concerns, and manufacturers made efforts to label their products (especially plastic water bottles) as "BPA-free." We've noted that many of the water bottles we used early in our outdoor careers were manufactured with BPA. While not the only harmful chemical used in the production of plastics and resins, BPA has been linked to endocrine (hormone) system disruption, ADHD, anxiety and depression, early onset puberty in women, diabetes, obesity, and heart disease.

All trends moving in the wrong direction. Phthalates, a class of toxic chemical, used in plastics manufacturing (commonly found in polyvinyl chloride, or PVC), can negatively impair brain development and increase risks of learning difficulties and ADHD and other behavioral disorders.[21, 22]

Last, PBDEs were found in 100% of the samples (as mentioned earlier, these are primarily found in flame retardants). Exposure has been linked to hormone disruption, neurodevelopmental issues, and tumors. A 2022 longitudinal study from the College of Medicine at the University of Cincinnati found PBDE exposure in mid-pregnancy mothers was associated with adolescent anxiety.[23]

This snapshot of common toxic exposures is not meant to scare readers or express futility about efforts to protect our children. But we want to be very clear about the significant burden these toxins pose to the developing body. This, we hope, will encourage those working with and raising youth to focus on preventative and protective factors that can help youth develop in a world worth engaging in. With all this research readily available, why is preventing harm the afterthought to causing it?

Geoffrey Rose proposed the *prevention paradox* in 1981 when he argued for broader societal interventions to reduce the overall burden of disease.[24] *Burden of disease* is the impact any health issue has on society. It can be measured by mortality, financial costs, or other indicators. Most people assume those who are thought to be at higher risk—because of their genetics—are responsible for a large proportion of the burden of disease. If we know a person's genetics make *less* of an impact than environmental factors, Rose's paradox is that even when equipped with the knowledge about potential harm, we still do not remove the cause—toxins, for example. Ideally, the preventative approach would decrease the likelihood of the disease for all. Small changes for a larger population can reduce the overall number of people who will be negatively affected, and consequently, society will bear less financial and social burden. As we have seen in our reading of research from several environmental health experts, the call for prevention—from the adults in the room—continues, but the funding focuses primarily on genetics. The status quo puts the problem within the person, and the goal is finding the cure, which is the moneymaker. It goes from *interference* to *intervention*. Bottom line: Small reductions of environmental toxins in the environment can create large reductions in disease and disorders.

Ignore the Cause, Find the Cure

We're taught numerous examples of prevention in everyday life. Wash your hands. Wear a hat and a long-sleeved shirt and avoid peak sun hours to protect your skin from burns. Avoid smoking tobacco, and limit alcohol. Limit your exposure to toxins to prevent a range of cancers. Still, most research dollars go to expensive medical interventions and treatments. Surgery and pharmaceuticals have been the primary interventions of the medical system since the early 1900s. Many examples prove this point. Smoking is an obvious one.

The American Heart Association (AHA) reported that smoking contributed to over 8 million deaths globally in 2020,[25] and the US Surgeon General reported that more than 840,000 deaths nationally could be attributed directly to smoking, with an additional 41,000 from second-hand smoke. We do not need to convince anyone that smoking is harmful to human health.

Cigarette warning labels may be the most obvious example of a public education campaign to reduce the incidence of harm from smoking. Backed by government mandates and data from health authorities across many nations, warnings and disturbing images are now placed on tobacco packaging across the globe. In this case, prevention has been taken some-what seriously.

One study published in the *Journal of the American Medical Association* in 2021 suggested educational labels on cigarette packets *do* lead to increased negative perceptions of smoking and to thoughts of quitting, but they *do not* actually reduce levels of consumption.[26] Regardless of the impact on smoking cessation, the public is informed by the campaign, and, as this study showed, the preconditions for quitting (that is, thinking about quitting) were triggered by the labels. This is an example of preventing the harm from outside of the person. Not looking within.

A 2024 commentary in *Psychiatry Research* contributed by psychiatrist E. Fuller Torrey—a controversial figure in his own right, given his support for the forced treatment of people with schizophrenia[27]—provided a cautionary tale about genes and mental health.[28] In June 2000, the Clinton White House announced the conclusion of the Human Genome Project, a multi-billion dollar initiative designed to fully map the human genome for the first time. One of the main goals of the project was improvements in medical research and practice. Advocates dubbed it the most significant, historic, and even God-like initiative in medical and scientific history. Funded by the US National Institute of Health to the tune of $3 billion, press releases would announce a "major breakthrough" every few months across the thirty or so years of the study's lifespan. There were findings related to genetic causes and psychiatric diseases, but these have never been replicated. (This is an important scientific measure. If research findings cannot be reproduced using the same methods, results are considered unreliable.)

Part of the initiative was targeting schizophrenia, a spectrum disorder categorized by diminished emotional expression, disorganized speech, delusions or hallucinations, and a disturbance in levels of overall functioning.[29] Despite decades of research, the billions spent on genetic research by the National

Institute of Mental Health found nearly nothing to help clinicians treat schizophrenia. While some genes were linked with schizophrenia, no causation was found. As Torrey points out, some "risk" genes "make it more likely that the person will get the disease, they can also be protective and thus make it less likely that a person would get the disease." Do you find this as confusing as we do?

Dr. Lanphear built on this irony of federal regulatory agencies and charitable organizations both claiming to do "the right thing." The CDC states clearly that smoking causes cancer, diabetes, stroke, and heart and lung disease.[30] The cause is known. Yet, the AHA reports they have funded more than $5.7 billion in research since 1949, *searching for the cure.*[31] While we are prevention advocates, we, of course, know how crucial effective treatments are. Prevention becomes a moot point when cancer, ALS, dementia, and other conditions are diagnosed after years of possible exposure to toxins.

Will lost his father, an Eastern European refugee, lifelong smoker, and drinker, at too young an age. It was called cancer. Will's mother is a breast cancer survivor who, we are happy to say, is cancer free today, due to the availability of effective treatments. Her sister did not survive the horrible disease. Neither knew the cause of the cancer. Between the interplay of genes (*nature*) and the environment or upbringing (*nurture*), we wonder why more funding isn't allocated to prevention.

The AHA is just one of the many nongovernmental organizations raising countless research dollars to address treating and curing cardiovascular diseases related to smoking. Of course, we don't wish for any premature death and acknowledge all adults have the right to live their lives as they see fit. That said, we'd need another chapter to evidence the paradox here when examining where the majority of funding is allocated. Let's add the American Cancer Society (ACS), another leader in cancer research, that invested $145 million for cancer research in 2022 alone. What specifically does the ACS study? The following is from their website (italics are ours):

> What does it take to *outsmart cancer*? Research. The American Cancer Society has helped make possible *almost every major cancer breakthrough* since 1946. Since then, we've invested more than $5 billion in cancer research, making us the largest nonprofit funder of cancer research in the US, outside of the federal government. We remain committed to finding more—and better—*ways to improve the quality of life for cancer patients*.[32]

While part of the funding for these organizations stems from tax dollars, much of it comes from personal and corporate donations, often from friends and family of those affected by the horrible disease, and those who have seen the devastating outcomes of toxic exposures. The AHA and ACS combined have put more than 10 billion dollars toward cardiovascular disease and cancer research over the last seven decades, yet by their own admission their focus is on treatment and cures. While environmental and genetic factors are at play related to the causes of disease, we find it hard to accept that the elimination of known causes isn't a primary agenda of these highly successful fundraising organizations. Where have we gone so wrong in that we can easily identify some causes, yet fail so miserably by not investing in prevention?

We find other confusing examples, such as the American Diabetes Association (ADA) being funded by chocolate and soft drink manufacturer Cadbury Schweppes, especially when the ADA states that 100% of their donations are "directed to research" with the goal "to support innovative scientific discovery that will translate to life-changing treatments and eventual cures."[33] Let that sink in. Research for treatment and cures for diabetes are funded by corporations that produce ultra-processed snack foods and soft drinks?

We know nutrition affects child and youth health. We could have included an entire chapter on food alone, but the bottom line is that adults simply need to be critical and mindful of what kids are eating.

Coca-Cola was busted for its activities a decade ago for funding academic researchers to divert attention away from its products; they wanted obesity and diabetes to be blamed solely on lack of exercise. Numerous analyses of Coke's "research" activities between 2008 and 2016 revealed they funded 907 authors to publish 398 articles in 169 journals. And these are just the articles that acknowledged Coca-Cola's funding. Researchers investigating Coca-Cola's transparency found the corporation itself only acknowledged funding 42 authors (less than 5%) and that most papers "disregard the role of diet in obesity."[34] Serious interference.

Former BBC producer Margaret Heffernan explored the reasons why people tend to ignore obvious dangers at their own peril in her aptly titled book, *Willful Blindness*.[35] She wrote, "The biggest threats ... we face often aren't secret or hidden, they're the ones we choose to overlook." Profit, prestige, ignorance, perceived psychological safety, conformity, information overload, and fear of retaliation are but some possible reasons limiting our capacity to make change. Yes, this is all shockingly obvious. We'll revisit these psychological and social barriers to change, the *intention-behavior gap*, in chapter 10, where we tackle how to confront facts, reduce fears, and make meaningful change, but first, we'll revisit the legacy of one particular toxin, one significant to Dr. Bruce Lanphear's impactful career and used in everyday household products. Lead is a good example of how removing a developmental neurotoxicant can spur decades of improved health benefits, though its impact still lingers invisibly in many of us.

Lead's Legacy

Lead exposure has been convincingly associated with crime rates and youth violence. It is now well-evidenced that lead from fuels, paints, and other products is connected to these behavioral issues[36] as well being associated with lowered IQ and other negative health outcomes.[37] Dr. Lanphear described to us the decades-long latency period of effects, from the time of lead being banned in the mid-1980s in North America to the peak of crime and violent behavior in 1994–95. Yes, specific dates have been evidenced.

This was the same time newly elected Mayor of New York City Rudy Giuliani promised to "clean up the streets" of excessive crime. From the 1960s through to the mid-1990s, many New Yorkers felt they lived in a war zone. Crime rates were through the roof, and New York gained a reputation as a dangerous city with graffiti-covered subway cars and plenty of broken windows. The new mayor hired a no-nonsense police chief and took actions to support his promise of being tough on crime, but lead appeared to play an equal, and maybe more important role in this story than his aspirations and actions.

Crime rates plummeted in the mid-1990s. Studies of lead's role in violence, crime, and behavioral problems even dispel the idea that there is more crime in bigger cities. The city size–crime correlation has been reconsidered; crime rates don't seem to differ when controlled for population.[38, 39] Larger cities had more cars burning leaded gasoline in closer proximity before the US Environmental Protection Agency commenced working to reduce lead emissions in the 1970s–80s and the introduction of catalytic converters and cleaner car emissions.[40] The cause was removed. Disruptive behaviors diminished. Health outcomes improved.

"When adjusted for age, dementia peaked over the last decade and now its occurrence is starting to decline," Lanphear said, "and that is consistent with widespread lead exposure over the past two generations with a long latency period." Overall, however, the number of cases of dementia is increasing because of the aging baby boomer population. It is the *proportion* of people with dementia that is going down. While this is promising news, we know these trends will sadly result in more than 9 million Americans with dementia by 2030.[41]

This may suggest a longer latency period for a poison like lead, but a decline in dementia and other neurological issues is predicted. This is exciting news; anyone who has experienced the impacts of dementia or Alzheimer's disease knows how challenging and devastating the disease is—for all involved.

Research proving long-term harm, like in this story of lead, should be seen as victories, but evidence of harm has not always been enough to trigger our governmental regulatory bodies to act. We experienced this directly, on a very small scale, with our publications focused on the systematic harm of youth in the US's *troubled teen industry*.[42] We provided the evidence to demonstrate the harm caused by these systematically problematic practices—delivered and advocated for by licensed mental health professionals. Not only did the practices continue, but we were asked to stop pointing them out by researchers and clinicians involved in the industry. The industry, we know, was also funding research, but it was not always disclosed publicly.

Whether the blame lies with the government or the public's willful blindness or a lack of morals in the corporate sector, confrontation may be a necessary step to initiate change—not through violence or radical disruptions, but through transparency and education. Public education campaigns for change are often needed to get harmful chemicals and products banned, controlled, or at least to have warning labels applied, such as with the smoking example above. The legacy of lead poisoning is not common knowledge, but thankfully, lead exposure and related illnesses are expected to continue to decline over time in North America—although they remain stubbornly high in industrializing countries. And there are *many* others to worry about.

For now, we'll shift our attention to one of the examples of a contemporary invisible and predatory toxin. The Merriam-Webster dictionary defines *predatory* as "anything that is inclined or intended to injure or exploit others for personal gain or profit." Humans evolved in close contact to many predatory animals—lions, tigers, and bears; today, we're surviving amongst many invisible toxic predators.

Atrazine: An Invisible Predator

Lists of environmental toxins are long. Most are dangerous individually, some worse in combinations, and others require interactions with our genetics to become real issues. They are not all unfamiliar sounding, and some are, or were, commonly thought of as safe at supposed "allowable limits"—asbestos, lead, arsenic, mercury, chlorine, fluoride, etc. Yet, we continue to purchase and use and eat products with other, lesser-known toxins in them. Fun fact: The European Union allows more than 300 additives (chemicals) to food.[43] The US allows more than 10,000![44] All have passed safety testing for "allowable limits," but there is an obvious discrepancy in what those limits are.

Atrazine is an example of where the concept of allowable limits remains significantly in question. You may have not heard of this toxic herbicide, but it is one of the most widely used globally, even though it was banned by seven European nations to protect their inhabitants from its dangers. Most other nations, like Canada and the US, where corn producers claim to rely on this product, have yet to bring the use of this poison to a halt.[45]

Atrazine can harm humans and other species. The evidence of harm is well-established. The *cause* is identified. Yet, the profit is too significant for the average farmer to speak out, to be the adult in the room. The global atrazine market, estimated by *Market Research Future*, is closing in on $2 billion annually and is anticipated to grow significantly in years to come.[46]

As with the example of tobacco above, the atrazine narrative presents another potent example of what Jewish chemist and Auschwitz survivor Primo Levi called the *functionaries*—the unquestioning common man—in this case, the people working for the corporations producing atrazine. Primo Levi considered the acts of the functionaries worse than dealing with monsters. Functionaries believe and act without asking questions. So, what's the fuss about atrazine?

Tyrone Hayes, professor of Integrative Biology and National Academy of Sciences Fellow at the University of California, Berkeley, built a compelling body of research on the topic of atrazine. This class of chemicals can interrupt, block, or mimic the proper functioning of the endocrine system in humans and other species, hence they are referred to as *endocrine disruptors*. Our endocrine system is important. It's responsible for growth, fertility, and reproduction; small hormonal disruptions can lead to significant developmental and biological disturbances. Atrazine exposure can lead to early puberty (which is happening today, especially with girls), reduced sperm counts (now common across the Western world), and disturbances to sexual development.[47] Long-term effects may include cancers, reproductive impairment, cognitive deficits, and obesity—all on the rise.

In 2002, Dr. Hayes's research received public attention.[48] After years of studying amphibians, Hayes found atrazine messed with frogs' reproductive systems, even at low levels of exposure. Agricultural runoff is where one would expect to find atrazine in the environment, and it certainly appears there, but it also appears in groundwater, surface water, and even in treated municipal drinking water in many places in North America (more so where atrazine is actively used). Dr. Hayes's previous sponsor and former atrazine manufacturer, Syngenta, one of the world's largest agribusinesses, was not impressed with his findings![49] For bringing attention to the harms of atrazine, Dr. Hayes was the recipient of a well-funded smear and intimidation campaign. Syngenta aggressively protected its best-selling product.

It wasn't just the frogs. Dr. Hayes discovered that endocrine disruption also occurred in other amphibians, fish, reptiles, and mammals.[50] Even low levels were found to have disastrous results. At .01 ppb (parts per billion, like a grain of sand in a sandbox), male frogs were showing signs of demasculinization (the degeneration of the testes) and hermaphroditism (developing both male and female reproductive organs). At 25 ppb (2,500 grains of sand in that same sandbox), male frogs had a tenfold decrease in testosterone, and partial or complete feminization of some species, ultimately impairing sexual development and reproductive ability. Atrazine interferes with the endocrine system by increasing the expression of the enzyme aromatase. Aromatase converts testosterone to estrogen.[51]

The literature clearly shows that this poison causes harm. The EPA in the US conducted a human health risk review on atrazine in 2018.[52] Their detailed review was based primarily on animal studies, a normal procedure in this type of research, and they very clearly outlined neuroendocrine disruptions and negative reproductive and developmental issues. What they didn't do was extrapolate those to human concerns. The EPA concluded, after reviewing *"all available scientific data,* including published toxicity and epidemiology literature," that atrazine poses "no risks of concern when evaluating all dietary exposure sources, including drinking water." Tyrone Hayes's research was absent from the review, although one sentence in the EPA's 212-page report, albeit without citing the researchers, mentioned reduced testosterone levels "in a number of studies in mammals, as well as other species." Atrazine should not be on the market. Europe is ahead of the US on this.

The CDC's 2003 Agency for Toxic Substances and Disease Registry report found atrazine to be "one of the most widely used herbicides in the United States."[53] Glyphosate, found in Bayer's (formerly Monsanto) Roundup, now holds the lead as the most used herbicide globally. This product has its own troubling history. Google "glyphosate" and come to your own conclusions.

In February 2023, Health Canada's Pest Management Regulatory Agency (PMRA), with knowledge of atrazine's endocrine disruption, carcinogenicity, and harms to aquatic species, reapproved its continued use, stating the "use of atrazine meets the requirements for the protection of human health and the environment."[54] This decision to continue its use was made based on evidence that atrazine levels found in Canadian drinking water and groundwater were lower than the allowable limits set by Health Canada. These allowable limits (.05 ppm), however, are *50 times higher* than allowable limits for drinking water in the European Union (.001 ppm, for *any* toxins), and 40% higher than US standards (.03 ppm)![55] In all of North America, drinking water limits for atrazine are higher than the low-level amounts that were found disrupting amphibians and other mammal's endocrine systems. We cannot ignore these findings and policy decisions if we are to protect the health of kids these days.

When the PMRA's study came out in 2023, Dr. Bruce Lanphear was cochair of their Science Advisory on Pest Control Products (SAC-PCP), formed to ensure government transparency. Bruce resigned after the regulatory agency blatantly ignored the PMRA's recommendations. Health Canada chose to restrict just one use of atrazine in Canada, and decided to add "environmental precaution statements"—basically, just labeling products like cigarette manufacturers were forced to. However, warning labels won't be seen on kitchen faucets or the rivers we play in, let alone food products exposed to atrazine. Buyer beware!

In the case of atrazine, the evidence is there, and top environmental health researchers and advocacy groups are speaking out against its use, yet change appears slow in North America, or not at all. Atrazine is another predator hiding in the shadows. Atrazine studies from Dr. Tyrone Hayes and others indicated significant risks to reproductive and hormonal health. But, even with twenty years of research literature available, public awareness lags behind. Human health warnings are listed on regulatory agency websites, yet few researchers are willing to engage in research agendas that will bring negative attention to themselves from formidable industries with interests to protect. In a review of corporate influence on researchers, scholars from the Faculty of Medicine and Health at the University of Sydney concluded that "corporate funding of research with commercial implications drives the research agenda away from public health priorities."[56]

The reader may question why a book focused on the well-being and mental health of youth is discussing endocrine disrupters such as atrazine. We learned from Dr. Bruce Lanphear that if we're going to take mental health rates seriously, we must examine the environment much more closely. We found a 2022 study in *Frontiers of Endocrinology* that detailed the increased levels of antidepressant chemicals running off from wastewater into our freshwater streams, and ultimately back into our drinking water. Similar to the work from Hayes, the researchers found endocrine disruption in fish due to antidepressants found in the runoff. They concluded that "early-life exposure to these compounds has the potential to alter the developmental programming of the endocrine system."

So, we are left wondering, how are these toxins affecting kids these days, especially when we're medicating them more than ever? Is atrazine, like lead or BPA (primarily used in the lining of various plastics), impacting the development of children and youth? What trends do we notice in the hormonal and reproductive health of young adults? Why has male sperm count dropped 56% in Western countries since the 1970s?[57] Why are teens and young adults engaging in less and less sex? Is it the phones or social media? Is it the environment? Is it our sociopolitical climate? Why are we seeing more and more youth struggling with their identity? Could atrazine and other endocrine disruptors play a part in the struggles young people face today? We can't be positive, but it seems likely. Why have some nations banned substances to protect their populations while others resist doing so?

Scouting a Path Ahead

Days without cloud cover are usually brighter. Clouds are clearly implicated in blocking the sun and reducing the air temperature. This is a *causal* relationship, and one simple enough that it is unlikely to be contested. But a scientist going deeper into it might ask questions about seasonality, prevailing winds, and other weather phenomena that could be involved. These factors are sometimes called *third variables*. They provide clues for drawing conclusions about how one factor influences another. Looking even more closely at the sun/cloud effect, the researcher might also ask what clothes we were wearing when we reported on the weather, what our body composition and general health conditions are, and a variety of other, maybe not-so-obvious questions to better understand the relationships between variables. Proving absolute causal relationships is hard. There are many wicked problems that cannot be reduced to causal variables. While scientists will continue trying, the good ones are aware of how difficult the challenge is.

As we wrote this book, this chapter kept creeping toward the front. Originally, we just thought it interesting and thought-provoking, but in talking to Bruce and reading the research, it emerged that important environmental variables were missing from attempts to find causation about kids these days. As we explore in the following chapter, discussions about mental health are everywhere, and the prevalence of mental health diagnoses is growing exponentially, but we find only a few mainstream voices asking, "What are we *not* talking about that we need to?"

Parents, teachers, and those of us who are engaged in young people's lives are offered insights into possible causes of harm, so we may have some control over the environments we work, live, and raise kids in. As outdoor educators, we know well to be prepared for a wide range of environmental conditions and how to best help young people learn to care for themselves in those challenging spaces. Stashing a rain jacket near the top of your backpack and paying attention to when it should be put on is maybe the most obvious example. One has to learn to keep the body dry and warm and reduce the likelihood of hypothermia in conditions where it may be difficult to warm up again once the body's temperature drops. This is prevention and preparedness.

Although Bruce tells parents to be cautious, many of the toxic predators, only some of which were mentioned in this chapter, remain unseen, increasing the challenge of minimizing exposure. It's a difficult message to hear when lead, mercury, atrazine, and other toxins are showing up in the blood of most children in the US.

"You can only do so much as a parent, but you have to figure out how to deal with all these harmful toxins and addictions," Bruce advised.

Whether a young person is getting too much exposure, be it microplastics, pesticides, heavy metals, TV, gaming, social media, porn, or drugs ... parents should be aware of the harms and do what they can to mitigate them. (Regarding heavy metal, however, we'd like to point out that countries with more metal bands do experience increased happiness scores![58] Does heavy metal music cause happiness or does happiness cause heavy metal? Claiming causation is hard.) Adults in the lives of kids these days need to step up as guardians of our children's health because our governments and regulatory authorities are dropping the ball.

The corporate profit motive is stronger than the demand to protect human health. Bruce shared this cost-benefit narrative in his "Crime of the Century" lecture at John Hopkins University in 2016.[59] Well worth the watch.

Lead exposure and harmful consequences were truly preventable. Lead was a well-known neurotoxin long before it was broadly dispersed into the evironment. Then, it became responsible for immense wealth at the expense of public health. Further, lead has been identified as the major risk factor for incarceration in the past half century, a fact mostly unknown by the public. It is clear that health research needs to shift from its current focus on potential cures for what is *in us* (genetics) to what is in the *environment* (the destructive causes) and how those two factors collide. Dr. Lanphear closed his "Crime of the Century" lecture with a few chilling statements. He told us that toxins are released into the public sphere often without adequate research on children, pregnant women, or the general population. And, since the children are most vulnerable, they are, in essence, used as "biological indicators" of how these toxins interact with human beings—just as canaries were formerly used in the coal mines.

This is not a "wait for the politicians to make change" scenario. No more willful blindness. We know toxins affect human health and well-being. Primo Levi warned us we cannot trust the functionaries, those who benefit from manufacturing, selling, and approving these poisons. Many working in these large systems of food, pharma, technology, and education believe in what they do and may not realize their role as functionaries. Or they may have been so spoiled by profits and corporate interests with a legacy of harm to human health that they carry on. Either way, they maintain the status quo.

Clearly, the way forward requires being vigilant and speaking out, together, for our children's sake.

PART II

INTERVENTION

5

IDENTITY POLITICS

If you begin to understand what you are
without trying to change it, then what you are
undergoes a transformation.
—J. Krishnamurti

"I'm borderline," declared Sarah, the 17-year-old high school student referred to therapy due to her parents' concerns about her social anxiety.

Borderline personality disorder (BPD) is typically diagnosed when a person experiences some or all of the following: abandonment, unstable relationships, an insecure sense of self, impulsivity and self-damaging behavior, suicidal behavior and self-harm, intense anxiety, feelings of emptiness, inappropriate anger, and/or paranoia. While the DSM initially rejected BPD as a condition worthy of inclusion alongside ADHD, bipolar disorder, and generalized anxiety, advocates, such as neuropsychiatrist Roy R. Grinker Sr., strong-armed the professional associations and third-party payers to acknowledge the diagnosis in the 1970s.[1] The most common justification for its inclusion was that the diagnosis would help clinicians to provide effective treatment—but many advocates are working toward eliminating such broad labels, especially with youth.[2] A diagnosis of BPD is a slippery slope, pushing a young person toward increased intervention and pharmaceutical treatment, as we'll describe throughout this chapter.

If we surveyed one hundred therapists about the best treatment for BPD, the majority would suggest *dialectical behavioral therapy*, which focuses on helping people accept and then change behaviors and emotions. People labeled as borderline are described as unusually resistant to traditional talk therapy approaches, and interventions, including medication, often lead to markedly negative results. So, psychotherapy is still a good option. Still, most people with the borderline label are prescribed a cocktail of pharmaceuticals, though we have limited research on their effectiveness or safety.

A recent large study in Sweden reviewed the data from 22,601 patients diagnosed with BPD over 16 years.[3] Only stimulants typically used for ADHD decreased the risk of suicidal behavior (these medications can reduce impulsivity). Antidepressants, mood stabilizers, benzodiazepines, and antipsychotics did not. Moreover, those given benzodiazepines such as Valium or Xanax (designed to slow brain activity) experienced a significant increase in suicidal ideation.

It gets worse.

Many therapy providers refuse to work with people diagnosed as borderline. They describe these patients as frustrating, manipulative, and oppositional to treatment plans; practitioners often just find these patients annoying, as do most people in these patients' social circle.

Sarah was not benefiting from therapy. But really, she hardly exhibited anything warranting a borderline diagnosis. Raised in a suburban town in a middle-class community, Sarah was a good student and maintained a good standing among her peers. She played soccer on the weekends, liked art, and became a vegetarian—fitting for her passion for animal rights. Sarah spoke of these things during her therapy sessions but also described an ongoing battle with social anxiety. She self-harmed with a razor, making small cuts on her thighs and upper arms where no one could see them. She had no desire to end her life but struggled immensely to regulate her emotional state when she felt distressed or anxious.

Most self-harm remains hidden from society. One recent study reviewed the global prevalence of self-harm from 2010 to 2021.[4] Sixty-two studies were included in the review. Researchers found that self-injury is becoming increasingly prevalent. They also found that today's adolescents are more likely to self-harm without suicidal intent. It is hard to understand what really drives self-harming behavior; it's context dependent.

In our clinical work, we find it helpful to view certain behaviors as clues to the way people are attempting to solve their problems—notwithstanding the positive or negative consequences. Many adults enjoy a beer after a hard day of work, smoking a cigarette on a work break, or indulging in substance use a bit more than necessary on the weekends. It can feel like lifting the lid off a pressure cooker. This is a sentiment many teenagers describe when discussing their self-harming habits. It's self-regulation and self-medicating to lift the lid off of whatever pressure it is they are so acutely feeling. It's adaptive self-protecting behavior, whether conscious or not. It can serve many roles. Physical sensations of self-harm may provide comfort to a youth coping with big emotions or provide a sense of control over their body. Those struggling with their self-worth may feel the urge to punish themselves or express anger inward. For others, it is a call for help.

Whatever the form of self-harm, whether it be cutting, burning, hitting, scratching, or excessive rubbing, adults engaged with these youth must remain present. No matter how difficult, we should resist pathologizing and medicalizing low-risk behaviors, especially because we know adolescents these days are using them more frequently for self-regulation, as Sarah was doing. However, we also know that, in general, adolescents who struggle to self-regulate their emotional states have a higher likelihood of getting involved in other high-risk behaviors, such as hard drug use or risky sexual activity, or exhibiting more extreme behaviors.[5] These are statistical relationships, though—correlations, not absolute truths. We need to resist labeling or diagnosing what may also just be normal adventurous adolescent exploration in their search for identity.

In the session with Sarah, Will reached for the bookshelf and handed her *Cognitive-Behavioral Treatment of Borderline Personality Disorder: Diagnosis and Treatment of Mental Disorders*. The dense book, written by the BPD treatment creator Dr. Marsha Linehan, describes borderline as the most challenging condition for the average clinician to treat. Will showed Sarah the diagnostic criteria. While she acknowledged having hardly any of the conditions to warrant such a label, she remained reticent to consider letting it go.

"I don't know," Sarah proclaimed. "My Instagram account is dedicated to my diagnosis." *Her* diagnosis—not a professional's.

She sought Will's affirmation of the diagnosis.

For years, Sarah maintained a social media account (hidden from her parents) dedicated to her depression, which then evolved to focus on her anxiety, then her self-harming, and most recently, her self-assigned BPD. She showed Will the online and public pictures of her self-inflicted scars and videos detailing the everyday struggle of living with one self-identified label after another. Followers flocked to the account, leaving comments telling Sarah to "stay strong" and other words of encouragement.

During the counseling session, Sarah acknowledged not wanting to lose the social network—the social network and peer orientation keeping her sick. The self-label and connection to people she only knew through a tiny screen provided acknowledgment and validation for Sarah's lived experience; social media offered superficial attachments alongside a neurological drug to the brain through tiny bursts of the human feel-good chemicals, such as dopamine. For someone feeling lost and out of place, this can feel significant. But these wildly inaccurate and ever-changing labels were not truly helping Sarah. Despite her parents' attempts to seek professional help, Sarah's online activity was giving her exactly what she wanted—but not what she needed. She was starving for social connection and support, and she was gorging on social media to get it. This is digital interference.

Sarah's social media experience isn't unique. Rebecca Johnson, a senior correspondent from *Vox*, a US news and entertainment website, first downloaded TikTok in 2018.[6] Within days, the algorithms found Rebecca to be someone with ADHD, and an influx of new videos came to her stream with seductive titles: "Hidden Signs You're ADHD" and "What My ADHD Brain Feels Like." As Rebecca engaged with the content, she realized that if we "consume too much of the mental health internet ... it becomes difficult to understand what anyone is saying." Between mixed messages, vague descriptions of mental disorders, or distortions of concrete concepts, navigating the maze of mental health terminology and labels is a challenge for even the most seasoned clinician. Now, Rebecca describes social media as "WebMD for mental health."

Anyone who has taken a course in psychology, even at the high school level, should have experienced a teacher's warning about internalizing the subject matter. It is an odd phenomenon, but when we read the symptoms of a mental disorder through our own lens and lived experience, we can suddenly feel we suffer from that disorder, be it ADHD, OCD, or depression. Teachers warn students to avoid what social media was encouraging Sarah to do, and what Rebecca Johnson warns against: Internalizing mental health labels to one's identity.

In this chapter, we examine labeling and self-diagnosing in relation to mental health and youth development. Another factor in this wicked problem. Our concern here is chiefly that adults are categorizing, medicalizing, and in many ways limiting the experiences of kids today more than ever before. This is *othering*—treating someone or a certain group as different from ourselves. This labeling mania can interfere with identity formation and make addressing serious mental disorders more difficult. If numerous students in a classroom are hastily labeled depressed, anxious, or attention-deficit, how do we identify and help those really struggling?

And You Are?

While the body undergoes its most drastic changes in the first years of life, the adolescent brain also evolves rapidly. To become faster and smarter, the brain facilitates a massive *synaptic pruning*,[7] shedding neurons and connectors deemed unnecessary. Teenagers can lose 15–20% of these synaptic connections—like emptying the trash can on your computer and clearing out inconsequential information. However, some of the brain's useful bits get dumped as well. In the pruning process, teenagers become more forgetful and disorganized. Communication often deteriorates into one-word responses.

"How was school today?" you ask.

"Fine."

Sometimes, you're lucky to get a coherent word like this in response as opposed to a short grunt, or that contemptuous look.

During these years, teenagers become increasingly insecure, and adults can help by understanding that this is a natural developmental process. If we kept in mind that the journey toward the most efficient brain comes with just a few years of challenging teenage behavior, we'd all be more tolerant. But here's the tricky part: As the brain is changing, identity is being formed simultaneously. Developmental psychologist Erik Erikson, who coined the phrase *identity crisis*, argued that the sole purpose of adolescence is identity *formation*. The blueprint for growth and identity formation is there, but if the settings aren't right for young people to form a secure view of where they fit in the world, through interacting with their environments, taking risks, and developing connections, they experience role confusion.

If youth do not experience secure adult relationships, they will attach elsewhere. It's the *Lord of the Flies* effect. And they may follow the path of least resistance. Substance-using groups often have a low bar of entry for connection—everyone is welcome—as does social media, and even gang involvement. In this time of synaptic pruning, teenagers have a small window of time where teenage beliefs can become irrational, especially surrounding their identity.

Adults are important here. Their purpose in these times is to provide a safe-enough place for big questions and challenging emotions and to test assumptions. Asking insightful and provocative questions can help teenagers juggle new ideas about who they are and what they can contribute. We want teens to try on different identities to explore their emotional and psychological world. This helps to develop a sense of self-concept (who we are in the world). If we center interventions on specific identifying labels, they risk becoming entrenched in the adolescent's identity. No longer is it something they experience or part of their developmental adventure, it's who they are!

The exploration to simply understand who we are, as Krishnamurti reminds us, allows for the transformation of mind—hence, growing up and into who we will be as adults. It's important to learn who we are well before intervening and trying to change it. As Gordon Neufeld will explain more thoroughly in the following chapter, an adult orientation is critical in these teen years for the healthy development of values and beliefs. While we should provide more opportunities for unstructured and unsupervised play, youth should not be left to teenage peers or social media to help sort out their identity. This is *not* the work of adults who don't have a close relationship with the developing young person. Parenting, and being an older, wiser presence in a child's life is a responsibility with gravity, to be undertaken with the child's best interests and care in mind. This is an area where we have witnessed conflicts between parents and *systems* (schools, child protective services, etc.) when labels are used to describe, define, and influence a child—often in unproductive or unhealthy ways.

Relevant to the topic of self-labeling and self-diagnosis, we are witnessing self-identifying becoming part of everyday conversation. Consider a 2024 study in which 72% of female and 67% of male 12- to 27-year-olds reported: "Mental health challenges are an important part of my identity."[8] This was significantly higher than other age groups, such as boomers who scored around 30%. Clearly, there is a cultural shift in the West to adopt mental health labels and use them to inform our identity. Some may argue the statistics represent increased awareness, improved access, and reduction of stigma, or that they help us to embrace human diversity. We aren't so convinced.

Redefining Normal

Take, for instance, the popular new term thrown around in schools, university campuses, social media, and workplaces: *neurodiversity*. Originally introduced in a sociology honors thesis from the University of Technology Sydney in 1998 by Australian sociologist Judy Singer,[9] the term was meant to convey a "biological truism that refers to the limitless variability of human nervous systems on the planet, in which no two can ever be exactly alike due to the influence of environmental factors."[10] Singer hoped the term would spur a movement for people on the autism spectrum akin to what women's suffrage and gay/lesbian activists accomplished. But the term *neurodiversity* became a label to differentiate and "other" certain groups of people. Not the intended goal.

Neurodiversity was never a diagnosis. Your adolescent can't suffer from a bad case of neurodiversity. Similarly, one human is no more neurodiverse than another. If a person is labeled as autistic, they may wish to be referred to as autistic, or possibly neurodivergent, but this does not make them any more neurodiverse than anyone else. According to Singer, terms such as neurotypical, normal, or natural have no place in discussions about neurodiversity. Two people make any setting neurodiverse. One can see how an important sociological understanding of our diversity quickly turned to ideology. A concept used to bring everyone together in learning and workplaces became a term to describe who is typical, or normal, and who is not.

From forming a binary of either neurodiverse or neurotypical (as if each individual is *not* neurologically diverse) to the oversimplification and categorization of mental illness and gender, educators, therapists, policymakers, and politicians are now asserting identity formation *onto* children and adolescents, whereas the process for millennia has been about kids observing, exploring, adventuring, and mimicking, and then finding and developing their identity for themselves. And they've been doing it in relationship with family, caring adults, peers, and community members.

Constructing an identity is a process, a developmental adventure, no different from the process of the infant learning to crawl, and subsequently, walk. Identity cannot simply be prescribed, diagnosed, or self-proclaimed. During childhood and adolescence, it is imperative that parents and other caring adults protect their children from labeling, whether the source is other adults or via self-labeling. (We'll provide some techniques for this further on in this chapter.) Recent evidence supports this assertion. One area of concern is that the youngest students in classrooms are the most likely to receive diagnoses, such as ADHD, indicating the potential for a youth's immaturity to be mislabeled as disordered, often with a pharmacological intervention unnecessarily prescribed.[11]

A recent study in the *Journal of Health and Social Behavior* explored self-labeling and self-diagnosis. The research illustrates the harmful impacts of labeling on the young developing mind.[12] The self-labeling phenomena grew as the general public adopted psychiatric language in everyday use, learned the names of all the common mental disorders, and used this language to articulate their own distress, often erroneously.

"I'm so OCD."

"I'm depressed."

Here's our concern:

Researchers from the University of California-Riverside's Department of Sociology collected data from 427 sixth-grade students over two years. The team provided students with a self-esteem measure and asked if they described themselves as *having a mental illness*. A mental health checklist was used to explore how symptoms varied during the two years of the study.

The findings were intriguing. The authors found self-labeling did not lead to increased self-esteem. Self-labeling did not help. It was destructive. The researchers found that it is when a child *begins* self-labeling that they are most vulnerable to *internalizing* the label. This was possibly what was happening when Sarah created her secret Instagram account. Though the labels and mental health terminology changed over time, it was her demonstrations of being sick and hopeless that her followers flocked to. Self-diagnosis, in general, appears to have surged in part due to increased and unsupervised social media use.

Additionally, we are currently witnessing rapid increases in self-identifying in the realm of gender identity, which can lead to life-altering consequences. We approach this topic with care and compassion, especially as this divisive and contentious topic is difficult to convey in writing. We encourage you to follow the literature and the evidence we cite and to trust our best intentions when discussing how we can protect kids from unneeded intervention and possible harm.

The Risk of Medicalizing Lived Experience

Data from the US Behavioral Risk Factor Surveillance System (BRFSS) were analyzed by researchers at UCLA's Williams Institute in the School of Law to better understand rates and changes in the occurrence of gender self-identification.[13] They found the number of adults identifying as transgender remained quite stable over the previous decades, while 13- to 17-year-olds are today significantly more likely to identify as transgender. In 2022, youth and young adults (13 to 24 years of age) identifying as transgender made up 2.74% of the US population; those 25 or older made up 0.77%.

Of course, a slight increase in these rates could occur from increased awareness and reductions in stigma that allow people to freely express themselves; the same factors may account for increased autism and ADHD diagnosis rates. However, we must also consider how the expression of self and identity can lead to harmful and dangerous interventions.

In July 2024, *New York Times* columnist Pamela Paul consolidated the evidence about this recent phenomenon and the associated medicalized interventions likely to follow.[14]. She wrote: "Imagine a comprehensive review of research on a treatment found 'remarkably weak evidence' that it was effective. Now imagine the medical establishment shrugged off the conclusions and continued providing the same unproven and life-altering treatment to its young patients." She asked this hypothetical question after reading accounts of recent gender-affirming interventions.

In March 2024, hundreds of messages were leaked from the World Professional Association for Transgender Health (WPATH) to Environmental Progress, the independent not-for-profit organization with "the mission of achieving nature, peace and prosperity for all."[15] Dubbed "The WPATH Files," the leaked messages revealed that there was virtually no evidence base for the medicalized care and intervention of transgender children, otherwise known as *gender-affirming care*.[16] Environmental Progress published a 241-page report on the leaked messages. It was revealed that doctors acknowledged that children are too young to comprehend the consequences puberty blockers and hormones could have on their future. They also said that hormone interventions could result in serious health problems, such as sterility or cancer. The report shared examples of harm, including one 16-year-old transitioner who developed large tumors on their liver after receiving a year's worth of hormonal medications to suppress menstruation, along with testosterone.[17]

We found this troubling since puberty-blocking hormones (gonadotropin-releasing hormone, or GnRH), according to the Cleveland Clinic, were being used for adult prostate cancer treatment and occasionally in extreme cases of early puberty.[18] Research on how these chemicals interfere with normal child development remains scarce, yet common side effects, such as erectile dysfunction, decreased libido, and fatigue, are well known. Research also suggests long-term use correlates with reduced bone density (osteoporosis) and metabolic abnormalities.[19]

What became clear from the WPATH Files was how adults and trained medical professionals failed to protect youth from medical experimentation. Some youth reported the inability to orgasm after early use of puberty blockers. Others experienced pain during intercourse, and some will live the remainder of their lives with surgical damage to their reproductive systems. The Files uncovered surgeons conducting procedures for some patients to live with both sets of genitals (i.e., phallus-preserving vaginoplasty), double mastectomies, removal of the nipples, and a rare procedure called "nullification," in which the genitals are removed and people are left with only smooth skin.

In October 2024, *The New York Times* uncovered how National Institute of Health-funded research about the negative impacts of puberty blockers was going purposefully unpublished. They reported that the lead researcher said, "that the drugs did not improve mental health in children with gender distress and that the finding might be weaponized by opponents of the cure"[20] and withheld making these findings public. The *Times* pointed out that the researcher in question was also the medical director of the nation's largest youth transgender clinic at the Children's Hospital in Los Angeles. This scenario illuminates how identity and politics can motivate individuals—those functionaries and their willful blindness—to limit the evidence of harming children to *protect the intervention*. The study's findings, funded by millions of US tax dollars, should be public knowledge for parents and youth, allowing them to make informed decisions about medical interventions.

Helen Joyce, former staff writer and editor for *The Economist* magazine, provided an in-depth analysis of transgenderism in her 2021 book, *Trans*, covering everything from historical events to the details of transition surgeries.[21] Helen took abuse from activists, while simultaneously receiving public praise for her work. *The Telegraph* endorsed and applauded the book stating, "A superlative critical analysis ... With this fact-filled, humane, and brave book, a grown-up has entered the room." Joyce's thorough writing included a review of the relevant research literature and the voices of proponents and critics of transgender activism and practices.

Joyce's review of the research suggests young people experiencing cross-sex feelings (now referred to as *gender dysphoria*, formerly *gender identity disorder*), if left to just feel those feelings and are compassionately supported by caring adults, often grow out of the dysphoria. No social transition to another gender. No puberty blockers. No cross-sex hormone treatments. No surgical interventions. No medical experimentation. In school settings today, teachers are compelled to affirm self-identifying youth and provide resources for further support, usually in the form of gender-affirming care from counselors or doctors. This adult influence may, with good intentions (the virtue of being inclusive), redirect the adventure of child and adolescent identity development toward irreversible harm.

What stands now as a primary concern is that gender ideology, which suggests that gender and sex are socially constructed, sometimes conflated, and have fluid properties, is being taught in schools and communities to young children. Teachers and other professionals are encouraging and affirming self-identification, and are likely to influence, if not promote, earlier transitions. As social scientists, we understand the notion of gender *roles* being described as socially constructed. However, when social constructions lead to medical intervention, we have a problem. When ideas are treated as objective realities or natural law, harm is likely to follow. Many parents and youth remain unaware of the known harms of using puberty blockers and cross-sex hormones, let alone the dangers of surgical interventions. Helen Joyce reported that many parents are told social transition and puberty blockers are easily reversed, yet physicians suggest they are elements of a "cascade of interventions." Surprisingly, many teachers we speak to are not aware of the relationship between their in-school support of social transition (the affirmation of a child or youth's self-identification of gender) and the next two levels of intervention: chemical and surgical.

Another recent study tracked 317 young people's (208 transgender girls, 109 transgender boys) gender identity over five years. [22] These youth had already socially transitioned (identifying as other than their sex at birth, pronoun and name change, often clothing and hairstyle change), yet the *average* age at the start of the study was just over *eight years old!* This suggests earlier social transition and actions had been taken, primarily the use of pharmaceuticals. By the end of the study, 32.3% of these youth had begun gender-affirming hormones and had moved through and beyond the initial phase of social transition.

Living in times of increased rates of self-labeling and mental disorder diagnoses, we must consider broader moral, social, ethical, and developmental implications of how these labels may impact children and adolescents. Again, we're talking about kids here, not adults. Of course, adults, if not harming anyone else, should do whatever they wish, but youth are being left unprotected from harm by chemical and surgical intervention.

There has been a link found between the intensity of gender dysphoria in children and the persistence of gender dysphoria in teens. [23] In more practical terms, children exposed too early to concepts of sexual orientation and gender fluidity, and when invited and encouraged to self-identify, are simply more likely to struggle with sexuality in the hormonal teen years. So, maybe Drag Queen Storytime, which according to Wikipedia is "geared for children 3–11" to "capture the imagination and play of gender fluidity of childhood," despite good intentions, might simply complicate kids' lives.[24]

Child Protection: A Moral Obligation

Associate Professor Dr. Sophie Isobel, at the University of Sydney's Faculty of Medicine and Health, focused on the moral implications, accuracy, and the effects of psychological and medical treatments for diagnosed mental illnesses with a critical lens in the peer-reviewed journal *Children & Society*.[25] Dr. Isobel argued that because of children's dependence on families, caregivers, the education system, and the community or state, the "need to protect children can be considered a sanctioned obligation, a moral imperative and a population survival instinct." Like Dr. Martin Brokenleg's writing of the buffalo in chapter 2, children need to be able to rely on the adults and experts.

As a clinical researcher, Dr. Isobel also critiqued the numerous checklists of symptoms clinicians use to identify potential mental disorders. Although not claiming mental illnesses don't exist (although some cannot be proven scientifically given the absence of common biological indicators), she challenged tools used for mental health diagnoses, such as the use of the PHQ-9 (the rapid patient depression questionnaire developed by the marketing team for Zoloft we described in the introduction). The problem remains, however, a diagnosis is required to facilitate the intervention, the therapy, or psychopharmacological treatment, though the diagnosis is rarely predictive of a positive outcome. This isn't a new problem.

In 1961, the Hungarian-American psychiatrist Thomas Szasz published the classic text *The Myth of Mental Illness* raising concerns about mental health providers adopting language sounding similar to medicine while most conceptualizations of mental disorders are more akin to pseudoscience or astrology.[26] Szasz argued for the need to accept a scientific definition of disease that would identify "a pathological alteration of cells, tissues, and organs." Mental illness, based on this concept of science and illness, is not a disease, but a metaphor of human distress or differences likely to increase discrimination, institutionalization, and intervention.

Like Szasz, Dr. Isobel's primary concern is not only one of what constitutes good-enough science, but a moral one. She argues psychiatric diagnoses provide fabricated boundaries about what is behaviorally right and wrong. The labels can become criteria for morality in society—like homosexuality's label as disordered or how long a person should grieve the loss of a loved one before being prescribed antidepressants. Again, we are questioning the consequences of medicalizing these terms. Children and adolescents inherently rely on adults for safety, security, and protection; they now also require adults to protect them from socially defined mental disorders and the treatments that may follow, some of which may have harmful side effects and potentially lifelong consequences.

When we searched for "psychiatry" books on Amazon in November 2023, the search returned telling results. Of course, psychiatry's bible, the DSM, was at the top of the list. The second was a newly published book: *Psychiatry for Kids: A Fun Picture Book About Mental Health Illnesses and Developmental Disabilities for Children.*[27] Yes, this title, authored by three medical professionals, does sound like they're pulling our leg, but their work appears to belong to a series with similar titles such as *Plastic Surgery for Kids* and *Obstetrics & Gynecology for Kids.* The book says very little about what psychiatrists actually do. It focuses more on defining normal and abnormal. Come on.

Efforts to reduce stigma should be applauded, and teaching children that it is OK to ask for help does reinforce good coping skills. However, we ask at what cost does this come, with what ideas are we priming today's youth? The self-proclaimed "charming, easy-to-understand" book with "beautiful illustrations" teaches children about anorexia and bulimia, body dysmorphic disorder, depression, anxiety, OCD, and ADHD. Remember, when learning about mental health, every undergraduate student across the globe should be warned about the risk of internalizing or overthinking their own symptomatology. *Psychiatry for Kids* is troublesome because it introduces advanced concepts to developing and easily influenced minds that might not be ready for such big ideas.

Upon learning about the *Psychiatry for Kids* book, we asked ourselves whether it is a good thing for children to be indoctrinated to psychiatry. Wouldn't it just produce more ideology about the big feelings needing to be felt in childhood? (We pursue this focus on emotions further in the following chapter.) Shouldn't we first figure out if a young person could benefit from professional intervention before molding them with concepts far too complicated for the young mind to fully understand? Adults should protect children from this interference and the interventions promoted by these texts.

To foster a secure sense of self, youth require role models and connections with adults who they can imitate, look up to, and learn from. Regulated, secure adults listen as teenagers explore their goals, values, and their identity. They understand adolescence is a time for exploration, to dress and behave differently, to deviate and push back, to follow the fad of a new hairstyle, and to seek connection with peers. This doesn't mean affirming—a verb meaning *to declare the truth in something*—or the opposite, ignoring these behaviors. In our role as clinicians, our professional standards would never support us affirming a client with anorexia when they claim to be living at a healthy weight or a substance user stating their regular use of crystal meth is appropriate and safe. We don't argue with them either. We listen. We ask questions to hear more of the story. We aim for a *thick, not thin*, description of what they're experiencing to move beyond bland definitions and explanations of lived experience. Thick descriptions go beyond simple, surface-level explanations of behavior or human action to consider the context within culture, environment, and society. We want to learn about their life, not just how they classify themselves. Self-labels are typically an easy response for a young person. By asking what their descriptors mean, we learn who they really are and where these ideas came from. We connect.

Externalizing Lived Experience

Narrative therapist Alice Morgan used an example of thick descriptions when she offered her self-imposed label: "I am a good driver."[28] Some will take Alice at her word. However, if we asked for proof, Alice might self-select certain events, such as never having run a red light or declining to drive under the influence. Alice's self-reported history of competent driving stems from her own worldview and her preferences for how she wants to be seen. But fuller narratives are never clear of sociocultural influence and other people's perspectives.

"What about your partner?" we may ask. "What evidence would they provide about whether or not you're a good driver?"

"Well, they don't like to drive with me so much," Alice might respond. "They say my driving makes them anxious." This might leave Alice with a revised idea about her driving capabilities.

Driving is obviously a somewhat shallow example we've used to show how there is so much more to the stories we tell ourselves about who we are. There are also the stories of our friends and family members, and those from society. We need to pay attention to the stories and descriptions young people are creating for themselves. Caring adults in the lives of identity-forming adolescents should embrace the nuance of self-labeling and ask for more information to build a thicker description of who they are and who they are becoming.

"Oh yeah? Tell me more."

"Tell me if I'm hearing you right, you're saying that..."

"That's interesting. I would love to learn more about this."

"Are there times you aren't...?"

Lean into what youth are experiencing. How are they seeing the world and what does it all mean to them? Better yet, do it at the dinner table, during a walk, or while kicking a ball.

We wondered about Sarah. Even with no changes to her symptomology, had she been encouraged early to explore or even drop the self-label would her self-esteem have been more likely to improve? Increased self-esteem may have improved emotional regulation and protected Sarah from self-injury during times of distress. Improving one's self-esteem can, after all, lead to improvements in mental health, quality of relationships, school performance, and physical health.[29] It is the role of adults to learn enough about a child to be able to stick up for them when harmful interventions threaten. Only then can they stick up and protect youth from potential harm, as our next expert did throughout his productive career.

Sticking Up for the Underdog

"If you can believe this ... from the age of five," Simon said, "I felt the discrimination of people was unjust. All people should be treated equally."

Simon grew up embarrassed and ashamed by the discrimination he witnessed in his everyday life.

His parents, whom he referred to as liberal white South Africans, maintained Black servants of their own. While they didn't like apartheid, and they paid their servants more than others in their community, Simon recognized his parents still benefited from segregation. He described how he and others his age were more often connected to the maids than their own parents. But their maids still lived in sheds in the garden.

In 2011, Simon was invited to deliver a keynote presentation in Toronto about why he chose a career in child psychiatry. He opened the presentation for the Canadian and American Academies of Child and Adolescent Psychiatry by showing beautiful pictures of South Africa. First, Table Mountain in Cape Town, followed up with the amazing wildlife—the lions, elephants, and rhinos. The audience was captivated by the natural beauty and the wild environments Simon presented. They oohed and aahed, one photograph after the next.

Simon then showed a picture of a beach with a posted sign: *For Whites Only*, printed in both English and Afrikaans, the two mandatory languages in South Africa at the time. The scenic white sand beach with rugged mountains and large rocks in the distance was spoiled by racial segregation so brutal, horrible, and unjust even a 5-year-old could see it. To add insult to Simon's youth, he was conscripted into the South African Army to enforce apartheid on Black South Africans. It would be the hardest year of his life. He soon after departed for Canada, and has not returned to the country of his birth since the 1970s. The wildlife, Simon says, is the only thing he misses about South Africa.

Dr. Simon Davidson completed his doctoral residency in psychiatry at McMaster University in Ontario. He eventually became the regional chief of Specialized Psychiatry and Mental Health Services for Children and Youth at the Children's Hospital of Eastern Ontario and the Royal Ottawa Mental Health Centre. He is a past president of the Canadian Academy of Child and Adolescent Psychiatry and the former chair of the Child and Youth Advisory Committee for the Mental Health Commission of Canada. A prolific career!

Motivated by his upbringing in segregated South Africa, Simon pursued the world of child psychiatry to "stick up for the underdog." He knew the impacts a mental health label could have on a person's life.

"The minute a diagnosis is on a chart, the discrimination that occurs is profound," he said. For example, research suggests the stigma results in a lack of emergency room care for people labeled with a mental disorder.[30] "That's one part of the problem, but the more important part is *borderline personality disorder*," Simon said, "a diagnosis I refuse to make."

Dr. Davidson is not alone. In April of 2024, Sir Norman Lamb, the former health minister in the UK wrote an open letter titled, "Children Should Not Be Diagnosed with a Personality Disorder in the UK."[31] More than one thousand concerned professionals signed the letter, and support for the cause was given by the British Psychological Society, the Royal College of Nursing, and the Royal College of General Practitioners.

A BPD diagnosis can affect the level of care offered by the medical industry. Hospital staff may perceive patients attending the ER with BPD as high risk, high needs, and demanding more service when in fact this is only sometimes true. As a result, a mismatch of service is experienced by patients and carers. Even Dr. Marsha Linehan, the creator of the most-used therapy for BPD, is said to have urged people with a BPD diagnosis to *not* tell medical professionals about the label. Studies of emergency room visits highlight the complexity and comorbidity of this label, as well as the failure of community services and the likelihood that an ER visit will be crisis-driven, such as an acute psychotic episode related to substance abuse or self-harm.[32]

Nevin worked with a young man in residential care in the mid-1990s who would, on occasion, be admitted to the ER for episodic care. Well-known to the doctors and nurses in the small local hospital, the youth would be assessed, then often left in an examination room near an exit, unsupervised, with his clothes and shoes on the bedside table. It seemed like they were encouraging him to leave. With no one monitoring his movements, he would dress quickly, slip out of the ER, and return to his high-risk peers to self-medicate with any substance he could get his hands on and continue his dangerous lifestyle. The community service wasn't adequate. Many thought more intense psychiatric care was the only option to keep this young person safe. In the hospital environment, this young man was described as attention-seeking, a manipulative burden. He was treated as such. How we think about kids these days and their labels will influence how we behave as adults.

Dr. Davidson shared a story of working with a young woman, Stephanie, who was a patient at the Children's Hospital. Stephanie's hair was dyed a flaming red color and presented as extremely manic (this is usually defined as highly energized or abnormally elevated, though the condition can also come with extreme mood changes). Her father had recently been diagnosed with bipolar disorder. Stephanie's chart showed the same diagnosis. Stephanie and her father hated each other. She was upset about being placed in the same diagnostic category.

In her first meeting with Dr. Davidson, Stephanie plopped a pile of paperwork on his desk. All of it printed from her internet searches. Each sheet of paper contained information about why her bipolar diagnosis was wrong. Stephanie felt what she really had was BPD.

"Hey, hey, hey, hang on a minute here," Simon recalls saying, "You really don't want to have a borderline personality disorder. If you want to choose a disorder, don't choose that one! That's the worst in the world!"

Dr. Davidson's approach involved protecting Stephanie from not only a dangerous diagnosis but also the internet's conception of it. He wanted to help her understand who she was without labels to lean on. "As soon as any healthcare provider sees that diagnosis," he continued, "the discriminatory treatment of the person is intense. This self-diagnosis thing is one hell of a problem."

Labels become harmful when they become internalized into a young one's identity, as they did in Sarah's journey. Of course, there are times when a client has come to us with a diagnosis provided by another licensed professional. They may even experience a sense of relief that their distress can be labeled and understood. However, when labels are internalized—especially self-assigned labels—mental health interventions and efforts to alleviate distress can become more challenging.

"I *am* depressed."

"*I'm* anxious."

"It's *my* ADHD or autism."

"*I'm* neurodiverse. *You're* neurotypical."

These are broad examples, but consider what it means when a child says, "I'm a little depressed." While a person may say, "I am sick," when they have a virus, cold, or worse, the verbiage is seldom internalized like it is with mental health. A person overcoming an illness usually does not identify themselves with that condition as they go on with their life. For example, many of us had chickenpox as children but do not identify ourselves as "I am chickenpox." Nor do we say, "I am a little chickenpox."

Understanding the detrimental effects of self-labeling, many approaches to psychotherapy and counseling aim to help people *externalize* their problems, a concept introduced in family therapy in the 1980s. To sum up this approach, we like to say, "The person is not the problem, the problem is the problem." Although this may seem overly simplistic or like it's just semantics, externalizing can help people understand that their problems are not located within themselves. It's not the *kids these days*. Their problems are better understood as a product of their environment, culture, and history.

Externalizing Conversations

The late Australian social worker and family therapist Michael White was one of the leading contributors in creating *narrative therapy*, which focused on helping patients, young and old, to externalize their problems. We don't identify ourselves as narrative therapists per se, but we appreciate how narrative therapy scholars and practitioners have aimed their work at protecting their therapy clients from dominant labels becoming parasitically entrenched into their identity.

Humorously, Michael White explains his approach to externalizing people's problems with one of the most distressing—and potentially embarrassing—problems a parent or child can face: *fecal soiling* (aka pooping your pants). White wrote the foreword to the children's story *Beating Sneaky Poo.*[33]

The illustrated children's book tells the story of a child named Minky and his efforts to gain control over Sneaky Poo, a poop trying to sneak out of Minky's tummy and underwear. What the story makes clear is that the problem isn't the child. The problem is the problem. In this case, it's a sneaky poop. By externalizing problems away from one's identity, problems become clearer, and creative solutions may emerge. We just have to catch it when it's on the move. Many children experience immense shame when unable to control their toileting habits.

"I am a loser," they might say.

Accidents at school are embarrassing, and parents can grow frustrated when the parenting tips gleaned from books, experts, YouTube, or doctors don't produce the desired outcomes.

Externalizing the problem *away from the person* aims to, first, help people understand that their problems aren't associated with their inner self. It's best to avoid using the distress and problems people experience as adjectives to describe their worth or personhood.

One technique we may use is to change the adjectives. For example, when a young person says, "I am depressed!" as if the depression represents something about their character or worth, the therapist may ask, "How long has this depression been impacting you?" Depression doesn't describe the person. Depression is experienced.

Facilitating externalizing conversations helps to develop a story beyond labels. We acknowledge that these labels may, at times, help someone understand and normalize the problems they experience. However, we remain focused on the *outcome* of our work first. We consider:

"Who is this label for?"

"Who is it designed to help?"

"When will we know if this label is leading us toward a better outcome?"

Mental health diagnoses aren't the only labels youth encounter in their day-to-day lives. Kids these days are faced with more choices about who they are, who they want to be, who they want to be around, and how they identify themselves. These choices demand labels because they are being expressed in words, on the internet, or in job or school applications, etc. As a result, there has been a rise in compelled self-identification. We've seen it, particularly in the universities, but it's true in many aspects of modern lives. Preferential job hires, access to certain grants, and inclusion in special interest groups require declarations of which categories one fits into based primarily on gender, race, and disability. Instead of adolescence being about the construction of a secure sense of self, children at younger and younger ages are *asked* how they identify. The very essence of adolescence—the formation of identity—is blanketed by identity politics.

Most people won't find it surprising to see labeling embed itself given our current sociopolitical climate. For two decades, 24-hour news cycles have perpetuated the divide between who is right-wing and who is left-wing. Today, we argue with friends and family about whether mainstream or alternative media is more trustworthy, or which news outlet is driven by less identity politics, a term used when politicking becomes focused solely on issues pertaining to a person's identity. The labeling mania has moved beyond the counseling room and into our everyday lives and the educational system.

In a study geared to the understanding of the cultural and political nature of self-diagnosing, it was found that younger, more politically liberal youth were most likely to self-diagnose.[34] The researchers claimed this is due to "concept creep," where certain ideas broaden their meanings over time and offer new perspectives on mental illness, thus possibly leading to the increased prevalence of these labels. The researchers concluded, "Self-diagnosis in the narrow sense can foster help-seeking, but can also promote overdiagnosis, overutilization of services, and maladaptive coping and loss of perceived control over one's condition."

In April 2023, Emma Camp published a guest essay in *The New York Times* about the autism diagnosis she received at 20 years of age.[35] We reached out to Emma.

"It was a pretty classic case of the kid who doesn't have many friends until they get to college," Emma described to us. "I desperately wanted close friends—I'm a 99th percentile extrovert—but I tended to feel 'off' in most social environments. For some reason, I didn't quite fit in and I found it maddening."

Emma read about autism and thought it was the perfect fit. A clinician agreed. At first, the diagnosis gave Emma permission to accept her insecurities and quirkiness. Quickly, however, the diagnosis crystallized into Emma's self-concept. She no longer "had autism." She *was autistic.*

Social media didn't help. Mental health influencers "accelerated the integration of medical labels into identity," Emma wrote. Like Sarah, the algorithms found Emma. Not only did companies try to sell her everything from fidget toys to coloring books to weighted blankets, but her social media feeds—and the ubiquitous, gamified infinite scroll—became flooded with information targeted to a person with a diagnosed neurological and developmental disorder. Reading the comments on posts, Emma felt many therapists weren't taking the condition seriously, inspiring a rise in self-diagnosis. Emma saw identifying as autistic was becoming similar to publicly identifying oneself by gender identity, sexual orientation, race, or any other categorical label.

Emma began using "As an autistic person..." to start her sentences. It was becoming a way for her to assert authority into a conversation—or to dodge claims of wrongdoing. As identity politics mushroomed during the pandemic, Emma took note of how many people strained to collect as many identifying labels as possible. It became a means of positioning every conflict as between the oppressor and the oppressed—as if it were a competition. It's the same risk we see occurring with people using neuro*diverse* to mean neurological disability or otherness, positioning themselves against the neuro*typical* (whoever they are).

In her essay, Emma described how her mental health label was providing her self-worth and identity, similar to another person starting a sentence with: "As a [Insert Marginalized Group Identifier] person..." It did not compute, and Emma summed it up in her *New York Times* article nicely: "But mental health diagnoses, along with most other categories up for examination under our identity politics, are accidents of birth. To make them central features of our identities is to focus on the things we can't control ourselves—an approach that is ultimately disempowering."

Though the diagnosis seemed helpful at first, 20-year-old Emma wasn't disempowered. "The social difficulties that I had assumed were a permanent part of my life pretty much went away on their own," she shared. "As it turned out, once I found the right friend group, I wasn't so socially awkward anymore." While autism may describe some of her "idiosyncrasies," autism is not who Emma *is*. As Emma wrote, "Making my identity revolve around a neurological condition began to feel limiting."

"I think I had a fairly common experience," Emma shared with us. "Unhappy teenager becomes a satisfied, well-adjusted adult ... I don't think I was misdiagnosed, necessarily, but my current relationship with my autism label is that it just isn't a useful way to think of myself anymore. I don't need it to make sense of myself or to explain my problems."

Dr. Simon Davidson would say that the growth and development of young people would better occur without limiting or categorizing labels; it's more important to focus on discovering our diverse identities in relationship with each other. He suggests that "Who am I?" and "Who do I want to be?" are more valuable questions than "How do I identify?" And those valuable questions should be asked and answered slowly, over time. Self-identity being claimed or suggested (or affirmed) by the adults in a child's life, Dr. Davidson suggests, "creates tremendous difficulty for young people."

Emma was a student at the University of Virginia and studied both philosophy and English. In 2022, Heterodox Academy, the nonprofit organization dedicated to progressing the philosophies of open inquiry, sharing new ideas, and challenging popular assumptions awarded Emma Camp with the Exceptional Student Award for her "consistent bravery in championing the principles of open inquiry ... despite social and professional costs."[36] Despite Emma's award for *open* inquiry, not everyone was impressed.

The parent of a child diagnosed with autism, Kate Lynch, wrote a direct response to Emma's article, writing that Emma was "living in a dream world of extreme privilege."[37] This was an interesting approach for critiquing someone with the identical diagnosis Kate Lynch intended to advocate for. Lynch described reading Emma's *NY Times* op-ed with "increasing fury." And she referred to Emma throughout as "Ms. Camp" (an acknowledged rhetorical device that attempts to demonstrate superiority over another). If her response were written with compassion, it was compassion well camouflaged. The words Emma penned were simplified into a thin description. If Emma didn't use the diagnosis as her identity, she was being privileged. Speaking up about her lived experience was criticized. It appears Emma was only supposed to have one lived experience.

Emma's friendships eventually grew, and she found the boyfriend she would eventually marry. The anxiety that motivated Emma to seek the label "melted away with time."

Opposing Views, Shared Humanity

We described in our introduction that we have been fortunate to work in various cultural contexts. Despite growing up in liberal, progressive Washington DC, and going to high school in Massachusetts, Will's work has taken him to Alaska, West Virginia, and Arizona—states commonly described as right-leaning. Our collective work experience has also involved experiences in rural Canada, urban and remote environments in Australia, and trips to Europe and South America.

Now, we know how some of this content can be interpreted. Some readers may think we are living in our own dream world of privilege. Afterall, we are two white fellas. And, while we have our own social quirks, we do not have an autism diagnosis. Will is, however, quite attention-deficit, and Nevin's ability to mix up numbers and letters might have earned him a dyslexia diagnosis as a child. That said, we remain incredibly cautious of this whole enterprise of entering into the identity politics of mental health, and ask you again to trust our intentions.

Will married his partner Renée in 2013 in Abraham Lincoln's cottage in Washington DC, the very place Lincoln penned the *Emancipation Proclamation*. During the reception, Will had time to chat with one of his oldest friends, Kevin. Kevin had recently finished his second tour of Iraq with the US Army and found himself with time on his hands as he adjusted to his life post-military service. Renée and Will convinced Kevin to come to Australia, first for a working holiday and then to work in the outdoors with Will's nonprofit.

Kevin was raised in rural Maryland, his backyard sprinkled with musket rounds from the Civil War. His views on politics, gun ownership, and taxing the rich diverged from Will's and Renée's. One evening in South Australia, the gun debate presented itself at the dinner table. Both Renée and Kevin were animated. For thirty minutes, the two argued, debated, laughed, listened, and contested the other's argument.

"Do you two agree on anything?" asked Isabella, the 11-year-old daughter at the table. Everyone laughed.

As Isabella and the year-younger Lucas were tucked into bed, they shared how fun it was to watch adults with drastically different worldviews talk out their differences. Now young adults, they still remember the night. It's a memory of friends with polarizing views breaking bread over a good, old-fashioned debate. And we are still friends to this day.

This example illustrates what Dr. Simon Davidson says: "Respect is reciprocal." Although he took a lot of heat from his colleagues, Simon "worried more about being an anchor for the youth than diagnosing and prescribing medications."

The foundation of social work and experiential education has philosophical roots related to democracy. Democracy involves participation from everyone, including those in marginalized communities and those who disagree with us. The more we can lean into the places we haven't explored—the people we haven't met—the more we can learn. Democracy also requires open inquiry; society will evolve through continuous open dialogue and critical thinking. Education is the foundation of democracy as young students are treated as active participants in the classroom, which serves as a laboratory to test new ideas, problem-solve, develop relationships, and act in creative and curious ways.

Despite all the medical degrees and high-ranking positions in psychiatry, Dr. Davidson's clinical work was about building relationships. This can be harder, and in some ways, slower. Parents, teachers, and the courts typically want answers right away.

"What's the diagnosis?"

"What's the intervention?"

"When will it work?"

Dr. Davidson, however, cared more about what mattered most: youth living more fulfilling lives with improved connection. Labels risk becoming barriers to connection. Labels are *othering*. Placing youth into identity silos furthers the disconnection they may experience in their everyday life.

Censorship

During the pandemic, the scarlet letter was whether someone was vaccinated or an identified anti-vaxxer. Friendships were lost, families divided, and people's private medical choices became public knowledge. Even more recently, in the arguments about who should be allowed to use traditionally gender-exclusive bathrooms or locker rooms and who can participate in women's sports, people were labeled as allies, transphobic, or anti-feminist. Social media has become a place of social control ruled by call-out and cancel culture, and labels have become weaponized. This style of labeling and attacking isn't a thick description of complicated ideas, it's *othering* those who simply see the world differently from you, and these attacks lead to self-censorship, both by those called out, and those not wanting to suffer the same treatment.

Self-censorship breeds conformity; people believe it necessary to suppress sharing their views to be accepted societally. This is not democracy in action. We have seen this play out many times. People have been shamed. Jobs have been lost. People seem much less interested in learning about how people are experiencing the world or where they are at in their lives. Today, it's about the labels each side applies to themselves *and* to their opposition. While politics is not our arena of expertise, we see the current divisive labeling in the political climate as also causing a direct—and negative—impact on the well-being of adolescents. We see students who are cautious about speaking in class for fear of reprisal for saying something wrong, or sharing a perspective that someone else may dislike. Self-censorship is on the increase, and some consider it the end of open debate and advancement of developing ideas. It is dangerous because it pushes opposing ideas into echo chambers that can strengthen rigid beliefs at the extremes.

Educators in British Columbia have been taught to deliver a set curriculum related to Sexual Orientation and Gender Identity, or SOGI.[38] In 2023, Nevin was teaching a cohort of future clinical counselors. Most were currently middle and high school teachers instructed to deliver the SOGI curriculum. Phase I of the SOGI curriculum is affirmation, or "social transition." Phase II includes medical/pharmacological transition, and Phase III is surgical transition. As teachers, they could only confidently speak to phase I, social transition—the phase that covers changes to pronouns, hair, clothes, and name, and the expectation that others treat and refer to the individual as they self-identify.

When asked to put on their counselor's "hats," there was a sudden drop in confidence on the topic. When pressed as to how they would respond, one student said quietly and unconfidently, "Affirm them?" There was a moment of silent pause before Nevin asked if we as counselors ever affirm other self-proclaimed identities or self-diagnoses.

Most counselors are not doctors. We do not diagnose unless trained and employed to do so. But we have difficult conversations about difficult topics all the time. That is our job. We remain curious, open, and ready to help our clients make meaningful decisions for their future. Clients share many things with us and describe having many ailments, but we do not accept these as identities. Open dialogue about these controversial topics inspired those students who then went on to discuss the pharmaceutical industries involved in Phase II and ultimately cosmetic and reconstructive surgeries in Phase III of transitioning. These interventions come at a significant cost to the child. When lived experience and identity become medicalized, the line between careful and careless can blur quickly.

Youth are a captive audience and should be protected from ideologies that can interfere with positive youth development and lead to potentially harmful interventions. Especially when social media maintains a stranglehold on youth attention, adults must stand up to create safe-enough places for youth to take risks with their identity, explore, and be curious—to undertake the adventure and discovery of learning about themselves. Adults should be the lighthouses youth can look for and reach out to when needed. We do not need to impose our ideas onto them. Raising awareness of diversity and inclusivity is admirable, but should not become a promotion of ideology, especially with the captive audience of children and youth. This ultimately undermines their evolutionary neurological ability to make sense of the world in relationship to the environment and caring people around them.

Nothing Strengthens Authority So Much as Silence

Staff writer for *The New Yorker*, Katy Waldman, described how therapy language left the counselor's couch and entered the real world.[39] Examples: *projecting, triggers, feeling seen, heard,* or *unheard* to *OCD, ADHD, depression, anxiety,* and the newest term de jour, *traumatized.* She asked where the line is between sharing one's experience of mental health or the label one identifies with and draining certain words and ideas of their meaning, as appears to have happened with the term *neurodiversity.*

We don't offer our critique of self-identifying and the need to protect young people from internalizing potentially harmful labels without suggesting an alternative. Many mental health and medical professionals spend their careers attempting to categorize lived experience. Humans are pattern-seeking mammals. Is someone *actually* depressed because they took five minutes to complete the PHQ-9? We're not so sure. Wanting to group and classify people is a natural human effort, but one that has inspired historic evil and further othering in society. When it comes to youth mental health, understanding lived experience is a problem philosophers have been tackling for centuries.

Humans find safety in understanding what they experience. The upset stomach before a job interview is common due to nervousness and may be unsettling when first experienced. A friend acknowledging how normal the feeling is might be reassuring. The biggest moments in life, however, we still struggle to describe. Love, grief, trauma, or existential crises are more difficult to categorize and sometimes doing so doesn't come close to grasping their intensity.

In chapter 7 we will introduce Dr. Scott D. Miller, a leading voice on the evolution of psychotherapy. In one conversation, Scott described human beings as wanting *freedom* and *safety.* Both, however, are not compatible for all. Freedom fosters a sense of risk, and safety requires a tribe of like-minded people who may avoid speaking up against conflicting ideologies. We could immediately see what Scott was describing in our own research and writing experiences.

We conducted a few studies revealing some of the inside workings and undisclosed conflicts of interest related to the legalized kidnapping of children that is a staple of the Troubled Teen Industry in the US. Some wilderness therapy practitioners and researchers affiliated with the small (but decreasing) number of organizations endorsing this practice thought us unkind, demonizing, and even irresponsible. Behind the scenes, people reached out to say they agreed with our efforts but couldn't publicly support our work. After the death of a 12-year-old boy on a wilderness therapy program in 2024, we asked friends to publicly condemn the institutional child abuse occurring in this industry—in the name of therapy. The responses we got were mostly a form of: "I'll be more effective as an insider." They needed the safety of their "tribe." But this came at the cost of the freedom to speak out against the systematic harm of thousands of youths.

"Nothing strengthens authority so much as silence," as Leonardo da Vinci is reported to have said.

Ninety percent of psychologists profess to have ethical concerns about the DSM—psychiatry's bible. Yet the book endures as the backbone of the mental health industrial complex. The safety of the profession protects the industry from progression. Those who may want to deviate from the status quo are left in a challenging position. It can feel lonely to continue pushing new ideas or identifying harm in a progressive direction. "Has any of this made a difference?" we may ask ourselves. To enact change through deviance, we need to find the unique positive outcomes, where against the odds or cultural norms, small changes helped to make progress in an arena where change had stagnated. It's hard to measure what is progress if we aren't counting or observing what we hope to impact first.

What appears progressive in intention, such as books like *Psychiatry for Kids*, can be far more regressive by returning to labeling and othering people into thin descriptive classifiers. These books suggest ideas about what it means to experience childhood, but they preserve the assumption that labeling and medicalizing of lived experience is important for understanding and supporting youth mental health. This strengthens the authority of those already in power (insurance companies who pay for services, professional associations, policymakers, etc.). Learning from those who deviated, like Dr. Simon Davidson, helps to shine a light onto another way of supporting youth mental health.

I Hear You

It might simply be our psychological makeup that helps the two of us feel comfortable embracing the freedom of meeting those we work with as a blank canvas and figuring out what they need as most important. Maybe it's just our rebellious spirits. In his writings, Indian philosopher and author Jiddu Krishnamurti warned us to not follow doctrines, ideologies, or authorities; they may limit our awareness, our potential for growth, and the development of thought or ability. He argued that no matter the size of our following, we should reject feeling as though we are the experts of another person's lived experience. In our clinical work with youth, we adopt the stance of not-knowing. We are a beginner on each therapeutic adventure with each person we meet. It is through understanding that we do not have all the answers that we connect.

Personally, we have no desire to keep searching for what is "wrong" with someone. We are privileged in that we don't work in a system requiring us to diagnose and pathologize our clients or students. They do, however often arrive with adult-inspired identities or labels. We inquire into their whole being and learn about their motivations, who they love, and where they want to go. If a label appears useful, sure, we'll discuss it.

But we aren't handcuffed by it.

As we lifted the veil on how these identity labels became commonplace among youth, Dr. Simon Davidson shared multiple stories of the adolescents he's seen in his extensive career as a psychiatrist. He talked about his role as the adult in the room to protect young people from inappropriate or unnecessary diagnoses and overmedication and provided insight into his aims in working with people. He asserted the importance of hearing more of the young person's story. Dr. Davidson embodied sticking up for the underdog, both with his patients and in society. We end this chapter with Simon's wise words to one of his clients. It's worth repeating to many kids these days:

"I totally hear what you're saying. Please know that I've heard it. But I need to understand who you are, how you became who you are, and how you decided where you want to go in life. I am going to be here to support all of that in the best way I can."

6

TEACHING ZEN TO FIVE-YEAR-OLDS

Children are great imitators, so give them something
great to imitate.
—Anonymous

Sue joked about being raised, and learning about people, in a small-town working-class pub in England. Spending a considerable amount of her childhood in their family-owned establishment left her educated in the emotional dynamics of human relationships. From 4 years of age, she spent hours on a stool behind the bar. Sue washed, rinsed, and returned pint glasses to their racks, and most important to her future career, she observed her father's relational work with members of their community. She witnessed adults—often quite inebriated—laugh, flirt, disagree.

On Friday nights, she said, she might be lucky enough to see a fight! Sue was amazed when her father would come around from the bar to "sort them out." As many bartenders do, he also provided a listening ear, a pat on the arm, or a reassuring look to those sitting on stools across from him. Call it accidental counseling. He would even offer a bit of horseplay when it seemed necessary for that level of physical human contact within the cultural restraints of two men in an English pub in the 1950s. Her father was, in many ways, an expert in how people connect. He always provided some form of attachment.

Sue became her dad's "apprentice," and her internship continued through grade school, where she was taught by nuns. She trained in the art of good debate, learned to think critically, and developed personal values for life. Listening to Sue, whether on a podcast, during a university lecture, or having a personally engaging conversation, it is easy to understand how she became a leading voice, scholar, and psychologist dealing with human emotions and bonding in relationships.

Dr. Sue Johnson remains globally revered for her work as a clinical psychologist, researcher, author, and founder of Emotionally Focused Therapy, a modality concentrated on helping people develop and maintain healthier relational bonds. While not seeming as radical today as it was in the 1980s, Sue fiercely advocated bringing attachment theory and a developmental and relational theory of personality to the forefront in psychotherapy.

Early in her career, Sue noticed psychology and the helping professions were infatuated with *cognition* and *behavior*. In essence, therapists would look at how one's thinking about life events influenced how one acted. In simple terms, this is how cognitive-behavioral therapy became so popular. And we're still dealing with the effects of what British psychotherapist Farham Dalal called the *cognitive-behavioral tsunami*, due to the dominance of this one particular modality in mainstream psychotherapy, which Dalal argues emerged due to "managerialism, politics and the corruptions of science."[1]

Dr. Johnson saw what was missing: *emotions*. Her colleagues weren't convinced, but she is not a person to back down or give up.

"My father said to me, 'There are certain fights in life you have to have, and if you don't have them, everyone pays,'" she shared in an interview about women in leadership.[2] "When you go into the fight, you don't say, oh I'll fight until I get hurt." Sue never cowered from conflict.

Her peer-reviewed articles were blocked. Experts dismissed her ideas of attachment, relationship, and love. Yet Sue's persistence, leadership, and willingness to endure the discomfort changed the world of couples therapy, and her work eventually received the recognition it deserved.

In 2016, Dr. Sue Johnson was named Family Psychologist of the Year by her division of the American Psychological Association,[3] and the following year she was inducted into the Order of Canada, the highest civilian honor in Canada, awarded for outstanding achievement and dedication to career and society.[4] She attributes her success to her early years—that formative internship in her dad's pub and her education under the tutelage of the nuns.

Unfortunately, Dr. Sue Johnson passed away as we were writing this book. *The New York Times* called her the "psychologist who took a scientific view of love" in their piece about her seventy-six years on the planet.[5] We're sad she won't be able to see her contribution to this project, but remain thrilled for the opportunity to bring this larger-than-life personality and legend into our work. Nevin's recorded dialogue with Sue Johnson was rewatched many times to remind us of her humor, direct style of communication, and wonderful smile.

She recounted her father's impact on her understanding of human relationships, and she described the cultural nuances of English society during her childhood. "No one spoke openly about emotions," she said. "They'd rather spend time together talking about nothing."

Sue gave one example of how a recently widowed man, living alone, would come to the pub at six o'clock every day. Her father served him the same drink every time, and they'd engage in the same routine conversation. Every day. Talking about nothing. Every so often on one of those evenings, her father would reach across the bar to hold the other man's hand.

The man's face would change, his voice soften, and he would say something special, something difficult, about how it was to be in the house alone without his wife. Young Sue felt in her chest that what was said was qualitatively different and deeply meaningful. Her father would take a deep breath, withdraw his hand, and without another word, pour the man another drink.

These grown men, shortly after the war, habitually following the stoic cultural code, were in fact communicating emotions in a deep way. Sue learned this at a visceral level, and it began to define who she was. These experiences informed how she treated others, and eventually became the basis for her celebrated legacy as a couples therapist and a leader in the understanding of attachment and human connection. Dr. Johnson had a great adult to imitate.

When asked about what she thought was happening today in terms of youth mental health, Dr. Johnson responded with conviction: "To grow up successfully, children need a secure sense of connection with self, and this only gets developed from having a loving, trusting relationship with at least one other person in your life." She adamantly added, "This is totally true as far as I'm concerned. It's not up for grabs. It's a scientific fact."

Humans require secure loving relationships with trust, care, and reciprocity. Dr. Johnson saw this becoming compromised today, in families, at school, in community, and elsewhere, as Dr. Martin Brokenleg did. Her concern was that these relationships are *essential* and should never be just *incidental*. Her fears were that many children today suffer from two ends of a spectrum: one in which young people are deprived of essential care and do not have safety, and the other, where young people are over-protected and not having a full human experience. In many ways, Sue's convictions embodied the central thesis of our book!

As clinicians, we, too, see the contradiction in the complexity and simplicity of raising healthy young people. When concerned parents call us, they want tips, ideas, techniques, and strategies. In some sense, we can provide hundreds, if not thousands of strategies. The range of ideas is endless and ever-growing. Parents might read one of the hundreds of parenting books published each year. We're inundated with advice and tactics. At the same time, the cruel truth is that there is no one solution. No magic wand. But we are convinced that if the strategy is the canoe, love and connection are the paddles. We write in the following chapter about how all the therapy tricks in the world *can* work, sure, but tips and tricks are moot without healthy relational bonds. Relationships aren't done through techniques. They live in a sanctuary where feelings can be felt and life experienced.

Sanctuaries for Feelings

Hold On to Your Kids. The title alone sounds like overprotective advice for parents.[6] When getting to understand the thesis of Drs. Gordon Neufeld and Gabor Maté's book by this name, we came to agree with their easy-to-understand and sound approach. The thesis is quite simple, but profound in its application and implications. One of its most fundamental points is that youth require meaningful attachments to adults who provide care, values, and guidance. Peer culture is a strong influence, and youth who don't have healthy adult attachments will find attachment and influence among others in their age group. This peer orientation can stunt and hinder healthy development. It will also undermine parenting. Children need adults in their lives—adults who have the young person's best interests in mind. Adults provide love and offer more mature perspectives on the world. Beyond being present, adults need to be involved. Peer orientation offers much less care and involvement, and more often than not, it misdirects healthy development.

Dr. Gordon Neufeld is a developmental psychologist and author from Vancouver. He is internationally recognized as a parent educator and professional trainer, and many refer to his work as *Neufeld's attachment-based developmental approach*. While training in psychology, Dr. Neufeld became interested in how the brain worked, although, at the time, his education was heavily influenced by radical behavioral learning theory, a view that says *everything* humans and other organisms do is *behavior*. It was the same status quo Dr. Sue Johnson faced. Behaviorism ruled the day. Feelings were ruled out.

In its simplest terms, behaviorism is quite similar to how we are taught to train dogs. Reward good behavior with a treat or praise and ignore or punish unwanted behavior. Dr. Neufeld quickly realized he was being trained as a technician, not a therapist—working from the outside and not the inside. He was taught to drive change through the application of structure, doctrine, and ideology (the concept we grapple with in this book's third act). Suspecting there could be a more heartful, naturally emerging approach, Dr. Neufeld spent years dismantling the veil of illusion that was his profession's elevated claims of expertise and capacity for reducing human suffering. Trust in experts had been compromised. Bolstered by his deep knowledge, research, and experience, or simply by paying close attention for his nearly eighty years on the planet, Dr. Neufeld can confidently say "Don't trust the experts!" Obviously, Dr. Neufeld's perspective resonates with ours!

Relative to our focus on youth evolving into healthy, functioning adults, the adolescent developmental stage could be, as Gordon Neufeld and Gabor Maté clearly say, guided by peer *or* adult attachments. Deeper in their thesis is the importance of feelings in human development, and quite simply, that a full expression of and learning from feelings is less available to young people in peer relationships. With peer orientation, youth do what they can to fit in, get along, and be liked, and, as Dr. Neufeld stated, "those who matter to you most, have the greatest ability to wound you." When peers matter the most, youth may avoid conflict and not get to play fully in the *emotional playground*. As we will explore later in more detail, Neufeld and Maté made clear that the experts—the teachers, mentors, and coaches—following research on self-esteem, mindfulness, regulation, and other constructs, have been trying to get youth to get along, be conflict free, increase social-emotional capacities, and be capable of their own self-care. Have kids' lives been made too "safe?" Are we intervening in a way that interferes with child development?

"The issue is that I hear parents talking about self-regulation and self-control," said Dr. Neufeld. "Go to your room. Get a hold of yourself. We're not gonna have a talk until you can manage this." These strategies place children in the position to work through their emotions, and get regulated, all in the absence of attachment. While many struggle to manage their own emotions, we must consider conditions conducive for children to feel and express their emotions fully.

"What are the conducive conditions?" Gordon asked. "Adults must take care of attachment needs when children experience conflict."

Of course, emotions and feelings are different. Every mammal on the planet has emotions, the neurochemical activation of the body. Humans, however, attribute subjectivity to these emotions with names for the emotions they feel, hence *feelings*. Dr. Neufeld said we can do no more to prevent emotions than stop the sun from rising each day. Emotions arise during our interactions with environments and are usually instructing the body to move in or out of a certain situation. Emotions need to be *felt*. In fact, the human brain develops language to feel emotions. For young children, feeling emotions requires space to express what they're feeling in the presence of a healthy attachment. This way the brain experiences a "mixing of emotions" helping the "thinking before doing" areas of the brain—the cortex—to fully feel and express the emotion.

"This creates prefrontal cortex growth," Gordon explained, "and that enables us to be able to have some kind of steering wheel to take up a relationship in life and self-control; it's always been the fruit of development. ... If conditions are conducive, the worst thing we could do is to teach self-management of emotion and self-regulation."

Emotions are going to happen no matter what. To tell us to avoid emotions means we are pushing back against our own natural neurological processes. We are telling youth that if they are frustrated, they must not be frustrated. If they are alarmed, they must not be alarmed.

"We are actually doing the worst thing we could do for emotional health and well-being," Gordon said.

"Trying to teach kids to regulate themselves?" Nevin asked.

"Yes!" Gordon proclaimed. "Our social-emotional learning programs are about the most harmful thing we have done in eons!"

Gordon believes many of the interventions delivered to children in school for mental health "are terrible and often exacerbate the problems." His perspective on the ideas of self-care is equally critical. He considers the messaging and services "just dreadful in that it makes kids responsible for their own mental health" rather than the way we as humans are meant to be, nurtured in a matrix of cascading care where we look after each other based on maturity, responsiveness, and individual capacity.

"As soon as you start teaching mental illness, you will get mental illness!" Gordon said.

This is exactly what we discussed in the previous chapter about the mushrooming of self-diagnosing among youth and in mainstream pop psychology.

Dr. Gordon Neufeld, in parallel with what's to come from Dr. Michael Ungar in chapter 9, argued against the idea presented by many experts that the individual child must be taught to grow and develop themselves. This is the premise of the entire self-help movement. The strength of Ungar's conviction on this front is obvious; his entire book, *Change Your World*, questions the billion-dollar self-help industry and its failings.[7] Dr. Ungar's antidote to the ongoing lack of thriving for individuals is systemic-level change, which is aligned with Dr. Neufeld's focus on adult bonding and attachment as primary to child flourishing.

Mindfulness Without Context: Unintended Consequences

Popularized in America by professor emeritus and author Jon Kabat-Zinn, meditation and mindfulness concepts and practices have become widespread and are well entrenched in the self-help industry.[8] Kabat-Zinn is often credited for integrating science and mindfulness and bringing this perspective to a broad audience in the West. Strangely, when the Buddhist practices of mindfulness and meditation, which date back centuries in Eastern spiritual traditions, were brought to New England and San Francisco in the 1970s, there was little mention of culture or spirituality. Kabat-Zinn and his cohort developed the practices into a program that aimed directly at *stress reduction*, a new non-pharmacological sedative to cope with difficulties in the world. He called it, simply enough, *Mindfulness-Based Stress Reduction*, known as MBSR. We don't have anything against mindfulness, and we may practice our breathing or do our own body scans throughout the day with hopes of remaining grounded and focused, but the proliferation of mindfulness as an "evidence-based" practice, void of cultural context, is a concern we explore throughout this chapter. Trying to force kids to be mindful doesn't work any more than telling every parent what the specific steps toward improving attachment are. And the research is clear in this regard.[9] Again, what isn't working is *shockingly obvious*.

Teachers in many schools are implementing meditation and mindfulness programs in classrooms, often with the intention of improving self-awareness and social relations and—hopefully—addressing mental health problems.[10] In her guest essay in *The New York Times*, psychologist (and previous contestant on *Who Wants to be a Millionaire*), Dr. Darby Saxbe wrote about the surprising failure of mindfulness-based programs in schools focusing on mental health.[11] Also citing how social media became the WebMD for mental health, Dr. Saxbe's article presents the research in a clear and engaging manner.

Take the social-emotional skills training program called WISE Teens. A clinical psychologist comes to the classroom for eight sessions to teach students how to manage emotions. Their techniques and principles are informed by Buddhist practices and the wrongly declared gold standard for psychotherapy, cognitive-behavioral therapy (CBT), and its offshoot, dialectical behavioral therapy (DBT).[12] (We dive deeper into the mania and hype about specific therapies in the following chapter.) In October of 2023, a group of researchers published their findings from a large-scale evaluation of teaching "Zen" and stress management to children.[13] Five hundred sixty-three teenagers did the therapy stuff at school, and 508 went to school as usual. Not only did those in the WISE Teens program report worse parent-child relationships, but they also measured markedly more depressed, anxious, and likely to be struggling with managing emotions. Dr. Neufeld was right. The students receiving the intervention were worse off!

The next study Dr. Saxbe referenced was another large evaluation of school-based mindfulness training (SBMT).[14] Schools were chosen to participate at random. This time, 4,144 students from 42 schools in the UK participated in the mindfulness training. Their outcomes were compared to 4,232 students who just went to school as usual. Again, anxiety and emotional problems were worse for those in the SBMT, and, most ironically, the students receiving the intervention reported *lower* levels in their mindfulness skills!

And here's another randomized controlled trial published in *Psychological Medicine* in 2023.[15] Twenty-five hundred students were placed in either a CBT-informed program called Climate Schools or in a control group that simply went to school as usual. (The Climate Schools organization is now referred to as the OurFutures Institute.[16]) At the end of the study, students in the CBT group were *more* distressed. The authors found their results "consistent with recent findings that universal school-based, CBT-informed, preventative interventions for mental health have limited efficacy in improving symptoms of anxiety and depression."

So, why don't these universal programs work? Remember when we talked about the universal ban of phones in schools or other broad mandates. The clue is in the question: *universal.* When interesting ideas, such as mindfulness or CBT, become mainstream, we see universal applications that are the result of a short-sighted belief that what worked for one should work for all. They become ideological. And when practices are ideological, they can then become popularized and politicized. When we zoom out from these assumptions, we see no way to predict what will work, or for whom. Universal approaches homogenize people, treating everyone the same. It's an odd twist of fate given how rampant today's divisive identity politics have become. Packaging therapeutic ideas into short, marketable programs misses the real point. What is important are relationships and attachment and the bonding and belonging that naturally follow.

"I have nothing against mindfulness," Dr. Gordon Neufeld said to us rather bluntly.

He acknowledged these efforts in the classroom are driven by good intentions, but it's not for children to learn to meditate, self-regulate, and control or suppress the big emotions they experience. It is the responsibility of the older, bigger one—the teacher, parent, coach, aunt, uncle, or other adult in the child's life—to provide safety, care, and compassion, allowing feelings to be felt and growth to come from the experience. Role model and care. Give youth something to imitate.

The intentions of many theorists, educators, and parents are driven by wanting children to grow up into healthy, happy, and contributing members of their community. This has somehow translated to those same adults placing grown-up expectations on children, rather than just being present in their lives, caring for them when they need it, and protecting them from harm. Our experts seemed to have comparable criticisms of this expectation for childhood personal development, and darts were thrown at social-emotional learning, meditation, and mindfulness equally.

"Self-care is not enough," Dr. Sue Johnson said to us. She reminded us of the Dalai Lama's famous quote: "We can live without religion and meditation, but we cannot live without human affection." Social connection, comfort, and belonging fulfill our need for human connection.

"Meditation can be another phony form of self-reliance," Dr. Johnson continued. "We need to know how to reach for and rely on other people. Our minds operate in a context, and that context is primarily our human relationships."

Dr. Johnson described herself as a nonconforming Buddhist. She agreed that the ability to focus on one's breath and mind is a powerful skill to possess. However, meditation in schools can be used as a substitute for the emotional playground children need to feel and express their emotions. Another regrettable substitution.

We should teach children and youth to be in a genuine relationship with caring adults so they feel safe enough to express their feelings and take action. More importantly, we need to encourage adults in children's lives to take the lead on this front and not expect children to initiate relationships. We stand up and take care of kids, so kids can feel safe in relationships and, eventually, learn to take care of others.

Dr. Neufeld was equally critical: "You don't teach Zen to a five-year-old!"

It is not only that Sue Johnson, Gordon Neufeld, and the other experts we spoke with see unintentional harm coming from children learning these self-regulating skills. Our critique is about the application and expectation of this "training." It stems from the assumption that if they are given the right skills, children can look after themselves and not experience conflict with other children. This is a safety trap. Children *need* the experience of life, including frustration, disagreement, and sadness, along with responsive care from a compassionate adult. Eventually, young peers, too, can provide this care as they observe, relate, play, and explore in settings where fruitful learning and growth develop through adult support, resourcing, and role modeling of behavior.

Teen Spirit and Emotional Playgrounds

In *Hold On to Your Kids,* Drs. Neufeld and Maté argued that society has surrendered to the myth that adolescents need each other and that they need to push away from their parents—that peer orientation is equally or more important than adult orientation. Neufeld agrees that teens do need each other to develop, but a caring adult-teen attachment is more critical for healthy development. They first laid out this argument in 2004, and it seems to be truer now more than ever. Social media is sure making it harder for these attachments to form, but Neufeld and Maté saw it happening well before smartphones became commonplace.

Teens need to be embedded in a context of caring relationships. They first need to feel cared for, a necessary condition for relational safety. Then, new and challenging experiences provide what Dr. Neufeld refers to as an *emotional playground,* the space to be able to feel emotions, to feel safe and cared for. We agree. Saying that, we want to be clear that we are promoting safety in child-adult relationships—not the ideological safety, or *safe spaces,* that are currently being promoted that "protect" everyone from differing values or beliefs. We have experienced the negative effects of so-called ideological safety in our universities, where language and behaviors are being heavily influenced by call-out and cancel culture rules.

We all need feelings to be able to respond, to adapt, to recover, to become fully human and humane, and our adolescents are losing the contexts in which to have their feelings. The research is unequivocal in that sense. Longitudinal research—in which people are studied over a longer period—is quite convincing that the single most important factor in adolescent development is a strong emotional connection with a caring adult.[17] Remember the happiness study cited in chapter 2? Happiness is love. Full stop.

In the absence of healthy parent-child relationships, an attachment void is created. The human condition dictates that this void will be filled. We are social animals. Like Dr. Brokenleg, Gordon Neufeld's coauthor, Dr. Gabor Maté, addressed how these voids are filled when human development goes awry.[18] His case study of addiction shows that suffering humans will seek relief from anything, no matter the context or consequences. "It feels like a mother's hug," one of Maté's patients said when describing the sensation of heroin. In this realm, when we want to intervene with a child's negative behavior or emotional pain, we should first consider "Why the pain?" instead of "Why the problem?"

Along with filling a void with substances, the child deprived of healthy adult attachments will seek connection elsewhere, often with peers. This is adaptive behavior, and we as therapists recognize this as self-preservation behavior, which isn't always entirely negative. Further, complicating the world for young people today is social media and electronic devices, which can distract from burgeoning adult-child relationships. No one could have predicted the level of disconnectivity nor the impact on individuals and societies brought forth by these technologies (developed to "improve" connection!). We are still trying to figure out how to live with these disruptive technologies, as we learned from Dr. Mari Swingle in chapter 3. Online communication and connections are often superficial, with limited emotional and psychological depth. They are no substitute for real human attachment.

Neufeld and Maté noted that our new technologies mean that kids these days have an extended amount of time they are involved with their peers. It now goes well beyond school and community activities. They now have evenings and weekends to remain in this shallower attachment; time which was often deemed as highly important and cherished by the kids them-selves. The child bullied at school has no respite. Now, the bul-lies, pornography, and addictive games and apps, all without adult intervention, are with our kids 24/7.

We know the radio, then the television, then the Walkman, the computer, i-tech, and social media all existed as the main scapegoats for their time. Artificial intelligence is the latest thing to blame. The calculator was thought to be the mathematician's cheat code. The television rotted our brains. Now, social media is accused of "causing" an epidemic of youth mental illness. His-torically, we seem to repeat the same pattern: First there is moral panic, then we overcome the initial fear, and then we adopt and adapt to the new technology. Adults, however, should be more attentive than ever in our busy day-to-day lives to make sure our focus remains on *connection before correction.*

Technology has become a persnickety and pervasive reality in all our homes. Traditional family time and familial relation-ships have been disrupted. Distractions displace conversations and social interactions in family and community; these activ-ities are crucial for growth and are yet another place where developmental phases may be missed. Dr. Neufeld spoke of how adolescent peer orientation is based on inherently insecure and immature individuals connecting (even if virtually) and influ-encing each other's development. Peer orientation will lead to missed growth and development opportunities, which ulti-mately become the *fractures* Dr. Michael Ungar will describe in chapter 9. Again, peer orientation can be the interference resulting in the lack of adult attachment. Trying to smother the feelings through universal programs in the schools is the intervention. All of this is cloaked in an ideology we continue to explore in this book.

Losing Their Feelings

Fractures in development become more apparent in relation-ships and times when people face challenges and struggle to respond effectively. They may materialize as a lack of skills or knowledge. Imagine an individual is "caught off guard" by someone else's words or behavior and finds themselves aggressively defending themselves or attacking the other person verbally. How one responds is reflective of their development. If a person is capable of adapting to the situation, whether infuriating, embarrassing, or any other big emotional reaction, and responds in a way that balances the need for self-preservation (say, defending your position) or dignity (standing up for yourself) while remaining mature or respectful, then the person doesn't become a victim of the situation. Consider today's identity politics, cancel culture, and the contentious social media environment, and you see how insecurity interacts with differing world views. To be the adult in the room, we must remain secure and build our attachments with youth when speaking up for youth well-being.

An ability to adapt comes from having had enough time in the emotional playgrounds of your earlier years. Ideally, we face challenges and difficult situations in the company of an older, bigger person (sibling, parent, coach, auntie, etc.) who can provide the support and care we need to learn from and grow through. Through these intimate and caring relationships—where modeling, mimicking, and practice occur—the younger person increases emotional awareness and openness to experience.

Dr. Sue Johnson told us about the significant brain activity occurring when we look into each other's eyes, read facial expressions, and interpret body language, and that these learning opportunities are lost when the caring adult is not present, or worse, when the adults in the room expect the child to struggle through difficult situations on their own. Whether seen as skills or maturity, these growth opportunities are often missed when a child or teen is deep in peer orientation versus parent or adult orientation. How does the immature teen get emotional and psychological support from another equally immature teen when faced with a crisis? Can they provide unconditional love, care, and ongoing resourcing and support for each other? Not likely. In this regard, peer orientation stunts growth, and learning opportunities are sacrificed, which may lead to a lack of skill in dealing with the world as one grows up. Worse, maladaptive behaviors may result, pushing the child further away from a pattern of healthy growth and development.

"The sanctuary for feelings is in emotional playgrounds," Gordon Neufeld repeated. "So, you take the kids to drama, to theater, or you take them for a walk in nature. The other sanctuary is a safe human relationship."

Quite simply, Gordon believes adolescents today are not experiencing their feelings. Through his work with violent and suicidal teens, he saw that these kids had no safe place to feel sadness, so instead, they didn't feel anything.

"They are losing their feelings and their feelings can only catch up to them with safety," he reminded us. Safety is not about overprotection, stranger danger, trick-or-treating, or being home by dark. More on that later. When we are safe, we can take risks. Sure, it might be uncomfortable and, at times, painful. But we take risks in the context of healthy relationships. How do we, the adults, ensure our kids get to play in the emotional playgrounds enough to become healthy and happy adults? It may start with us.

Harvard Professor Emeritus and psychologist Robert Kegan proposed that how we make meaning in the world is related to how we have developed into adults, beyond the ages and stages of childhood and adolescence. Kegan suggested there are increasing *orders of consciousness* which, when achieved, will determine how well we successfully navigate learning, relationship-building, parenting, our working career, and healing. Kegan theorized that many adults are stuck in an adolescent developmental stage due to our hurried and overwhelmingly complex modern lives. He even titled one of his books *In Over Our Heads!*[19] Kegan may be right.

We need to develop the ability to balance our values and beliefs with those of society's and others in our lives. Beyond this ongoing struggle to "grow up," which many parents, teachers, and adults experience, lies the capacity for self-authorship, more independent thinking and acting, and eventually the ability to hold multiple perspectives and appreciate diverse viewpoints. These elevated orders of maturity allow the adult to navigate complexities, to speak their truth while remaining empathetic to others, and to not self-censor or be recruited into others' dramas or ideologies because of external pressures.

The issues we encounter in relationships, work environments, and societal structures often demand a level of self-awareness, adaptability, and understanding that surpasses our current developmental stage. Kegan suggested that to effectively manage these challenges, individuals must continuously cultivate and evolve their cognitive and emotional capacities to better align with the demands of the world around them. What kids need these days is for the adults in the room, as Dr. Neufeld says emphatically, "to step up and take care" and to be responsible for their emotional safety, belonging, and developmental trajectory.

In short, our experts are troubled by the attempts to raise consciousness about issues of mental health. There is too much talking *about* and identifying and labeling, and not enough effort to simply be in caring authentic relationships. The sentiment that has been expressed in numerous ways is true: Where our attention goes, energy flows. And with energy, things grow. If we look toward attachment, resilience, and growth, instead of spending so much time talking about mental illness and safe spaces, our investments of time and energy will yield more positive outcomes for kids these days.

Conclusion: Seeking "Better" Help

Dr. Gordon Neufeld has been openly critical of putting "self-help" initiatives onto children and youth. Most nations have kids helplines, which youth are encouraged to call (or even text) directly for support from someone they don't know and may never see (or whose voice they may never hear if they are texting). Again, there is no bad intention in those initiatives and we're sure they have helped many distressed youth. But let's dig a bit deeper.

If you've listened to popular podcasts in the recent past (we wrote this in 2024), chances are you've heard an advertisement for BetterHelp, an online platform providing mental health services by phone or text. After all, BetterHelp spent nearly 8 million dollars on podcast ads *in December 2023 alone*, second only to the juggernaut Amazon.[20] Apple was third. Big Therapy is now positioning itself with Big Tech.

The service was founded in 2013 by Alon Matas, who had struggled to find an available professional therapist on his own. Through BetterHelp, people seeking therapy can have virtual sessions online, billed monthly through online payment options such as PayPal or Apple Pay. Access to adequate mental health services is a problem around the world. On paper, BetterHelp appeared to be a noble approach to improving access to adequate care. BetterHelp benefited from the COVID-19 pandemic as therapists around the world quickly learned how to deliver therapy online (and outdoors!). Of course, leave it to therapy to remain dreadfully behind the ball and slow in catching up with practices already delivered worldwide. We were not surprised by the heightened interest in our work during the pandemic as providers utilizing the outdoors. There was nothing to clean, and open spaces made health mandates easy to work around.

Now under new ownership, BetterHelp has been slapped with multimillion-dollar fines for releasing consumer information that allowed other companies, such as Facebook, to use algorithms to target BetterHelp's users. Yeah, your therapist can't do that. The American Psychological Association and the National Association of Social Workers took legal action when

BetterHelp used deceptive and manipulating business practices to lure people to BetterHelp from the website CareDash, a now-defunct healthcare referral and review website. BetterHelp distanced themselves from CareDash, and the lawsuits were dropped. As of November 2024, the US Trade Commission, better known as the FTC, reported BetterHelp "agreed to pay $7.8 million" due to charges surrounding users' private information being shared for advertising purposes.[21] The consumer's trust in distance counseling, however, took a hit. Improving access to mental health professionals is an honorable idea. However, increased intervention requires ethics and oversight and should be secondary to close caring adult relationships in a child's life. Adults must actually be in the room.

Just as bringing Zen and meditation to the classroom appears like a progressive idea, so too did BetterHelp. Psychotherapist Dr. Scott D. Miller, who we talk to in the following chapter, warns that improving access to mental health services must be approached thoughtfully and carefully. Outcomes cannot be ignored. Consider knowing you can access BetterHelp whenever you want versus knowing the best therapist for your child is across town. Ask yourself, which option would you take? Would you take access over outcomes?

The experts we spoke to got to where they are by standing up for their ideas and pure persistence. Dr. Sue Johnson knew when the fight was worth it, especially in the face of uncooperative men advocating that psychology and couples therapy remain in the status quo. She stayed focused on progressing her field in the face of protectionist ideologies and agendas. The result? She has been proven correct over the years. It is now understood that attachment, bonding, and belonging are the essential ingredients in child development and relationship recipes. Dr. Gordon Neufeld watched as schools adopted social-emotional learning programs (still well-intended and still quite common today) that he identified as detrimental to youth emotional well-being, but he still carried on with his teaching to counter the trend. He continued editing his books and teachings as new evidence emerged.

It remains unclear why some people can take a stand—like the people whose ideas have been presented in this book. Their unrelenting passion for helping people thrive seems unwavering in the face of fads, bad ideas, and stupid policies. What Drs. Johnson and Neufeld have in common is their passion for human-to-human, heart-to-heart connection. It's something every human living on planet Earth is capable of.

As Dr. Sue Johnson summarized at a public talk a couple years ago, "Once you recognize there is a map to emotions and relationships—because emotions and relationships have structure—and you realize you can reach people, tune into people, and help people grow, that is exhilarating." Modern, hurried lifestyles leave the adults thinking they need to always defer to expert opinion and guidance, when in fact we all have deep understandings and impulses.

"Our innate knowledge and wisdom doesn't matter if we don't use it," Sue reminded us.

The key points we heard from these two experts are to not let situations become overly complicated, but rather to focus on being in authentic and caring relationships, and to help our kids see, hear, and feel safe and cared for. Growth and development will follow. And they prompt us to remember that it's not about teaching all children self-help methods or how to calm themselves or keep them from feeling uncomfortable or to become one with the universe—at five years old!

7

THE TALKING CURE

Know all the theories, master all the techniques, but as you touch a human soul be just another human soul.
—CARL JUNG

In 2016, the government of South Australia, where Will lived and worked, concluded an extensive review of child protection services and determined the need to overhaul the entire system. In the 856-page state government inquiry into child protection, four young people were featured. Nathan was one of them. His life is one extensive case study of interference, intervention, and ideology.

Nathan was first removed from his parents at eighteen months of age. Nathan had spent most of his life up to that point confined to a car seat while his parents filmed homemade pornographic videos which they sold to sustain their crystal meth use. Traditional developmental markers, such as crawling and walking were missed. While the government workers tried to keep Nathan in contact with his mother through supervised visits, she became emotionally and physically abusive, so attempts for family reunification were abandoned.

Nathan's parents were eventually arrested in a drug sting.

Frightened by the impending criminal charges, they fled to Western Australia—along with Nathan's four older siblings. Nathan remained disconnected from his family. Now a child of the state, Nathan was placed under a long-term government order that would remain in place until his eighteenth birthday.

He was diagnosed with *reactive attachment disorder* (RAD), a relatively uncommon affliction characterized by a child's inability to form healthy emotional bonds. Nathan was four years old at the time, and he appeared to never show positive emotion, love, or happiness. Kids with RAD often avoid physical touch and eye contact. They express fear, anger, and sadness, and disciplinary approaches often fail. Kids like Nathan are motivated by their fear of caregivers and adults. They may have no desire to please anyone.

Nathan was moved from school to school due to his violence and from one foster carer to the next as each adult burned out dealing with his behavior. With limited options available, Nathan was placed in commercialized, government-funded care and provided a multidisciplinary team of caseworkers, psychologists, and clinical supervisors. In their notes, they wrote that psychotherapy was unlikely to help without a secure attachment to some caregiver—someone to provide for and protect him.

Safety and protection were not what Nathan received. One caregiver cut the heads off Nathan's teddy bears when he acted out. Another brought Nathan to his personal home for Nathan to sleep over during an Easter weekend because he didn't want to work in the residential facility. Professionally, this is an appallingly inappropriate decision, a reckless blurring of personal boundaries. The government intervened. Again. Nathan was then placed in emergency accommodations, a specialist care intervention costing $180,000 per year. Once more, adults moved the goalposts. Nathan was moved to another home—if one could call it that.

From 2014–2015, Nathan was hospitalized for medication abuse, and again after being abused by an older male, and again after a bicycle accident while intoxicated, and again while nearly dying from amphetamines. He was twelve. What followed were twenty-two criminal offenses over a six-month period and five incarcerations in youth detention. Nathan attended just 95 of 294 possible school days that year. By this stage, he had spent one-third of his young life waiting for suitable care that would never come.

In 2015, a "quarantine wing" was devised as part of a solution. The team believed that since Nathan reacted negatively to close relationships, he might be compelled to become more social if they "placed him in a wing of the unit by himself" with a team of professionals within earshot. Yes, that is a direct quote from the government report, not our writing. By the time the plan was ready for launch, the staff had changed; Nathan's favorite worker moved away.

That was it. No long-term plan existed. Stuck in a quarantine wing with strangers around the corner, Nathan's care team had just one person from the original plan, and that worker was transferred to a new position shortly thereafter.

That's when Will met Nathan.

Nathan's case file was over five hundred pages, with not one nice thing to say about this kid who had been parented by social workers, foster parents, therapists, and politicians—through budget cuts, left- and right-wing state leadership, new "evidence-based" policies, and the shifting ideologies that emerge when administrations and red tape dictate how a young person should experience the world. No matter the number of experts in the room—and there were a lot of them—nothing helped.

"Children like Nathan," read the file, "run and find each other." Kids these days. Of course they do. When connection to adults is lacking, children will attach to their peers. This is peer orientation, which we discussed in the last chapter. Where else will kids find connection? Nathan could have benefited from an involved, predictable, and present adult, but no one stepped up. When adults aren't maintaining connections, youth will attach to youth.

We read the seemingly endless documents to prepare for meeting Nathan. The notes argued that it was the *other young people* Nathan was forced to live with who encouraged his antisocial behavior. Not the adults. But we asked, *where were the adults?* The education system had failed him, and the transitioning adults in Nathan's life increased the effects of complex trauma that results from ongoing relational harm from caregivers.

The state government's inquiry concluded with the following, demonstrating a somewhat sympathetic view of Nathan's experience in care:

> Lack of understanding of Nathan's condition, combined with a rigid system which expected him to conform to its standards, prevented him from actively participating in education. Squabbles between agencies and unrealistic conditions placed on enrolment saw Nathan too frequently absent from schooling.

Nathan's experience, while extreme, demonstrates the importance of an engaging and supportive education system, the presence of secure adults, and stability in a home environment. In cases like Nathan's, education and child protection systems are intrinsically entwined in a child's experience. Mental health professionals were also central to the story. These professionals came up with ideas about which label fit Nathan in order to make decisions about what would work and what wouldn't. To raise healthy children, systems need to work together in supporting and maintaining the well-being of the child and helping them develop to their full potential. Prevention first. And if searching for a cure isn't working, it might be worth going back to the preventative approaches, such as those stemming from the *Circle of Courage* model before bounding to the next shiny intervention.

What Nathan experienced was a lifetime of regrettable substitutions. The result was a troubled and at-risk young person.

He suffered the effects of an endless search for a cure to fix him, though each intervention made for new problems and further harm. But we had hope for Nathan, if only for a moment.

In 2017, when Nathan turned eighteen, a new approach to helping him was launched and Will was brought in as a consultant and clinician capable of delivering some outdoor therapy. Nathan entered the run-down brick building of the under-funded nonprofit organization that would manage Nathan's case in relation to education and therapy. The front office was tastelessly placed in a strip mall between a thrift store and a gun shop. Nathan was introduced by one of the carers hired to provide live-in supervision in the new house the government bought Nathan—an attempt at reconciliation after more than a decade of unpredictable care and misguided attempts to stabilize his mental health and well-being. Will and the team around him were naturally saddened by this case, yet optimistic about the opportunity to rescript a tragic story of so many wrongs. So many people had washed their hands of Nathan; this new group was hopeful, even if naively so.

Barely five feet tall and developmentally delayed, Nathan walked with a slight limp and didn't have the facial hair you'd expect from an 18-year-old. His appearance resembled a pre-teen, not an adult capable of buying a beer or enlisting for military service.

As we shook hands, Nathan's eye drifted down the hall as Will's bulldog trotted up to meet the group. Though regulations didn't allow for unregistered service dogs in youth services or education settings, the stocky bulldog was Will's "employee." Maybe not a *therapy dog*, but the *therapist's dog*. Will brought the dog each week and signed him in at the front desk. To bend the rules, the receptionist made the dog, Ridgley, wear a visitor name tag on his vest. An acceptable substitution.

Nathan knelt to pet the lumpy dog, and, after the five minutes of play required to exhaust a bulldog, Nathan and the staff team were escorted to the consulting room. Nathan laid on the floor, gently using the dog as a pillow while everyone asked questions about his interests and described the services they could offer—school, outdoor therapy, life skills training, etc. For a start, Nathan wanted to be outside. He wanted to be like Bear Grylls, the former British SAS trooper and survival expert. This was interesting. Having read his file, it was clear to us that Nathan was already an expert in surviving. He also wanted an education. Nathan appeared motivated and kind.

The next six months were promising. Nathan enjoyed therapy outside. He also worked with an occupational therapist to improve his posture and walking to make up for other developmental delays stemming from his traumatic upbringing. Nathan spent a good part of his days at the school with a caring teacher, a salt-of-the-earth Australian raised in the country, one of those people who takes no shit, but students and colleagues love! The dynamic duo played Uno and Jenga between sessions devoted to learning how to budget money and talk to girls. Nathan still spent most of his free time smoking marijuana and playing video games at home while a government-funded worker sat in the adjoining room, although he did attend an alternative school every day for six months. He didn't miss a single session of therapy, which is uncommon for even the most well-adjusted adolescents. His attendance over this period was better than any other young person using the service.

Then, unsurprisingly in Nathan's life, disaster struck. Nathan was arrested. The crime had occurred prior to our first meeting. Lawyers warned that the sentence could be dreadful due to Nathan's history, which was plagued with crime and violence. Sure enough, Nathan was convicted and sent to live in a correctional facility. Despite our best attempts to advocate and present data on Nathan's engagement, his schoolwork, and the appropriate relationships he was building with numerous adults, it was too little, too late. Nathan was moved to another new home. This one had prison guards. What an irony, given this was the same government—a similar set of adults, paid for by Australian tax dollars—that had been telling Nathan where to live and who to live with since he was two years old. (For context, anecdotal evidence suggests it costs roughly one million Australian dollars per year for each child removed from home.)

We haven't heard from or about Nathan since our short time together, though we often think of him, how he is doing, and his whereabouts.

We became mental health professionals to help young people. Of course, it doesn't always go well, and uncooperative systems make our work exponentially more difficult—much more difficult than any of our young clients. Still, we believe in the work, and we are willing to deviate from the norms. Much of the research evidence supports this. In this chapter, we examine this evidence.

If you're a helping professional, we hope this discussion serves as a reminder of what matters most and how seemingly nice ideas, while lacking in any substantial evidence or proof of moving the needle in mental health outcomes, become so-called gold standards. If you're someone considering whether you should seek professional help for yourself or an adolescent, we hope to equip you with the knowledge to advocate for yourself and protect yourself from not only harmful labels, but from ineffective care, misleading diagnoses, and unneeded medications.

Mental Health and Clinical Excellence

Parents face challenging issues when sending their child for therapy:

"What diagnosis will my child get?"

"What if the therapist thinks I'm a bad parent?"

"Will my child be prescribed medication?"

Parents relinquish a lot of power and control when seeking external support for their children. In school settings, teachers may recommend therapy when a student is disruptive in class or inattentive. A doctor may provide a referral to a psychiatrist for a clinical assessment and possible pharmaceutical intervention, though some doctors forgo the psychiatrist and prescribe the medications themselves. And a parent can't know what to expect or who they should put faith in.

Of course, all helping professionals experience treatment failures—like the dozens of adults who came in and out of Nathan's life—and our work is no exception. Some research suggests it is the humblest of therapeutic workers who elicit better outcomes; those who refuse to overinflate their effectiveness as therapists and take responsibility for treatment failures (instead of blaming their clients for a lack of progress!).[1]

Failing to produce a positive outcome with an adolescent isn't always because of the egregious behavior of adults (though it was in Nathan's case). Sometimes we as therapists fail to engage a client to stick through emotionally charged conversations, or we do something to create a rupture in a collaborative relationship. For over a decade, our collective research has not shied away from seeing when therapy goes wrong and what therapists and clients need to know to make the most of their opportunities. To untangle what works in mental and behavioral health interventions, we examined the research and spoke with the leading researchers in our field. One of them was Dr. Scott D. Miller, the cofounder of the International Center for Clinical Excellence (ICCE).[2]

Scott grew up in sunny southern California in what he describes as a normal and uneventful childhood with a great family. Scott's father, an elementary school principal, insisted on the importance of a good education and made sure young Scott knew education was the path to opening doorways and ongoing success. After high school, Scott went on to study accounting, much to his mother's pleasure, as she thought regardless of her son's future income, Scott would at least spend his days in the proximity of money, capable of counting other people's cash, instead of making it rich on his own.

But his career took a different turn. After a year of studying at Brigham Young University in Utah, Scott met Professor Hal

Miller (no relation). Hal had studied under the famous behaviorist B. F. Skinner at Harvard, and Scott found Hal provocative and interesting. Scott became Hal's undergraduate research assistant, and he wanted to become a professor and researcher just like his new mentor. Hal, though, encouraged Scott to focus on therapy and put him in touch with a clinical psychology researcher, Professor Michael J. Lambert.

In psychology circles, Michael Lambert's name emerges (as does Scott's) when people ask who best understands what works in psychotherapy. Michael's career includes creating systems for identifying people who are *not* benefiting from the therapy they are receiving (something therapists routinely neglect to assess in their everyday practice!).[3] These are systems you would think every therapist on the planet would want to implement. But the majority have not. Motivated, Scott enrolled in graduate school under Lambert's supervision and began a nearly half-century journey exploring what makes therapists effective. Lambert and Miller remain friends to this day.

Dr. Scott D. Miller described himself as quite an anxious therapist early on. He could sense how much his clients struggled, and he struggled with *that*. He felt ripped off when his training didn't provide him with the secret to helping those who sought his counsel. Scott's peers, students with similar training and clinical experience, appeared more confident about how therapy was supposed to work. Other students rattled off the latest diagnostic criteria and applied the hottest so-called evidence-based practices without blinking. For Scott, his anxiety about therapy developed into his superpower. His careful and constant questioning and exploration have facilitated a prominent career. He is now a leading voice in psychotherapy.

Dr. Miller took us down the research rabbit hole, which ultimately provided us with a pragmatic understanding of what works when helping people in therapy. He alerted us to one of psychotherapy's most important pieces of research. It was a study that introduced the world to a new statistical method, and it is now widely used across professional fields. We find it troubling that neither of us learned about the study in our undergraduate, graduate, or doctoral training!

In 1977, psychotherapy researchers Mary Smith and Gene Glass conducted the very first meta-analysis, a robust research method for examining the effects of multiple, large-scale studies.[4] While originating in the study of psychotherapy outcome, meta-analyses are today used in medicine and a range of other scientific endeavors. At first, the compilation of large sums of data gathered from a range of studies on a certain topic was believed to put an end to certain scientific debates, such as whether or not psychotherapy actually works.

Ever since the emergence of psychotherapy—the *talking cure*—people have argued whether all this talking stuff truly works. Many will have firsthand evidence readily available to prove its ineffectiveness. Listening to our friends' *Very Bad Therapy* podcast might only reinforce those assertions.[5] Despite many bad outcomes (like Nathan's), there are also many good stories. It takes just one black swan to prove that not all swans are white, just as it takes one horrible or one particularly helpful account about psychotherapy outcomes to shift our narrative about its usefulness.

Smith and Glass thought they put this part of the debate on psychotherapy's effectiveness to rest. They found people who received therapy of any kind were better off than 75 percent of people receiving no therapy at all. It was the largest study of therapy to date, and the findings remain remarkable. For the average struggling person, therapy was better than doing nothing. Remarkably better!

However, researchers didn't only compare therapy against no treatment at all—a factor Smith and Glass didn't overlook either. In some of the studies, patients were randomly allocated to receive one of two or three types of therapy. This is what researchers call a *direct comparison trial*.

Imagine half the people in a study receive one kind of therapy, and the remaining are randomly assigned to a different type: *therapy A vs therapy B*. The therapy is compared to another therapy, not to no therapy. Using exercise science as an example, this could be having half the research participants go on a short run while the other half enjoy a brisk walk. In the therapy context, this could be half receiving behavioral therapy and the other half receiving some sort of Freudian psychoanalysis. While both involve sitting and talking in a therapist's office, they are somewhat distinct in the ideas informing what the therapist would ideally do. Of the nearly sixty forms of psychotherapy available in the 1970s, Smith and Glass did not find an ounce of evidence to suggest one therapy was more effective for a particular condition than another. In fact, everything seemed to work.

Fifty years on, we hear rumors of more than one thousand models of therapy, each brand named with a convenient acronym in the alphabet soup of therapy, such as CBT, ACT, DBT, IPT, CFT, EFT, PCT, or SFBT. The question remains, how does one choose which therapy to receive or know which is most likely to help?

We put this to the test in our own field of outdoor therapy. In 2018, we published a review of the available direct comparison trials where clients receiving therapeutic services in the outdoors were compared directly to those (in the same study) getting therapy indoors.[6] What did we find? We landed on the same findings: *no differences in outcomes*. Whether therapy included rock climbing, hiking, canoeing, or just time in natural environments, it did not make for more effective therapy. It didn't *hurt* outcomes either. Each type of therapy we investigated tended to work the same.

Top researchers in the outdoor therapy field weren't impressed. "Fuck that guy," said one prominent outdoor therapy researcher following a keynote presentation Will delivered in 2018 describing these findings. Our work apparently interfered with their pursuit of insurance reimbursement for wilderness therapy programs in the US. These are the same types of programs Paris Hilton has been campaigning against in recent years due to systematic abuse and harm caused to children in America's failed troubled teen industry, a debate we also never shied away from. We pushed first for ethical and safe practices, and second, for honest research and better outcomes. Based on the available data, we found it easy to identify the "My-therapy's-better-than-yours" vanity and self-righteous project of proving one's therapeutic acronym to be more effective than something else.

To have your therapeutic acronym stamped with the moniker of *evidence-based* or *empirically supported*, researchers must prove the therapy to be effective, safe, and cost-effective. Researchers had already found most wilderness therapy programs to be effective based on outcome data collected from the Youth Outcome Questionnaire created by Michael Lambert and colleagues (though we've publicly questioned the validity of these studies).[7] These programs were also found to be physically safe—though safety must be questioned when exploring psychological trauma, breaches to human rights, and unethical practices common to a lot of American wilderness therapy practice. All that was left to prove was cost effectiveness.

Despite public outcries from youth about the long-standing effects of harmful, involuntary practices, industry-funded researchers published a 2019 open-access article about cost-effectiveness for everyone to see. On the surface, the findings looked extraordinary. Ninety days in the woods had a cost-benefit ratio 60.4% higher than traditional therapy services. "Traditional" is often used to refer to *treatment-as-usual*—a tactful research tool allowing researchers to provide a control group without describing what treatment-as-usual actually is. Apparently, wilderness therapy provided $36,100 of societal benefits and led to "424% better treatment outcomes."[8]

Though many wilderness therapy programs have closed in recent years, we began to see "424% better treatment outcomes" marketed on residential programs' websites. The claim was a blatant attempt to recruit anxious parents to send their children away. The claim is simply bullshit.

The article was published in a substance abuse journal and focused on comparing wilderness therapy outcomes to a large sample of people receiving substance use treatment. They positioned their study by stating a true, but cautious, finding. People who complete their substance use treatment are mostly better off than those who leave therapy prematurely. For treatment-as-usual, only 37% completed their substance abuse treatment. Ninety-four percent completed the course of wilderness therapy treatment, and according to the researchers, outcomes and "costs were adjusted for actual completion rates." Of course, we are equipped with an insider understanding of this industry, and we know the hoops these researchers leapt through to get to their conclusions.

The researchers crafted quite a compelling narrative that was then used to market harmful therapy programs to parents. But scratch the surface and you find disturbing twisting of the facts. First, the wilderness therapy used in the study was an involuntary experience. Youth *could not leave*. (Wouldn't it be more interesting to know what the 6% of youth did to escape the program?) Second, these are mostly *for-profit* programs. Insurance coverage remains limited, and the median household income for participating families is well above $100,000 per year. Most of the participants were white, upper-middle-class youth.

We are not saying that certain youth do not deserve safe and effective treatment. We do argue, however, that claiming a "societal benefit" from treatment only available to families that can afford it is a bit of a bold assertion.

We share this story to showcase some of the detailed inner workings of psychotherapy research. There are those who want to own and sell their own type of therapy—the so-called *cure* that pads their wallets or improves their reputation—to become a gold standard. The problem Mary Smith and Gene Glass warned about (that was largely ignored) is that none of the sixty or so available therapies pre-1970 were 1% more effective than any other, let alone 424% more effective!

But we keep digging. Are all approaches equally effective when working with children and adolescents? Was there really no secret sauce? No magic treatment or technique we could provide to be more effective in our work? We turned to Dr. Scott Miller for answers.

Finding the Cure

In 2008, Dr. Miller was the lead author of another meta-analysis with another prominent psychotherapy researcher, Emeritus Professor of Counseling Psychology at the University of Wisconsin–Madison Bruce Wampold, who was known for his meta-analytic research.[9] According to Dr. Miller, "Bruce had published yet another groundbreaking meta-analysis" and, while perceived as radical for the time, Wampold believed therapies should be compared directly against each other if claims of superiority were going to be justified.[10] Wampold and Miller believed we couldn't learn much about psychotherapy, how it works, and what matters if we continued the century-long tradition of comparing those who get therapy of any kind to those getting nothing at all.

Scott believed in Wampold's work and wanted to apply it to working with youth. They invited Katelyn Varhely to the team, a doctoral student at the time and clinician working with young people.

The trio launched a search for relevant studies published from 1980 to 2005 that incorporated a clear, direct comparison of two or more therapies for participants under the age of eighteen being treated for depression, anxiety, ADHD, or conduct disorders. After reviewing more than one thousand papers, the team included twenty-three studies that met their stringent criteria.

Like the first meta-analysis in 1977, this research team found that when two approaches to helping youth were compared, the differences in outcome were small. But Miller, Wampold, and Varhely asked why *any* differences existed, knowing as they did that Mary Smith and Gene Glass found otherwise. One rationale for this was the different sample sizes. It is difficult to compare the results for treatment groups drastically different in size. For instance, the impact any intervention makes on fifty people will likely be statistically different when another intervention is compared to two hundred. So, the impact may be due to the statistical power of the findings. The next variable, however, was more interesting—and alarming.

Of the included studies, Dr. Miller and company found something peculiar when one of the study's therapies was developed by one of the study's authors (or the author's supervisor), or if the clinicians had been trained by the creator of a particular approach. When the authors or trainers held allegiance to a certain therapy, they accounted for 100% of the differences in outcomes! That is, the studies claiming to have found one therapy was more impactful in helping alleviate youth distress were conducted by those already believing in and practicing that chosen therapy! They created the therapy. The game was rigged. Miller, Wampold, and Varhely landed on a crucial finding we do not discuss enough. One's belief and allegiance to a specific therapeutic intervention influences the outcomes and subsequent promotion of evidenced mental or behavioral health care.

The popular therapies, those typically championed and hyped by a charismatic leader and their acolytes (and preferred by health insurers, grant funders, and third-party payers), find their way to the top, even though available evidence doesn't support privileging one approach over the next. Other therapies, like what we were delivering in outdoor therapy and other "alternative" therapies, like those involving music, horses, sports, arts, gardening, or board games remained overlooked. Parents are left navigating what will help their child the most. We wrote in chapter 2 how most adult attempts to curb unwanted adolescent behavior are likely to fail. Similarly, focusing solely on techniques or certain models of helping may eclipse the importance of connection and how people make meaning from their therapy experience.

Besides psychotherapy for specific phobias, such as a fear of spiders, no one can predict if an adolescent will benefit from a certain *type* of counseling or if they should see a psychologist, psychiatrist, social worker, counselor, marriage and family therapist, or even just a good friend. Mental health care has become so bogged down with processes, manuals, and evidence-based ideologies that we seldom hear anyone talk about *improvements* to outcomes. Psychotherapy outcomes have not improved since Gene Glass and Mary Smith's first meta-analysis was published in 1977. Not one percent!

Improving access to mental health care feels important. Some of the statistics we've presented throughout this book suggest a mental health pandemic at levels well beyond the coronavirus we all lived through. But we are left asking, what exactly are we improving access to? Remember, diagnosis and medication rates have skyrocketed in the last two decades for depression, anxiety, and attention-related issues. We've improved the access to that treatment exponentially, so what's the outcome? Let's look.

The UK's National Health Service created the flagship Improving Access to Psychological Therapies initiative in 2008 at a cost of around one billion pounds.[11] The program, now called NHS Talking Therapies, did improve access to psychotherapy. From 2008 to 2022, psychological services were accessed by 1.2 million people.[12] However, the most common number of sessions any person attended was *one*. One visit. And the sessions were free. Looking at it under the microscope, only 9.2% of therapy recipients entered into recovery.[13] Improving access is wonderful, but if we keep ignoring the evidence, it won't help improve overall therapeutic outcomes.

During the COVID-19 pandemic, therapy apps became a phenomenon; profits doubled from 2020 to 2021.[14] As stated in the previous chapter, psychotherapy practice has been decades behind on telehealth and online therapy options. We are all for improving access, especially for people in remote settings where therapists are few or, worse, unavailable. We question, however, the value and the consequences of improving access to mental health care when the promise of improving outcomes remains on the back burner.

According to the *Harvard Public Health* magazine, the number of mental health care apps is now estimated to be in the tens of thousands.[15] Once again, access to something that *might* help has increased. But the outcome? Interestingly (although maybe not surprisingly), ninety mental health apps were downloaded more than ten thousand times in 2019, though less than 4% of users had opened the apps after two weeks. It's like walking up to a therapist's door and not knocking.

Another emerging trend is biometric and health wearables, such as smart tech rings and watches, which many claim to be "the future of mental health care." Like a pedometer counting your daily steps, this new smart tech collects data on a person's sleep patterns and uses skin-sensing technology to show how one's brain impacts electrodermal activity through signals sent from our sweat glands, heart rhythm, skin temperature, and breathing rates.[16] These devices provide the user with information they often don't know what to do with. While seemingly useful on the surface, when these new technologies and ideas don't give useful information, people can get *more* anxious about their mental or physical health. Access improves, but outcomes don't.

And new trends continue to materialize. Stress balls and fidget spinners came and went. Art therapy coloring books can still be found in gift shops and airport bookstores. For youth, our question is not related to whether these ideas or technologies can help. We are not claiming they do not, and people should always do more of what works for them. Remember, all therapies tend to work about the same. The question is what works for whom, and to answer that question we must know who the who is. *Who* is seeking the help, and *who* is providing it? In the psychotherapy world, the relational connection continues to be eclipsed by evidence-based ideologies. The problem remains most people searching for help don't know who is most likely to help them. When they do, they often cannot get in the door.

In 2022, the American Psychological Association's survey of practitioners found that 60% of psychologists had no openings for new clients, 40% had waiting lists of ten or more people, and 20% reported an increased demand from youth and people of color.[17]

To get a foot in the counseling room door, people search for services that are nearby. As Scott Miller shared with us, many will choose the therapist down the road, as opposed to the one across town despite the farther therapist possibly being more likely to help. They choose access over the possibility of better outcomes. The medical establishment is not very good at matching people to the right mental health intervention.[18] This was an issue with the NHS's talking therapies initiative. Most people who saw a therapist left after one session convinced therapy wasn't for them and the clinician was unlikely to help.

Searching for Supershrinks

Improving psychotherapy outcomes is the foundation of Dr. Scott Miller's work. Thirty years ago, Scott threw a wide net to find the next generation of *supershrinks*, a term coined by Harvard researcher David Ricks in the 1970s to describe a class of extraordinary therapists.[19] Ricks's landmark study examined the long-term outcomes of a group of adolescents described as *highly disturbed*.[20] One group of these adolescents appeared measurably more well-adjusted in their adulthood than the others. The reason? They worked with the supershrink (one therapist in the small study appeared to elicit results above and beyond others). The others worked with what Ricks referred to as the *pseudo-shrink*, though we'd prefer to call them average therapists.

David Ricks's research found something everyone working in therapeutic settings or teaching institutions—or any job—already knows. Some people are better at their jobs than others. Some therapists are a cut above the rest. So, how does one find them?

Ever since the medical field adopted ideologies of evidence-based medicine, mental health has been trying to keep up. We've been told the industry is making data-driven decisions yet the evidence suggests they aren't putting their money where their mouth is. The first meta-analysis of outcomes showed therapy helped the average person, but not because of the type of therapy provided. What Ricks found was that some practitioners are more effective than others, leading to important considerations of how we evolve therapeutic practices. Half a century later, energy, funding, and resources are still being "directed exclusively toward identifying effective *therapies*." Like Dr. Bruce Lanphear's work described in chapter 4, psychotherapy research is a dog chasing its tail for the cure. The list of psychotherapy approaches has only grown. Again, outcomes have not.

Scott Miller suggested that no one in medicine would argue with the validity of a search for cures. We all want *problem-specific* interventions. Many of us find solace in knowing their doctor is administering an intervention specific to the problem or medical ailment they experience. In mental health, however, one hundred years of deliberating on how to classify what is wrong with people and identifying the best talking cure all but confirms that we have been asking the wrong questions for a very long time. It is not the type of therapy or the therapist's qualification that is the important thing. There is something much more human to consider. It's actually deceptively simple.

Who provides your therapy is far more important than the *type* of therapy provided.

According to another large study from Scott's colleague, Bruce Wampold, people who saw the most effective therapists improved at a rate 50% higher. The people those therapists work with disengage from therapy 50% less of the time. These are the supershrinks.

When medications, such as antidepressants, are used alongside traditional talking therapy, the impacts of the supershrinks endure. Bruce Wampold and colleagues found the combination of talk therapy and drugs was ten times more effective, *but* only when those clients saw the best therapists! The impact of psychiatric drugs disappeared when people worked with average or below-average therapists (as rated by the clients themselves). Even when chemistry and biology were involved in the mental health treatment, the power of medications still relied on who administered the treatment. The better the therapist, the better the outcome. Simple, right?

In therapeutic work, the practitioner is a *catalyst*. It's not the techniques, theories, disorders, qualifications, level of education, professional training, or anything else people spend thousands of dollars on to learn at university. Some things can't be taught. Our associate, Daryl Chow, found that it's also not how long a therapist has worked (that is, how "experienced" they are) that predicts how likely they are to help.[21] It's how hard they work at perfecting their craft of psychotherapy—pushing themselves to be better tomorrow than they are today. They are better at engaging with a range of diverse populations, repairing ruptures in relationships, and inspiring hope where a positive future had seemed impossible. (This finding got Chow's article, coauthored with Scott Miller and others, the nomination of Most Valuable Paper by the American Psychological Association in 2015.)

The endless search for new interventions and cures found its way into therapy. We've all heard people say, "That kid needs therapy." The statement indicates something is wrong with the youth, and the cure would be sitting on a couch and talking about it. We wrote this part of the chapter in the hope that we can inspire anyone working with, living with, or raising youth to become a firm yet guiding presence as youth navigate potentially turbulent teenage years.

A good place to start is to think of ourselves as a *lighthouse*. It's a role any adult can adopt in the life of an adolescent. Parenting expert Maggie Dent wrote that lighthouses are adults who "lean in with compassion and act as a safe, predictable base for a child or teen to help them to pause, regroup, recover, replenish, and grow."[22] If we all take a moment to think about who was there for us in a difficult time—and it may have been a therapist—think about what it was they did. How did they act? Did they actively listen? Provide advice? Maybe they shared an uncomfortable truth, but you had to trust their opinion to really listen and take it on board. Where did the trust come from? This is why connection before correction remains the best-tested theory in mental health care.

We often wonder if the youth we've seen thought to themselves after a first session, "Hey, I think Will's therapy stunk. I feel worse now. But hey, he's got a PhD, and he said what we did was evidence-based, so I'll keep my next appointment!" More bad therapy seldom leads to good therapy, and therapy cannot be done with someone disengaged from the process.

Snark aside, the world of therapy has privileged ideologies of evidence-based practice to prop up certain interventions and treat people as passive recipients of the therapist's expertise. The truth is, youth are still crew in therapy, not passengers. They are active participants, and they also tend to know best when therapy is working for them—and when it isn't.

As Sheldon Kopp reminds us, we must learn and trust ourselves and our experiences; we need to stop waiting for a guru (or a therapist) to resolve our problems or dissolve our pain. Kopp, a Washington, DC psychotherapist, is known for his 1972 book *If You Meet the Buddha on the Road, Kill Him,*[23] in which he clearly outlined the need to become responsible for ourselves and not trust the experts or the gurus.

Though attributed to Buddhist master Lin Chi in the 1800s, "Killing the Buddha" became a popular Zen story post-World War II in the West. Not recommending murder; the story teaches us to avoid turning spiritual symbols, rituals, and teachings into any sort of religious fetish.[24] Because the Buddha is thought to be *within* everyone, including each of his disciples, the disciple should look inward and avoid idolizing or aggrandizing him as a God-like figure.

Kopp used this story in reflecting on his career as a psychotherapist. Sure, the teacher, or therapist may be important in a person's change journey, but the therapist's skill is in understanding how this position of power can be used to help motivate a person toward a positive change. We can offer guidance and care and help the seeker gain an understanding of their difficulties, but change comes from within the client. Kopp wrote, "The most important things that each man must learn, no one else can teach him. Once he accepts this disappointment, he will be able to stop depending on the therapist, the guru who turns out to be just another struggling human being."

As Carl Jung told us: Just be another human soul. As therapists, we must suspend our know-how and what we believe is technique mastery to just be *present*—a person with our own failings, insecurities, and scars. This is the humility that helps to improve connection. To be most impactful in helping struggling youth, we need to actively listen, avoid providing too much advice, ask more questions, and partner with their worldview.

In Zimbabwe, for example, grandmothers with no mental health or medical training deliver therapy on what is called *The Friendship Bench*.[25] With large waitlists making mental health care difficult to access, six hundred grandmothers were trained quickly in some basic talk-therapy skills (asking open-ended questions, active listening, etc.) so they could meet and talk with people seeking mental health treatment. In 2017, these grandmothers worked with thirty thousand people across seventy communities in Zimbabwe. They were so effective that Friendship Benches have begun sprouting up in Washington, DC, New Orleans, Malawi, and Zanzibar. Providing a caring space and a listening ear to connect with youth is the secret sauce, and we don't need to wait for more clinicians, disorders, or interventions to start today.

This may feel antithetical coming from two qualified and experienced mental health professionals who cherish their work. For some, this may feel damning of their techniques. Therapy is a sociocultural practice, not a medical treatment. Sure, some feel shocked or inadequate when our techniques, therapeutic rituals, and diagnostic criteria don't live up to the hype we're sold on the news or during much of our professional training. We assure you: This is liberating.

The therapist, or *change artist*, as the late social worker Virginia Satir refers to therapists, is co-adventuring on a journey. They're also crew on a person's heroic pilgrimage, asking questions to direct their focus inward toward the changes—no matter how big or small—they want to make every day. And yes, anyone can be a change artist in a young person's life.

"The best therapists receive no thank-you notes because the client feels they did it themselves," Will's first psychotherapy supervisor shared. This echoes the classic Chinese text and foundation of Taoism, the *Tao Te Ching*, which says: "A leader is best when people barely know he exists. When his work is done, and his aim fulfilled, they will say: We did it ourselves."

In chapter 1, we heard Dr. Martin Brokenleg describe today's adolescents as starving for connection. Humans are relational beings. For a century, the talking cure has been in a fight for legitimacy, trying to survive in the shadow of medicine. Scott Miller had us imagine the possibilities when we stop asking about what "therapy" is and start to question what is "therapeutic" and "for whom." The options become endless. The caring hairdresser becomes a beacon for the socially anxious teen going on their first date. The groundskeeper at school sees a child sitting alone and offers a chat. The teacher doesn't punish or publicly shame a student for forgetting his books at home, knowing that a teacher can't know what happens in that child's home (this last example came from Maggie Dent). These people are lighthouses. The skill of a good therapist is in the heart of any human. But, we've been duped by the ideology of evidence-based practice, a false idol, and a bad approach to tackling wicked mental health problems that continues to prop up certain interventions.

Who Decides What "Works" in Therapy?

Here is one illustration of how entrenched some psychotherapy approaches can become in mainstream mental health discussions and social policy. Back in 2013, the WHO announced the expansion of its 2008 Mental Health Action Program to scale up services for substance use and mental and neurological disorders and to include care for post-traumatic stress disorder.[26] WHO Assistant Director-General of Noncommunicable Diseases and Mental Health, Dr. Oleg Chestnov, said providers "will now be able to offer basic support consistent with the best available evidence." Good idea. In the same breath, the WHO argued that "referral for advanced treatments such as cognitive-behavioral therapy (CBT) or a new technique called eye movement desensitization and reprocessing (EMDR) should be considered for people suffering from PTSD." Advanced treatments? These therapies may be well-researched, but are they more advanced? That's less than evidence-based. This is an example of following treatment guidelines, not the outcomes. Treatment guidelines are often cherry-picked from the vast canon of the literature.

CBT and EMDR have become remarkably popular over the last decade. Psychotherapy outcomes, however, remain stagnant. If the target remains finding effective *therapies* rather than training effective and engaging *therapists*—nothing will change. CBT and EMDR are two of the most researched interventions today. The human factor—what is most important to the therapeutic adventure—is overshadowed by treatment protocols and manuals. The provider's contribution to therapeutic progress continues to be ignored. The experts led us astray again. There is nothing wrong with therapies such as CBT or EMDR, but their hype is not supported by the evidence. Cognitive-behavioral approaches will not cure the coddling of the American mind as suggested,[27] and the new so-called *independence therapy* will not fix the Anxious Generation.[28] Describing these therapies without understanding who is involved misses the point. The therapist and youth are both treated as passengers, but the truth is *they* are the wild cards. Their influence is both unpredictable and uncertain, yet essential. Getting referred to a specialist based on the type of therapy they provide might help, but the evidence suggests this is not the best predictor of whether or not you will benefit.

Going to a therapist's website, many concerned parents will see a lot of descriptions of what therapy the clinician provides. There is seldom any presentation of how effective the therapist is or their values or any description of when a patient will experience change. How does one choose? One pathway toward change, described below, is a factor worth reflecting on throughout your or your child's therapy journey, and one that was central to child and adolescent psychotherapy one hundred years ago.

Making the Most of the Therapy Experience

At a 2022 conference in Norway, we began a dialogue about mastery among youth and decided to flesh it out into a *conceptual article*, a process usually undertaken before a new research project begins. It's an exploration of what's already known mixed with some current insights as to what we may yet want to discover in future studies. While not groundbreaking, we wanted to revisit a century-old understanding of how therapeutic approaches work. We reached out to our international colleagues for help and enlisted a brilliant cast of coauthors from Latvia, Canada, Spain, the US, Australia, and Ireland. Our challenge was to reexamine how the concepts of success and mastery were the focus of adolescent psychotherapy in its early days.

We suspected that therapeutic outdoor approaches with adolescents were focusing on the wrong version of success and mastery. For many practitioners in our field, success and mastery in therapeutic interventions are related to a young person's level of compliance with the therapist, defined by the young person climbing the mountain, listening to adult instruction, or blindly following the therapist's orders. Hardly the spirit of youth.

In Nathan's tragic story, every adult wanted Nathan to fall in line; they wanted to fix adolescent behavior. For the adults, Nathan needed to behave in ways the adults could describe as "masterful" and "successful." This is not how things work in therapy. No one cares what therapists and experts believe about mastery. The adolescent's view is most important. If they feel successful in overcoming their problems or believe they possess the capacity to overcome their difficulties—that is, a sense of mastery—they become more likely to mentally engage in the therapeutic process.

With colleagues, Harvard-educated psychiatrist Jerome Frank from Johns Hopkins University Medical School put mastery to the test in the 1970s. With mental health patients in Johns Hopkins's outpatient clinic, Frank and colleagues explored the impact of facilitating successful and masterful experiences with clients. The catch? They didn't do anything resembling classic therapy. There was no therapeutic relationship with the researchers. People simply completed a sequence of tasks containing certain responses to visual and auditory stimuli. These tasks contained no inherent therapeutic value and no association with the reason these people arrived at the celebrated Maryland hospital. The study allocated people to two conditions: a mastery group who were told their efforts were successful, and a placebo group who were told that a special pill (a placebo with no actual remedial ingredient) was responsible for their success.

As the study concluded, both groups, on average, appeared better off. Upon follow-up, however, the group told the placebo pill was responsible for their success reported significantly greater rates of relapse than those believing their success was due to their own mastery. Experts attributing change, growth, success, and development to anything other than the heroism of the active participant is predictive of relapse, a backward step.

What mastery looks like to one child or adolescent will be different from the next. Adults can keep an eye open for when moments of mastery arise and ask thoughtful questions to aid in reflection.

"How did you manage to do that?"

"What does this accomplishment say about you?"

"How do you think [person's name] felt when they saw you do that?"

Trust your instincts, trust yourself. If it works, keep going. If it doesn't, consider moving on. Mental health care is a relational experience, even when medications are involved. As we described in chapter 2, attempts to fix adolescent behavior are likely to fail. Youth asking for help from adults is wonderful, and the richness of different perspectives brings innovation and new ideas. Additionally, too much professional or unsolicited advice may increase uncertainty—for adults *and* youth—just as the decade of the parenting manual spurred increased anxiety for new parents.

As our dear friend Doug from Gippsland Adventure Therapy says, all of this work must be "fun, safe, and useful." Who decides that is the young person. Psychotherapy, counseling, and change in general is an experience. We must ask youth how they *experience* it. We cannot tell them what or how to experience. That could lead to an extinction.

PART III

IDEOLOGY

EXTINCTION OF EXPERIENCE

As cities and metastasizing suburbs forsake their
natural diversity, and their citizens grow more removed
from personal contact with nature, awareness and
appreciation retreat. ... So it goes, on and on,
the extinction of experience, sucking the life from
the land, the intimacy from our connections ...
people who don't know don't care. What is
the extinction of the condor to a child
who has never known a wren?
—Robert Pyle

Ellen loved exploring. She took risks and craved doing crazy things. She was a sensation-seeking child. Her parents, like many Norwegians, loved to play in the mountains and spent every free moment outside, a passion they shared with their young daughter, whether hiking the steep peaks on the western coast, skiing in the dark winter, or just getting involved in a range of competitive sports. Ellen has fond memories of the many positive experiences her parents provided. Her childhood matches the perceptions we developed over the years working with and learning from our Scandinavian colleagues.

Yes, in Scandinavia, you can see children rolling down grassy hills in parks or jumping in muddy puddles during recess. Rain, sleet, snow, or shine, you can witness children playing outside— even in the dark mid-winter months of the year!

Norwegians have a culturally embedded concept called *friluftsliv* (pronounced free-loofts-leev). Friluftsliv translates as *open-air life*; it sums up the Norwegian tradition of outdoor activity and the belief that health and happiness are defined within their connection to nature—a oneness with all things living. Our Scandinavian friends coined the term *frilufsterapi*— therapy in the open air. They combined their therapeutic work in the outdoors with the cultural lifestyle that may account for Scandinavian countries' rank at the top in world happiness reports.[1] Fortunately, we have witnessed and experienced friluftsliv, both personally and professionally, during our visits to Norway.

Yet, according to Ellen, friluftsliv is in decline, a trend we see in many ways across the Western world. A deterioration of meaningful opportunities, be it hiking in the mountains or other emotionally and physically engaging activities, has dire consequences for the health of kids these days, such as increasing the likelihood of missed developmental opportunities (fractures), increased social isolation, and emotional and spiritual starvation. And, as modern technology and entertainment displace time spent playing in nature, we can add the hijacking of frontal lobes to the list—with gorging likely to follow. We have watched disconnection grow in numerous ways over time; government responses to COVID-19 only exacerbated these ill effects.

Along with the pandemic's unpredictability and prolonged social isolation and disconnection, we saw reduced physical activity and sports participation and deteriorating mental health in youth.[2] While the US Sports and Fitness Industry Association (SFIA) report showed sports participation numbers in 2022 returning to prepandemic levels, there are lingering effects and differences in how youth are engaging.[3] Kids today are less likely to commit to a *team* sport. Instead, they dabble in *multiple* sports, which skews the numbers by falsely keeping up overall numbers for what we think of sports participation. The CEO of SFIA shared his insight that, during the pandemic, when kids were not playing team sports, they found other ways to be "with" their peers, and he reminded us that sports are, for some kids, a way to be with friends outside their love of the sport.

Again, the pandemic illustrated the priorities of our decision-makers. We saw how factors that can increase resilience and well-being were treated as incidental. We see this repeatedly in schools, organizations, and families when budget restrictions put play, outdoor activities, and physical education on the chopping block. As play and physical activity become increasingly endangered, we've also observed global metrics of reading, mathematics, and science scores deteriorating since 2000—and then dropping off a cliff in 2021. Coinciding with increased youth access to social media and i-tech,[4] these numbers continue their downward trend despite Western education having prioritized Science, Technology, Engineering, and Mathematics (STEM) in elementary schools over the last two decades.

As the Western world continues evolving its automated workplaces, it just kind of feels right for educators to push STEM curricula. However, the Organisation for Economic Co-operation and Development (OECD)'s Programme for International Student Assessment (PISA) found consistently declining STEM test scores since the early 2000s, that is, in the decade *before* front-facing cameras on phones and the entrenchment of social media in everyday life.[5] These numbers are averaged from across the world; numbers crashed at steeper rates since 2010, and the curve does not appear to be flattening. But if unstructured playtime is diminishing in schools, shouldn't reading, math, and science scores improve? It hasn't happened that way. As opportunity for play becomes an increasingly unimportant factor in the decision-making of adults, not only do mental health concerns rise, but academic performance continues to deteriorate.

A 2016 survey of twelve thousand parents from ten different countries reported about one-third of 5- to 12-year-olds were spending less than thirty minutes a day outdoors. About half of kids in the US were spending less than an hour outside. The study, funded by the German and UK laundry brand Persil, resulted in a clever campaign promoting childhood outdoor play. The campaign was headed by Sir Ken Robinson, a champion of childhood development through play. Persil (known as *Omo* in some countries) has held strong views on outdoor play, and has used the "Dirt is Good" slogan since 2005. While it may just be a brilliant marketing strategy to sell detergent to parents of kids with dirt-stained clothes, we applaud their efforts and love the series of videos they produced, now almost a decade ago. Especially poignant is the one where prison inmates, who get two hours of outdoor time each day, were informed of the research and were quite troubled by what they heard. "That is just not good" and "Something's gone wrong" were their responses.[6]

The nonprofit Aspen Institute's 2023 report on the state of play graded Norway's youth participation with an A, and government support of play, an A+. Sweden, Norway's Scandinavian neighbor to the east, received a B+ in participation and a B in government support. In youth sports participation, China received an F, the United States a C, the United Kingdom a D, and Canada a C+.

We know sports alone are not a panacea responsible for healthy communities, healthy people, or one's flourishing mental health. However, we do argue that the extinction of play, organized or not, and the reduction of outside physical activity has a drastic impact on kids these days.

Robert Pyle (quoted at the beginning of this chapter) speaks of this extinction in terms of loss of contact with nature, some

thing we recognize and see often in our work as outdoor therapists.[7] Based on the evidence we have presented, there is a very
real need for improved mental health support, and, our primary
field of research—outdoor therapies—suggests the benefits of a
more intimate connection with the natural world. We also see
and read about a loss of experience happening in other realms
for youth and young adults. Beyond lower levels of physical
activity and participation in sports,[8] there is less reading,[9] a significant decrease in teens learning to drive,[10] and (as reported by
the CDC) a historic drop in the number of high schoolers having
sex.[11] You only have to ponder each of these, reflect on your own
life and experiences, and think, what are the long-term effects
for youth who don't have these experiences? Are these experiences now endangered?

The young child raised in the Norwegian wild helping us
to explore the extinction of experience is Dr. Ellen Beate Hansen Sandseter. She is a professor specializing in early childhood
physical activity at Queen Maud University College in Trond-
heim, Norway. She remains a thrill-seeker and outdoor enthu-
siast whose research interests grew along with her children
and their development as playful sensation-seeking people.
Her work is focused on the importance of unstructured outdoor play—play that often includes elements of risk. We were
eager to connect with Sandseter to discuss her internationally
recognized work in education and child development circles.
Her research demonstrates the benefits of outdoor risky play,
such as child explorations of height, speed, dangerous tools, and
risky environments. This adventurous type of play is music to
our ears—climbing trees, cutting wood for a fire, or bounding
across a stream on boulders are activities we've used to engage
struggling youth throughout our professional careers. We met
with Ellen to discuss her work, her passion, and her views on
how kids these days experience *less.* Together, we examined the
impacts and what we can collectively do to address them.

Teen Competencies and the Antiphobic Response

After completing a bachelor's degree in sport education, Ellen went on to study adolescent risk-taking in her master's degree. The prominence of her research today is due to her subsequent focus on outdoor play, which became the subject of her doctoral research. Ellen found that youth need positive ways to seek sensations—or they'll find less socially acceptable ways for themselves. We've known this for more than a century.

The mother of professional social work and the first American woman to win the Nobel Peace Prize, Jane Addams, wrote in 1909 about the kids of her day in *The Spirit of Youth and the City Streets*. She argued the desire and *quest for adventure* seizes all youth—they need to feel more alive![12] As we described in chapter 1, Jane Addams was a founding member of the National Child Labor Committee and played a substantial role in reforming child labor laws. She knew some youth's acting out behaviors may be less about the act itself than the seeking of *experiencing*. Jane Addams wrote that a teenager's "very demand for excitement is a protest against the dullness of life, to which we ourselves [adults] instinctively respond." More than a century ago, Addams illustrated the *kids these days effect* with stories of youth being sent to reform schools or detention as punishment for thrill-seeking and petty crime. She argued these were not the sins of the child but the adults who "failed to rescue them from a life of grinding monotony which their spirit could not brook." Adults have been wondering for a long time how a child gets to be a teenager feeling so void and starved of novel experiences that they would choose petty theft or gorging to fill that emptiness.

Dr. Sandseter's scientific pursuits confirm a simple truth. Sensation-seeking experiences satisfy adolescent curiosities about personal competence and character. Children need rich developmental critical opportunities to explore and take chances in healthy ways to develop an *antiphobic response—* or in plain language, a natural ability for people to face and

respond to challenges. For Ellen, the antiphobic response is for-
tified through risky play and outdoor exploration.

Resilience is the ability to bounce back from difficulties or
adverse events. It's a rubber band capable of stretching and
adapting to different stimuli and states of being without breaking. Dr. Sandseter knows it's hard, if not impossible, to prove her
hypothesis of the antiphobic response. Studies would need to
include risky play compared with less risky or risk-free play.
University ethics boards are stereotypically risk-averse when it
comes to human research. Rightly so, considering the complex
history of harm inflicted on research participants in the name
of scientific discovery. Difficulties in research ethics increase
as the Western world privileges certain types of research, such
as the randomized controlled trials we described in the previous chapter.

A somewhat humorous example would be skydiving. Everyone knows parachutes are effective for skydivers, but we can
never really "prove" a parachute is the most effective option for
successful skydiving because we can't "control" for it in a clinical trial. To do so, half the research participants would have to
be randomly provided a parachute and the others a fake (placebo) parachute. The participants, who would have consented
to be in the study, would not be aware of which parachute they
were given. Using researcher lingo, those skydiving with the
placebo would be "falling-as-usual" (which is similar to "treatment-as-usual" in psychotherapy studies). Research ethics don't
(or shouldn't) allow us to place kids at risk, or conversely, to
deprive them of experiences such as therapy or medicine. This
adds difficulty for researchers looking for robust evidence. This
is why it is hard to test the meaning and impacts of risky play.

Still, it is not hard to conceptualize what Dr. Sandseter is suggesting: partaking in diverse challenging experiences will set
the child up with learned responses (through trial and error) to
better prepare them for more difficult experiences in the future.
This is a conditioned response to exposure and a classic expres-

sion, sometimes called *habituation*—simply building up the habit of doing something until one is more capable and comfortable with the habit. These repetitive explorations should involve supportive adults and be undertaken in conducive environments. Of course, these are essential elements in childcare, and any other setting where child and youth development takes place.

Dr. Sandseter has also explored how children think about and respond to challenging experiences. Whether kids feel supported by caregivers, parents, or other adults is just as important as the experience itself. As therapists, we meet many adolescents experiencing anxiety. It's easy to agree with Ellen's premise here; youth should process their exposure to risk as a growth experience, not a harmful one. Success in working through anxiety can come via increased exposure to the cause of the anxiety. Sounds simple, yet it's not the exposure, nor the talking about your feelings that really solidifies change.

Anxiety may provoke feelings of fear or increased stress response in the body, but it's what meaning one makes of it, and actions that follow that determine success with the intervention. For example, meeting a group of new kids is stress-inducing to a child. If they talk about how it made them feel, great. But it is in recognition that they didn't die or weren't attacked that will determine whether they will repeat the exposure, even if it was uncomfortable. This relates to the antiphobic response; skateboarding or climbing trees both contain inherent dangers, but we do them anyway. Habituation—forming habits—builds resilience.

Of course, risk can elicit feelings of fear and discomfort. Risky play should, however, not be equated cognitively with being dangerous. Our ability to persevere, process the facts, and describe our feelings is helpful and allows for better integration before our next exposure to risk. Sensing experiences as dangerous reinforces fear and increases self-doubt. The adults in the room must remain present while actively listening and caring for the child as they experience the world, allowing the child to feel their feelings and express them. This communicates and models a sense of safety to help the child recognize their skill development. Also, ask the child about their desire to repeat the experience for its benefits. With more repetition of similar experiences, kids gain in ability, confidence, and determination, and they psychologically fortify their perception of self.

In a 2023 article in the *International Journal of Play*, Dr. Sandseter, along with two coauthors, argued that risky play aids in emotional regulation, anxiety reduction, maturation, and competency in new social settings, and it increases psychosocial competencies youth bring with them into their adult lives.[13] For younger children, play creates a safe-enough "laboratory" to play with the big emotions we described in chapter 6. Kids play family, pretend to run a store, or be boyfriend/girlfriend well before "hormones and romantic feelings become too serious."

It's important to note that risky play can be misinterpreted to be literally dangerous play, which is sometimes endorsed by adults to make sure we're toughening up the kids these days. If you have any level of involvement with social media or online marketing, you'll see plenty of messages out there to *just do hard shit!* Do the authors of these messages recognize the preconditions required for being successful at completing said hard shit? Accomplishment reaps rewards. We get that. But completing hard tasks usually begins with doing similar, easier tasks successfully. Remember our discussion about how important success and mastery are to effective psychotherapy in the previous chapter. The specific task matters little. Self-esteem can be improved through mastering the basic open chords on a guitar, catching a fish from the river, or engaging with a new peer social group.

Progressional learning, or scaffolding (a term we also heard from Dr. Simon Davidson), sets up incrementally harder challenges that are ideal for growth and development. The idea is to start small and increasingly develop exposure to more emotional and physical risk-taking. Of course, this requires developmentally appropriate containers for youth to experience risk, which often requires adult support and guardrails.

Where youth are given space to explore and test themselves with others who are also testing themselves, you have what Dr. Gordon Neufeld calls an *emotional playground*. As they grow, their activities and roles change, capacities increase, and the ability to maintain healthy developmental trajectories is determined by how well the previous milestones have been achieved. It is in the absence of the previous developmental steps (the fractures) that youth find themselves struggling with capacity, and, by extension, their sense of self, especially through the neurotic teenage years. Physical activity and exploration are important for understanding one's body and emotional self-regulation in relation to others, whether that be adults or other youth. Social media and i-tech should not be the substitute classroom for puberty.

This brings us back to our concern about the reduction of team sports and the stark increases in individualized, structured "play." We've seen how when school budgets get tight, outdoor and physical education are often one of the first things to go, along with music and arts programs. Humans evolved over six million years, and it's only in about the past two hundred, or 0.000033% of this evolution, that children have been required to sit still in a classroom every day. The sedentary lifestyle is increasing mental and physical ill health. Sitting is quickly becoming the new smoking.

Active Healthy Kids, a global alliance of health researchers across fifty-seven countries, gives a failing grade for international physical activity, reflecting today's screen-centric, indoor, automated, and sedentary lifestyles. It is not the responsibility of children to be active. Given the right circumstances, they will be, which generally means socialized play. An active childhood tends to lead to an active adolescence, and not surprisingly, an active adulthood. This global reality of reduced physical activity in children has major implications for the health and well-being of societies. The Active Healthy Kids report points to factors such as parenting, family contexts, school policies, and government agendas failing to increase active play, provide accessible transport to organized sports, and create environments conducive to physical activity. While specifically looking at physical activity, and knowing its importance in child and youth development, how do these factors relate to less-happy, less-healthy, and increasingly anxious kids these days?

Dr. Sandseter has taught fundamental movement skills for decades. She knows children need to challenge their bodies. Through play, muscles strengthen, coordination improves, reaction times improve, and spatial orientation expands. She suggests there is every reason to believe these developments occur psychologically as well. Ellen believes the free exploration of landscapes, experimenting in social relationships, and risk-taking in play are all natural learning processes.

Resiliency researcher Dr. Michael Ungar calls this the *risk-taker's advantage*.[14] An advantage is gained by those youth who don't experience fractures in their development process. These fractures or inadequate skills and knowledge acquisition, says Ungar, can lead to further incremental gaps. In a climate where young people are kept *too safe for their own good*, developmental milestones are missed or not fully developed. Today, we have created an environment that caters to young people lacking resiliency. It's an interesting irony since our current education system evolved during the Industrial Revolution, which centered on producing effective workers.

Rough-and-Tumble Play

Dr. Ellen Sandseter has another major concern: the loss, or extreme endangerment, of rough-and-tumble play, particularly in childcare and school settings. This type of play may be one of the most important for children, especially for young boys. Rough-and-tumble play is slightly more preferential for boys—partly due to the higher levels of testosterone—and one of the few ways for all kids to learn and practice a combination of social and physical skills in a meaningful manner.

Ellen warns us that this is a type of play adults seem to have pushed to near extinction; it is now nearly forbidden in schools. She notes that rough-and-tumble play is banned in most kindergartens and preschools—ages when play is most developmentally relevant and needed. Empirical support exists for rough-and-tumble play as a developmental asset, shown to have positive effects, yet adults are depriving children (again, especially the boys) of a critical growth opportunity because this play is misunderstood or simply disliked by many early-years educators.[15]

When working with youth in the correctional system, Nevin used modified forms of wrestling, jousting, and tug-of-war games to dissolve tensions between the boys. On paddling expeditions, beaches provided a dynamic arena for gladiator or strongman sports with rules that allowed for tests of strength and other fundamental movement skills but limited the chance of anyone fighting or getting hurt. While not incident-free, the risk-benefit analysis was supportive of the activities and significantly improved group dynamics. However, as many adults are uncomfortable seeing any sort of youth discomfort during physical play, the quick fix is to remove and overprotect, diminishing opportunities for rough-and-tumble play (and teachable moments). Instead, adults should be providing guardrails and a container for this evolutionarily normal social interaction.

Overcontrol of kids' play has been described before in the literature. In 2007, Matt Hern wrote in *Watch Yourself: Why Safer Isn't Always Better*:

> The common and comprehensible rationale for adult domination of kids' play is safety. It is the overwhelming reason most of us intervene, supervise, and structure kids' play for them. Our interventions are justified by speeding

cars, abductions, concussions, eyes poked out, hurt feelings, being bullied, being scared, and broken limbs. Actually, it is not really these things; it is the specter of these things, the worst-case scenarios, the guilt, the fear. In the era of risk-reduction analyses, our cost-benefit ratios invariably tip heavily toward hallucinated potential injuries and other disasters and the light they would cast on our parenting. But how often do we consider the costs of crowding out play?[16]

Matt Hern was a teacher in alternative education. He wrote about this problem almost two decades ago, but we didn't listen. We are observing even more and more intense risk aversion now. It appears to be the behavior and ideology of adults that limit natural exploratory play in children's lives, including risky, unsupervised, outdoor, and rough-and-tumble forms of play. Most kids in America will spend about twelve thousand hours of their lives in school. We've seen movements toward more nature-based playgrounds and acknowledging the benefits of increased time for recess. Another factor worth considering could be the under-representation of males as leaders in the classroom.

The American Institute for Boys and Men reports that men only represent 23% of elementary and secondary teachers and as few as 3% of kindergarten and pre-K educators in America—and their numbers are dwindling rather than growing.[17] The gender differences are clear, and our experts are observing and trying to address the impact while focusing on youth experiences and the research evidence while avoiding the ideology wars stemming from these discussions.

"Most of the people working in kindergarten and preschools are women," said Ellen. "And they don't see the benefit of rough-and-tumble play. They actually don't like it because they interpret it as aggression."

A review of rough-and-tumble play in 2022 found differences in perceptions across genders.[18] The researchers found female educators may bring a "rather negative or at least ambivalent attitude" to risky play. However, training and experience reduced the impact, including understanding the beneficial outcomes related to competence and emotional regulation. Again, not a judgment, just an important finding when it comes to interpreting play.

Some adults trying to interpret rough-and-tumble play understand it as hostility; but often, it's simply playful. Neurotherapist Dr. Mari Swingle referred to this type of play as especially critical in the early years. The lack of it is a contributing factor to the endangerment of children's abilities in socialization. Much is to be learned through this physically interactive form of play. Children, it appears, are much better at interpreting their play than the adults protecting them from it. They are much more accurate in judging the difference between play and fighting or aggression—with no adult intervention.

"While looking at the research," Ellen continued, "rough-and-tumble play is probably one of the most important play types for younger boys."

Rough-and-tumble play is not just a human concept; it's a mammalian behavior. When observing a litter of kittens, or any young mammals play fighting, we can see how strength and movement are tested. Then retested. Roles of dominance and submission can switch between combatants. Children try their best to preserve the relationship with the care shown to each other during their playful version of a "fight." A give-and-take unfolds, and Ellen believes kids are masterful in designing their own play to best meet their own needs. Kids engaged in rough-and-tumble play are actively developing physical skills and assessing their own capacity for movement, strength, and problem-solving—all the while trying to develop and maintain social relationships with those they are playing with. It's not aggression, anger, or a fight. It's an evolutionary adaptive process. It's play.

Dr. Ellen Sandseter described an unwritten, mostly unconscious, social regulation system children use to maintain social competitiveness and keep play fun. Imagine kids playing soccer at a local field. No referee. No direct adult supervision. Kids often pick competitive teams because lopsided games are less fun. It's more fun to remain unsure who will win. They may want to win, but they also want the game to be challenging. When in rough-and-tumble play, kids will, with whatever social and emotional skills they have developed, work to engage in a fun way that hopefully allows for future play, too.

Much like fake-fighting kittens do, kids typically want to preserve friendships over simply "winning." In situations where adults are present, boundaries can be negotiated for safety and support to fit the circumstances, but this shouldn't remove or dilute the developmental opportunity. A certain amount of trust and understanding is necessary for an adult in any caregiving capacity that allows them to gift the children with autonomy and the dignity of risk.

Our experts agreed that adults need to recognize that children's previous skill development will be a factor in successful rough-and-tumble play. Children learning to have fun during a test of physical strength doesn't happen without incidents. The ability to negotiate boundaries and regulate emotions doesn't develop overnight. It is, however, the adult's responsibility to reflect on their own risk tolerance and keep in mind their role in these developmental opportunities during play, and to not simply extinguish opportunities, risky, or rough, or not. Rough-and-tumble play is the child's training ground to develop a repertoire of functional physical, social, and emotional skills and social boundaries.

Returning to the concept of an antiphobic response, Dr. Sandseter worries kids are missing out on unstructured and sometimes unsupervised outdoor play, in addition to experiences of rough-and-tumble play. Decreased opportunities to play can lead to social difficulties later in life.[19] She mentioned the example of teenage students struggling with social relationships in a Norwegian school. "Upon being sent to a psychiatrist, they were prescribed facilitated rough-and-tumble play, so they can get better," Ellen described, a bit cheekily.

Seems like youth simply must go back and work through missed developmental stages or fractures at some point. The factors associated with effective mental and behavioral health care appear to be the same factors for prevention—those similar to the Circle of Courage model and what works in effective therapy: *social connection, experience, success, mastery,* and *hope.*

Thankfully, the research supporting rough-and-tumble play is growing, and it suggests that educators, childcare staff, etc.—as well as parents—need to be shown how to let kids be kids in this regard. Parents and guardians need to understand and support the emotional playground children need for physical and emotional development. By facilitating emotional playgrounds, adults create environments, provide resources, and support developmental needs which may ameliorate future adolescent mental health issues: *the antiphobic response.* You may not see yourself in a role to assist on this front, but parents, aunts, uncles, coaches, neighbors, mentors, or any adult in the life of a child can contribute.

The "Risk Society"

We live in a climate of fear regarding litigation. We see this especially in custodial settings such as youth programs, community centers, and schools. No one wants to be blamed for allowing a student or child to get hurt. No one wants to get sued. Unfortunately, this *risk-averse culture* is dictating many decisions in these settings.

In the absence of a parent to take responsibility for their child's care, educators and providers of recreational and community-based programs make decisions about policy and practice that constrain childhood behaviors and eliminate some experiences common to previous generations. In the US, we know drive-through fast food restaurants have been successfully sued for serving coffee too hot. In one well-known case, significant burning occurred when a customer tried to open a cup while it was nestled between their legs. While many thought this was a frivolous lawsuit, it was later found in court that McDonalds was serving their coffee *intentionally* too hot, hoping customers wouldn't have time to benefit from free refills.[20]

Maybe that's not the best example related to child development, but the reality is we live in a *risk society*, a term coined by Ulrich Beck, a German sociologist, who saw modern Western nations after the Industrial Revolution turning away from the guidance of nature and traditions, and instead focusing on predictions to assess and manage risk.[21] Instead of relying on cultural beliefs and common sense, societies began to rely on science, technology, and a mechanistic worldview to calculate and quantify risk. Then, mitigation strategies were employed to "play the odds." Insurance companies do this every day. The insurance industry likes to define risk as *the potential for loss*, while we, and childhood experts such as Dr. Sandseter, acknowledge risk as having two sides, including *the opportunity for gain*, bringing a balance to the risk equation.

We know from neuroscience that the prefrontal cortex, the executive part of our brain, differentiates us from other animals, helping us with self-awareness, problem-solving, and learning. We develop our prefrontal cortex into our mid-20s. Insurance adjustors trust the science on this, calculate the likelihood of having to pay out for accidents, and set prices accordingly. This is why auto insurance is most expensive for drivers under 25 years of age. But the risk society extends beyond car and life insurance. Today, it dictates how carefully children are attended to.

Consider two major factors historically receiving considerable attention and heavily influencing parent decision-making: *stranger danger* and *fear of kids being hit by cars*—neither of which fully deserve the hyperbolic attention they get in the media, nor the resulting limitations put on children to protect them from these perceived dangers. Printing the faces of missing children on milk cartons raises the alarm that our kids are not safe. But the level of alarm is out of proportion to the actual threat.

Ulrich Beck did his best to educate the public about uncertainty and the ignorance of assuming that all risks and variables are controllable. It's just not possible. Modernity, he argued, has created a false sense of belief about risk, primarily through mass media and globalization. For instance, one child abducted somewhere in the world, as horrible as it is, ends up on TV screens across the globe, and families everywhere experience heightened levels of fear. It's the same with terrorist attacks. Our televisions and mobile devices bring these events into our living rooms. Increased anxiety by design. The likelihood of child abduction by a stranger, at least in North America, while still terrifying, is quite low; in the US in 2016 it was close to 1 in a million.[22] For those who struggle with that number and think occurrence is higher, remember this is abduction by a *stranger*. Missing children are much more frequently runaways or abductions by a family member or friend, such as in custody disputes and family conflicts, or even miscommunications. Many are often resolved within hours of reporting.

When it comes to strangers and the stranger danger myth, critic Warwick Cairns did the math: "...if you actually wanted your child to be abducted, you'd probably have to leave them outside for 750,000 hours."[23] When you combine the realities of stranger danger and children's safety due to traffic concerns, it is statistically safer to let your kids walk to school than any other means of getting them there. The American Academy of Pediatrics in 2007 advocated for children to take school buses, cycle, and even walk to school to save lives, as 75% of deaths and 84% of injuries related to school travel occurred in passenger vehicles.[24] Guidelines for improving the safety of children and teenagers walking or biking to school are also available.[25]

Will grew up in the suburbs of Washington, DC, and remembers Halloween fondly. Dressed as a zombie or Batman, Will would walk with his father around the neighborhood, collecting a pillowcase full of candy each year. Of course, this was a relatively safe neighborhood (if you ignore the DC sniper), where houses are packed close together with no fences to separate them. When Will was old enough, he'd trick-or-treat with his friends. Despite the best attempts of morning talk shows and the 24-hour news cycle to scare parents, the stories of poisoned candy or apples with razor blades were mostly debunked. Still, some families are taking precautions to protect their children.

There is a recent and now-growing American trend: *trunk-or-treating*, a sort of Halloween tailgating.[26] More and more parents are gathering in parking lots across America to allow children to walk from car to car to collect their Halloween candy. Why? In communities where houses are far apart, this makes sense. But for most parents? It's for safety.

Sure, parents are placing trust in their neighbors when their little ones ring the doorbell and shout "Trick-or-Treat!" And the evidence is clear that most neighbors do well with that trust. We're not saying Halloween is going to save the world; most countries get on with life without All Hallows' Day. But we are seeing activities that should be fun—one many adults remember fondly from their childhood—becoming more and more endangered in the name of safety and protection.

Lenore Skenazy, author of *Free-Range Kids*, penned a 2024 article about how Montgomery County Public Schools in Maryland revised their "Supervision Recess Procedures for Playground Aides" with a policy banning baseball, football, "haphazard running," chasing, and tag games on the blacktop. Students could no longer swing on bars or rings until the student ahead of them was done.[27] The Procedures advised playground aides to "caution children if it appears that emotions and excitement are mounting to a point where incorrect actions may soon result." This is the very definition of treating kids as passengers. No trust. Not crew.

In 2009, a lawsuit was filed against a municipality in British Columbia by a family after their daughter had fallen from playground equipment at summer camp.[28] The playground was supervised, and the kids were playing a common game of tag called "grounders" in which the person who is *it* (with their eyes closed) starts on the ground and everyone else tries to avoid detection and getting caught. The game involves kids running and climbing all over the playground equipment, not always as designed. (We could write another chapter on the extinction of experience with old-school playgrounds with high swings, steep slides, merry-go-rounds, and teeter-totters!) The point here is that a child got hurt during a child-led, semisupervised, and indirectly sanctioned activity. Adults were present, but not interfering with children's play. The suit called the activity and the adult supervision into question. Fortunately for child development, this outdoor play was seen by the judge as within the boundaries of normal activity. The case was dropped.

The judge suggested that by the measure of a reasonably prudent parent, the activity itself did not require adult supervision—nor consent—and that children's play, by its very nature, is inherently risky, be it running, jumping, chasing, hiding, or in this case, playing tag. While a bright spot for the judicial system's support for this type of risk, this case was cause for a flurry of editorial responses for and against the decision. The child injury prevention folks were adamant that the developmental psychologists and health promotion folks had it wrong—and vice-versa.

Those rallying in favor of outdoor risky play suggested that repeated and increasingly challenging types of play lead to development in many domains of the child's life, from movement skills to self-esteem and confidence. The injury prevention side argued back that their efforts over the decades to reduce childhood visits to emergency rooms to near-zero were being compromised. An obvious response to this back-and-forth debate is the question: If no kids are getting hurt, are they taking risks, and if the answer is no, then at what cost?

One developmental psychologist arguing on behalf of outdoor risky play, a recently deceased colleague of Nevin's at the University of Victoria, Dr. Chris Lalonde,[29] was passionate about the dignity of risk and believed that children learned their own boundaries through testing them, yet another way of articulating Dr. Ellen Sandseter's antiphobic response. As former adventure guides, we maintain a strong bias for the *right to risk* and its role in human development. It's important to encourage risk-taking in kids, but parents, educators, and therapists do need to remember that some young people already have too much risk in their lives. We shouldn't impose challenges or increased stress when more basic needs aren't being met.

In the 1960s, the director of the Swedish Association for Persons with Mental Retardation (outdated terminology, we know), Dr. Bengt Nirje, formed a club comprised of some people diagnosed with a mental disorder and some who had not.[30] There were no leaders and only a few simple rules. The members met to plan an outing, an adventure. They would go on the outing and then meet to discuss and reflect on the experience. Sometimes the activities involved risk. The people labeled as disabled were provided the opportunity to make their own decisions, even when mistakes might be made.

Dr. Nirje was called a radical. The medical community at the time believed people with developmental disabilities were incapable of decision-making and required protection at all costs. "To be allowed to be human means to be allowed to fail," Dr. Nirje responded. What he realized was that many of the people labeled incompetent by society actually wanted a *new role* in that society. They wanted autonomy, equality, and, most importantly, personal dignity. The approach spread internationally, and in the 1970s, a new advocacy group formed in the US called *People First*. (The name was inspired by the person who said, "I want to be known as a person first!") All people want dignity, which includes the right to risk.

Ordained Methodist minister Robert Perske, described in his eulogy as a champion of people living with mental and developmental disabilities, conveyed this idea of the dignity of risk.[31] He witnessed people living with mental disorders being convicted for crimes they didn't commit. He observed rising rates of people diagnosed with mental disorders being institutionalized. They would be sent to residential facilities where in everyday life, their decision-making was oppressed and controlled. As Dr. Simon Davidson described, many mental health labels come with discrimination. This is also why so many healthcare professionals and associations signed the open letter we mentioned in chapter 5 advocating for a ban on diagnoses of borderline personality disorder for children and youth in June 2024. "Until there is conclusive proof that this diagnosis does not harm children, we say it should not occur," the letter stated.[32]

In the 1970s, Minister Perske saw the limitations on risk-taking activities imposed on people with mental health labels. In 1972, Perske wrote:

> Overprotection may appear on the surface to be kind, but it can be really evil. An oversupply can smother people emotionally, squeeze the life out of their hopes and expectations, and strip them of their dignity. Overprotection can keep people from becoming all they could become. Many of our best achievements came the hard way: We took risks, fell flat, suffered, picked ourselves up, and tried again. Sometimes we made it and sometimes we did not. Even so, we were given the chance to try. Persons with special needs need these chances, too. Of course, we are talking about prudent risks. People should not be expected to blindly face challenges that, without a doubt, will explode in their faces. Knowing which chances are prudent and which are not is a new skill that needs to be acquired. On the other hand, a risk is really only when it is not known beforehand

whether a person can succeed. The real world is not always safe, secure, and predictable, it does not always say "please," "excuse me," or "I'm sorry." Every day we face the possibility of being thrown into situations where we will have to risk everything ... In the past, we found clever ways to build avoidance of risk into the lives of persons living with disabilities. Now we must work equally hard to help find the proper amount of risk these people have the right to take. We have learned that there can be healthy development in risk-taking and there can be crippling indignity in safety![33]

It isn't just those living with mental health concerns who are missing developmentally appropriate levels of risk. It's *most young people.* Parenting expert (2024 Western Australia's Senior Australian of the Year) Maggie Dent made a plea to the federal government to stop removing opportunities for play.[34] Writing to the federal education minister, Dent argued that rising rates of aggressive behavior in young boys was a direct—and normal—response to schools forcing children to read, write, and count at earlier and earlier ages. This was not a new idea; Jane Addams wrote about it in the first decades of the twentieth century. What these kids were missing was the development of social skills *through play.* Maggie leaned into the statistics regarding trends that could be associated with reduced risky play:

- Increased in-school suspensions for kids younger than six (mostly boys)
- Rises in meltdowns in the car on the way home from school
- School avoidance after just six weeks of preschool
- Rising ADHD diagnoses and consequent medicating
- Children as young as 4 having homework, and 7-year-olds with two hours of homework a night
- Increasing rates of autism

- Reductions in student autonomy
- Rising rates of self-harm and depression in children as young as 4.

To echo the title Maggie gave to her plea, we are *stealing childhood in the name of education*. The role of mental health providers appears to be focusing on the concerns of adults—the teachers, parents, politicians—in order to medicate, therapize, and even sedate children to fit into uncooperative and developmentally inappropriate environments. As we learned from Dr. Bruce Lanphear in chapter 4, if we remove something from a person's life in an effort to help, we must examine the usefulness and quality of the substitution. Maggie is describing a *regrettable substitution*.

Generational Amnesia

Just as adults rant about *kids these days*, they also, on occasion, refer to how much harder it was in the past or reminisce about how much better things used to be. "Back in my day..." is a classic refrain.

University of Washington Professor Peter Kahn Jr. put forth the concept of *generational amnesia*, specifically relating it to environmental degradation.[35] He described how each subsequent generation sees the world through its own lens. The implications on the environmental front are obvious: We may see, for example, trees being cut down in a residential area "over the years," but we don't have our parents' memories of when the region was mostly forest and only a handful of homes were present. Further, our grandparents may recall when a road was first pushed into a densely forested area and trees cleared for the first time to lay the foundation for the first homes. We treat Kahn's generational amnesia concept as transferable to many aspects of our lives and believe it fitting to apply here. We must consider the world kids grow up in and what they experience, acknowledging it was different from previous generations. This can help us to avoid the kids these days effect.

Our children today cannot imagine a time without mobile phones or Wi-Fi. Nevin's father grew up in a home without electricity. Much of life now could be called faster, more convenient, more efficient, and safer than a few generations back, yet we may have lost something in return. Is it possible, as Ellen Sandseter argues, that we are missing out on developmental benefits that previous generations had? While maybe not yet extinct, children's opportunities for growth through rough-and-tumble play may be on the endangered list. Another loss may be the unstructured and unsupervised play that offers children a variety of circumstances in which to develop their capacity for wayfinding, decision-making, independence, and maintaining social relationships.

Can you recall from your own childhood how far from home you were allowed to play unaccompanied by an adult? Researchers call this *ranging* or *independent mobility*. Our review of the literature suggests an extinction of experience on this front as well.

One study published in 1990 focused on changes over time in independent child mobility and safety.[36] *Ranging* is defined as a child's ability to be autonomous across a geographical area, hence, the range in which they have the independence to travel, get to school, visit friends, and so on. The comparison between 1971 and 1990 resulted in unsurprising findings. Although the mobile phone and i-tech are being blamed for causing most of today's problems with youth, the study showed that ranging and risky play were diminishing well before the internet fit into everyone's pocket. (A more recent Canadian ranging study showing 7- to 12-year-olds with more independent mobility [range] were less likely to experience mental health distress during the pandemic, lending merit to the premise of the anti-phobic response.[37])

Children and youth in 1971 took part in a wider array of activities, and more often traveled unaccompanied and much farther away than the 1990 cohort. Parents involved in the study echoed this reality; they believed they had ranged farther and more often, and they confirmed the reduced experiences of independent mobility of their own children. Equally, the study supported the notion that independent child and adolescent experiences of mobility had been reduced significantly within just one generation. What range do kids have today? Are we now seeing only supervised play (play dates) in fenced back-yards or indoors, where no ranging is available to the child? What does that mean if we take Peter Kahn's generational amnesia into account? What is lost across two or three gener-ations when we can only see the world through the years we ourselves have lived?

The Risk-Averse Safety Trap

After twenty-four years of teaching at Queen Maud University in Norway, Dr. Sandseter knows that her current young adult students have had much less diverse experiences outdoors, less unsupervised and unstructured play, less risk, and less rough-and-tumble activity in their lives than previous generations. Knowing the value of those exploratory and thrilling experi-ences, she is worried about lowered resilience and the growing trend of adolescent and young adult fragility. Again, while the extinction of experience progresses little by little, and we might not recognize the detrimental effects over time due to genera-tional amnesia, we are beginning to see clear signs of harm. The focus on safety in our risk-averse society resulted in unintended negative consequences.

Dr. Ungar called our society "too safe" years ago, as have others. In 2010, Lenore Skenazy's *Free-Range Kids* discussed the concept of helicopter parenting, warning the public about the dangers of overparenting, which is basically applying too much control and helping a child too much when the struggle of learning—including risk—is presented to them. Overprotec-tion may lead to reduced tolerance and resilience in kids these days (what some refer to as *fragile*). Additionally, if we continue to treat kids these days as if they require increased protection beyond the safety required to form a healthy attachment, we as adults may intervene in ways which are not resilience-promoting. The phenomenon of overprotection has gone beyond parenting and is found in classrooms, community centers, sports arenas, and elsewhere. Societally, we are risk-averse to a fault. Fear of litigation and/or being that one person who gets stained socially for allowing harm to come to a child in their care is just too much. Easier to play it safe. Let kids grow and develop through riskier forms of play with their own parents.

Although it will be hard to evidence how the evolutionary anti-phobic mechanisms engaged by children during outdoor risky play build resilience, grit, and self-efficacy, the concept deserves our attention. Kids these days deserve the opportunity to test it. It may mean getting school-aged kids up from their desks more, teachers taking a few more steps toward allowing free play, and changing societal beliefs and actions to support the dignity of a child falling off playground equipment during an exciting game of tag. It also may mean parents allowing more autonomy and trust to develop between them and their children to explore developmentally appropriate ranging, rough-and-tumble play, and adventurous thrill-seeking experiences.

9

THE SAFETY TRAP

I am not afraid of storms, for I am learning to sail my ship.
—Louisa May Alcott

Dr. Michael Ungar published the book *Too Safe for Their Own Good* in 2007, well before the negative impacts of social media on mental health became everyone's main concern. The first iPhone was released that same year. At the time, he identified a societal *glitch*: the overprotection of children had become too extreme. He saw how adults were letting the fear of litigation influence how they were parenting, and he saw school boards applying safety policies resulting in the removal of trees and rocks from playgrounds. Both approaches limited options for exploratory play. He thought the trend would pass and the anomaly would become obvious to all and a more balanced approach would emerge—driven by common sense—that would again allow children access to activities with elements of risk, such as ranging, climbing trees, or throwing snowballs. Today, we appear to have fully adopted the risk-averse standpoint. Maybe we collectively bought into the ideology that kids these days are too fragile to cope with risk, setbacks, or disappointment and need to be protected by adults. In this chapter, the safety trap is our focus.

Why do some children handle adversity better than others? The leading theory says it is *resilience*. As described in the previous chapter, resilience is often defined as the ability to "bounce back" from difficult situations, but it is much more nuanced than that. Resilience can include a few other characteristics, such as problem-solving skills, adaptability, coping mechanisms, being able to build connections with others, the ability to regulate one's emotions, and having a sense of self-confidence.[1]

Resilience is a desirable characteristic. Yet, we know our risk-averse society protects kids too much from experiences essential for the healthy development of resilience. We also know that some kids remain exposed to far *too many* risks and challenges. We know these kids; we work with many of them. Somewhere in the middle, where challenge is balanced with support, and caring adults are present, is where developmental experiences unfold to the child's benefit.

Dr. Michael Ungar is a resiliency expert. He shares the same passion for protecting childhood play and sensation-seeking we heard expressed by Dr. Ellen Beate Hansen Sandseter in the last chapter. Michael's decades of research, working with clients at risk, raising kids of his own, and teaching at the university level provided us with yet another well-informed perspective on kids these days and resilience. He has observed changes over time leading to where we are now, and he shares our concerns that society is headed in the wrong direction when it comes to the mental health and well-being of children and youth.

Risk Is Not a Negative Word

Risk provides opportunities for gain or loss, although most modern interpretations classify risk as a negative. Risk can be *imagined*, such as a parent imagining their child playing near a swift-moving river, falling in, and being swept away in the current; or risk can be *real*, such as when a child is actually trying to swim across the same river. A river *is* a hazard, but a child playing near a river, under the right conditions, can be a learning opportunity that will aid in the development of appropriate skills and positive psychological responses to challenges. We can support, resource, and sometimes supervise our children's interactions with hazards. We can allow for risk in their lives.

The picture in your mind of a child playing near the river may make some of you nervous. But the river itself is not the problem. It's our perception of it as a problem, and how we as adults allow children to play relative to it. A less extreme example of imagined danger is the height of today's playground swings. What happened?! They are less than half the height of those we grew up with. In fact, merry-go-rounds, teeter-totters, and tall swings and slides are more and more relics of the past. They were *fun*, and yes, sometimes dangerous. When children can explore height, speed, and other dangerous elements, they receive tangible and unforgettable lessons. There is dignity in being allowed to learn from our mistakes. The possibility for injury exists. We are not suggesting we intentionally put kids in harm's way, but more and more, we are limiting our kids' opportunities for adventurous exploration.

Michael Ungar's *Too Safe* was an early warning signal and call to action to not overprotect our youth, yet it seemingly went unheard. Lenore Skenazy's *Free-Range Kids* hit the bookshelves a few years later, and she received a lot of negative criticism for it. Her warning, as well, hasn't had its intended effect. Michael told us, jokingly, that he thought he'd write the book—published in 2007—and the *too-safe* problem would just fade away! "I had no idea at the time," he said, "that it was going to stick around and grow into such a thorny, wicked problem that we can't seem to get past."

The problem of *safetyism* carries on today, and we are still addressing it (in this book, for example). We, too, found plenty of evidence to support the thesis Dr. Ungar wrote seventeen years ago. We adults have done too much to keep kids "safe." Criticism of safetyism has grown in recent years, and we feel simple solutions could do a lot to help curb the trend of overprotection.

Even though the problem—overprotection of children inhibiting psychosocial development—has worsened, Dr. Ungar remains hopeful that kids these days can recover from the unfortunate trend and develop into happy and healthy adults, or, as Alcott wrote, learn to sail their own ship. The American novelist, Louisa May Alcott, is best known for authoring the novel *Little Women* in 1868—and the book serves as a testament to her own advice.

Growing up poor in Concord, Massachusetts (where she socialized with the transcendentalists Ralph Waldo Emerson and Henry David Thoreau), she worked from an early age to help her family get by. She worked as a servant, a teacher, and later, a Civil War nurse. Louisa's father saw her as an independent and wild child, and when her father didn't recognize her sacrifices, Louisa and her mother grew passionate about righting the thoughtless inequality and wrongs done to women. (Ironically, when Louisa penned her most famous book, it was as part of a deal to help her father get a publishing deal for his own book on philosophy!) She remains known as a social activist and abolitionist.

Alcott is an example of a self-confident and determined person. Not only was she a ground-breaking novelist, she was the first woman registered to vote in Concord. Tragically, she suffered from mercury poisoning due to medication containing calomel (mercurous chloride), a toxic compound used in many medicines in the sixteenth to nineteenth centuries. She died of typhoid fever and pneumonia contracted while nursing dying soldiers and assisting doctors in surgery during the Civil War.

We share Louisa May Alcott's quote and brief biography as an example of resilience in the face of the challenges of daily life—150 years ago. We know times have changed, in many ways for the better, but one area in which we are not witnessing improvements is in how we as adults allow children to experience challenge.

We spoke with Dr. Ungar about the safety trap. He is a family therapist, a social work professor at Dalhousie University in Nova Scotia, a world-renowned resilience researcher, and a prolific author on child development and family and community resilience. He earned recognition in 2022 as the leading scholar of social work. His written work, from books on working with troubled youth and from papers offered on his *Nurturing Resilience* blog on *Psychology Today*, is widely read and influential for parents, educators, and other practitioners in human and social development.[2]

Afraid of Storms: How Did We Get Here?

Dr. Ungar says the phenomenon of overprotecting kids has increased over the decades. He described these changes as being similar to a highway's on-ramp that is too long. Kids are on the on-ramp, but not getting to the highway. He suggests children and youth are suffering from increasingly fear-based and persistently restrictive approaches. For youth today, the on-ramp problem leads to dire consequences.

Michael is well aware of the statistics showing increasing rates of anxiety disorders among youth, their inability to function in workplaces, and other problems, such as those outlined in earlier chapters. What's even more concerning is youths' self-perception of fragility, exemplified by the assorted expressions one hears, such as "You're triggering me," or "Words are violence."

Understanding the mechanisms promoting or eroding resilience, Dr. Ungar found it troubling to see young people today in such a delicate state. He reflected that somehow, we've given messages that "there is this vulnerability, that basically everyone is helpless and that we are unable to cope with anything." This ideology is placed on many young people and translated into the idea that nothing at all, nothing ever, should make them feel uncomfortable—a message that, as Michael put it, means "the world is stress-free, and one that should never tax or push me." The safety trap.

The result of this messaging is that some youth and young adults feel psychologically vulnerable. This reality is reflected in high rates of anxiety and in youth who are not forming meaningful, healthy relationships.

As university educators, we have experienced what Michael Ungar identified back in 2007 as young adults being kept "too safe for their own good." We occasionally have university-aged students who are devastated by not getting the grades they feel they deserve. (More on that to come.) We also have university administrators telling instructors they need to include "trigger warnings" on course outlines and before lectures when content may upset students. (Even though research suggests trigger warnings offer little to no benefit and in fact may increase anticipatory stress.) We have had students say they don't feel safe because of certain words used in the classroom or upon hearing ideas they disagree with. But here's the problem: Those same students provide the faculty teaching evaluations that many university educators rely on for job security and promotions. This puts teachers (especially contract or adjunct faculty) in a perilous position. Their ongoing employment relies on getting decent evaluations from students, oh, and not having complaints filed to administration for saying—or not saying—something.

Of course, we're not saying any educator should be afforded the right to be, well, an asshole. Negative feedback on that front is, of course, warranted and essential to ensure a healthy learning environment. However, faculty are feeling pressured to perpetuate the safety trap, avoiding important and timely topics and missing the opportunities to create a democratic learning environment rich for free discussion about lived experience. Critical analysis of subject material, no matter the content, should be allowed, but more often educators may try to resist backlash by avoiding topics likely to inspire passionate discussion.

As outdoor therapists and educators, much of our work is informed by the American philosopher John Dewey, the so-called guru of experiential learning in the early 1900s. For Dewey, the most productive classroom is one that gives children things to do—together—not just things to learn.[3] Through reflecting on experience, the learning happens naturally. As educators, we never approach a student as some sort of empty vessel needing to be filled by our genius, books, or curriculum. Much like a healthy democracy where everyone, no matter their viewpoint, gets one vote. This approach to the classroom is to view every student as capable of offering a unique perspective or understanding of the content. This is the actual ideal "safe space" we've heard about in the media recently—the safe space for the big ideas, big mistakes, and big feelings we've been discussing throughout this book. However, the safety trap has become an ongoing conundrum in academia and elsewhere; it supports the belief that youth are fragile and incapable of dealing with stress or adversity. In this ideology, we must protect youths so they never feel big feelings or experience the emotional playground! Another extinction of experience. The safety trap—a regrettable substitution.

One side effect of the safety trap may be *grade inflation*. Students give faculty higher evaluation scores when they receive good grades. So an instructor doles out C's and D's at their peril. Grade inflation is a much harder problem to understand than this simple transaction, but there is evidence of it being one contributing factor to the safety trap, along with the economics and shifting ideologies of universities.[4]

Starting in the mid-1960s, grades in US universities have risen by 3.75% per decade, with the "A" grade becoming the most common given nationwide by 1998.[5] These numbers are seen equally in private and public institutions. Why is this happening? Has university become a service industry, and the consumers are demanding higher grades? Have faculty, as described above, put advancement and job security before academic rigor? The situation seems even worse now, postpandemic, as many institutions are fighting to stay alive in the face of distance learning that has made in-class lectures less relevant and student tuition seem unreasonable.

According to the US National Student Clearinghouse Research Center, enrollment numbers have been dropping since 2019, with 1.16 million fewer undergraduate students compared to prepandemic numbers. In 2024, enrollment across the nation had grown 2.5%, although most of these new students are in community colleges, graduate programs, and dual-enrolled high school students taking post-secondary courses. So, there has been some overall growth, but in different educational systems. It also seems that routine four-year undergraduate students are starting to come back, but much more slowly than the alternative types of educational systems.

Was it the do-it-yourself nature of people's response to the pandemic, where people took up baking sourdough, learning low-and-slow barbeque, gardening, foraging, home renovations, or even teaching themselves instead of going to university? Or, as some of the evidence suggests, youth may be more drawn now to direct-to-workforce training such as shorter, applied programs, trade schools, or online courses offered by private training institutions. The online world of learning was forced upon many of us in 2020, and institutions caught lagging on the technology front scrambled to remain viable.

Some were ready, such as Will's employer, Australia's largest school of social work, which had pioneered distance learning more than a decade before the pandemic. (Students were still required, though, to attend multiple face-to-face intensive teaching periods to practice their counseling, interviewing, and assessment skills with professionals from the field.) Many institutions are still adjusting to become more relevant to distance learners and students seeking shorter, more applied training.

So, higher education enrollments are down, and cost-cutting measures are in place at the same time labor, material, infrastructure, and maintenance costs continue to rise. Some education institutions will not recover from their lost revenues.

If faculty accept the idea that young people are vulnerable and need protection, they may be less likely to treat students as people capable of experiencing challenges, adversity, or possible setbacks. How would they fare in the nineteenth century alongside Louisa May Alcott? Would they be resilient enough? Will they be resilient enough to launch as healthy and happy adults today? Are they learning to sail their own ships?

These questions play into the classic generational trope that kids these days are not as tough as they used to be. Is that being too critical? The available research suggests many adolescents today are (1) not taking on and achieving the same developmental challenges as previous generations, and (2) experiencing more distress than ever before. Less achievement and more distress? Have adults overprotected children to their own detriment? We believe treating young people as fragile or incapable of engaging in difficult discussions will regrettably create a problem we are intending to avoid. This approach is hardly resilience-promoting.

Dr. Bruce Lanphear encouraged us to look for causes; we know there are many variables. Can we point to some and initiate change? As we learned from Dr. Mari Swingle, technology and entertainment through electronic devices can mess with our brains and result in less-than-favorable behavior and health. Dr. Sandseter stressed the extinction of experience. Dr. Miller shared the importance of shifting the narrative about what is harming kids these days, and Dr. Brokenleg showed how social connection and generosity can help. Dr. Davidson described how the mental health labels given to youth may not lead to improved outcomes, but instead to stigma and discrimination. These experts are all people whose work we respect. With all these researchers giving us all this information, we clearly see that no one factor can be pinned down for causing a youth mental health crisis.

Fractures, Fragility, and the Fall of Diverse Opinions

Greg Lukianoff and Jonathan Haidt argued that three particularly bad ideas have taken hold among young people, especially university students. They described them in an article in *The Atlantic*, "The Coddling of the American Mind." They then expanded their theories into a 2017 book with the same title. Their title recalls Allan Bloom's eminent book, *The Closing of the American Mind* from 1987.[6] Now in its fifth edition, Bloom argues that higher education is failing democracy (some of the same ideas John Dewey expressed one hundred years ago). For Lukianoff and Haidt, the bad ideas, which resonate with Bloom's, are: (1) that all bad experiences must be avoided, (2) that emotions are to be given priority over reason, and (3) that the world is constructed on dichotomies, such as good and evil, left and right, and that there is no in-between. These ideas, according to the authors, are further stunting the emotional growth of adolescents and young adults.

Lukianoff and Haidt suggested university faculty and institutional policies are the most established examples of this way of thinking and behaving, although we now see this phenomenon in the business realm and our communities across the world. These ideas, they argue, (echoing Dr. Michael Ungar) are shaping student beliefs that they are fragile and incapable of dealing with difficult conversations or experiences. Being uncomfortable has become unacceptable. If anyone feels uncomfortable (or simply disagrees with someone's opinion), there is an allowance in our culture for them to simply cry "foul" and correct the situation by "calling out" and "canceling." These social behaviors spell disaster for youth. Both actions are antithetical to our work as caring, attachment-based educators and therapists.

Calling out and canceling are destructive to relationships. They increase self-censure by promoting fear of retribution, and they reduce interactions between diverse groups. A more relational response was proposed by social work educator and Smith College professor Loretta Ross who proposed *calling in* instead of *calling out*.[7] Ross's approach helps "address harm while creating space for growth, forgiveness, and understanding" by focusing on caring for each other when having difficult conversations. Ross's simple message is that we need to build and preserve relationships rather than using approaches that create an outcast of anyone having differing opinions.

We have seen numerous universities initiate the creation of "safe spaces"; strong messaging from policymakers callings for increased equity, diversity, and inclusion. The policies usually require any and all differences to be recognized and protected. Conceptually, this is easy to support, and we have worked in human and social development long enough to know the intentions are mostly good. However, as these ideas of social justice progressed (or regressed, depending on how you look at things), we've seen the weaponization of ideas and subsequent harm in order to suppress open discussion and giving space to diverse opinions. Some have argued rampant social media use has only increased the cocooning over ideas. (We explore this in more detail below.)

We've seen this play out in our own work trying to protect adolescents from systematic harm. Our strengths-based approaches help clients establish, fortify, and exercise personal agency, and autonomy is a primary goal in the therapeutic process. But in our aim to improve youth safety in outdoor therapies, our gender, the country where we live, and the tone of our writing have been criticized, publicly and privately, to discredit the actual message of protecting youth from harm and human rights infringements. These *ad hominem* attacks (*ad hominem* means a logical fallacy in which an attack is focused on the person rather than the subject at hand—"killing the messenger," if you will—feel similar to how overprotection can sometimes lead to focusing on anything but the actual content or substance.

Social media makes it easier (and more societally acceptable) to cut down other's ideas by ignoring the substance of the idea and going after the messenger.

Safe Spaces and Echo Chambers in a Digital World

The coddling of university students may well be an extension of overprotective parenting. Lukianoff and Haidt suggested the evidence around declines in the quality of adolescent mental health, more negatively impactful for girls than boys, correlates well with social media use, specifically as it began to advance around the years 2010 to 2012. The authors blamed like buttons and the ability to repost as fundamental social media harms; these are the two main functions that converted networking sites into social media. The availability of likes and reposts ramped up the performativity of users. Digital interference. Haidt continued his exploration of the smartphone impact with *The Anxious Generation* in 2024.

Before 2010, smartphones weren't in everyone's hands. Apps such as Facebook and Twitter were just assistive technologies for work, networking, and lifestyle. Dr. Mari Swingle's proposed digital integration was easier in those days. After 2010, smartphone apps shifted the act of knowledge-sharing and networking into a competitive space for attention. In essence, social media users were given more options to engage, and they also saw the quantification of their posts through likes, number of comments, and reposts. Couple that with the constant self-comparison with others online, FOMO (fear of missing out), and the natural neuroticism of the teen and young adult years. The result is a storm of social and psychological intensity for youth. The flames were fanned by science-based algorithms that hacked into teens' developing brains and emotions. This could be seen as targeted exploitation—for which app developers should be held accountable.

How should we interpret social media's influence *and* the cocooning of young minds by adults and our educational institutions? Lukianoff and Haidt see the changes resulting from shielding young people from ideas and people they may disagree with, leading to a lack of practice in debate and dealing with conflict. Social media, an effective tool for calling out and canceling, has proven to be a formidable weapon in protecting ideas from challenge or discussion, and it shields the poster from having to sit and talk face-to-face with *anyone*. Social media *appears* to have the ability to connect everyone, but it so easily damages and *dis*connects. This is all unsurprising to those who have used the platforms.

Policies and behaviors in the universities, in some ways, have mirrored social media in the way they overprotect students from challenges that compromise the social fabric that should be holding diverse voices and beliefs closer together. Traditionally, and we'd argue more appropriately, differences should be expressed and shared in relationship, and that means together, in person.

We've avoided over-harping on social media as a causal factor of harm to youth mental health because the story needs a wider scope than graphs and charts of youth distress since 2010. So, what do the long-established resiliency researchers see as other causes of youth distress?

Dr. Michael Ungar suggests that the growing pressures of teen culture and the societal push for "success" champion individualism—a political, philosophical, and moral outlook that emphasizes individuals over community and social cohesion. This can lead to breakdowns in social connectedness. Dr. Ungar thinks that if we continue moving away from a society that values the notion of a collective and a sense of mutual dependency, and we move toward a world where everyone is doing their own thing and everyone thinks that the world should move around them as individuals, we will see the sacrifice of courtesy, decency, respect, and grace.

Michael is also keenly aware of the hyperindividualism of social media and entertainment kids are exposed to today.

Youth absorb a lot of messages that "everything is about me." This "self" that is portrayed outwardly is very performative but hardly ever represents one's *true self*. Further, he points out the lack of accountability and responsibility for what one says or does online, which further erodes mutual respect across those within a community. Instead of people communicating face-to-face, we are seeing generations of keyboard warriors. This over-protective "cocoon" or "bubble-wrapping" is, according to Dr. Ungar, "a fine formula to focus on vulnerability and individualism, and a further breakdown of decorum and mutual respect" resulting in an increased sense that "I matter, but others don't."

Handrails or Handicapping

Whatever the origin we ascribe to the problem, examples are not hard to find of individuals who claim to need protection from the words, thoughts, and actions of others. One example Dr. Ungar shared is the accommodations being demanded by students for support of disabilities in the classroom. Students have long been provided with the necessary support and resources to help mitigate specific learning barriers. Vision issues may be accommodated with brailed or audio versions of notes or readings. Physical ability accommodations may include alterations that improve access to buildings, classrooms, or activity adaptations. These are historically common and essential accommodations. Today, the accommodations being demanded suggest that many students have become incapable of dealing with traditional classroom settings, experiences, and expectations. While no one will contest the need to remove legitimate barriers to success, the rate at which accommodations are being requested is causing frustration for faculty and administrators in the universities.

Students request learning accommodations from campus support or independently from their course instructors. We are often not permitted to know the issues or barriers faced by the students. This protects the student from instructor bias and maintains confidentiality of their personal health information. Accommodations may be related to physical barriers, learning differences, chronic illness, "neurodiversity," or mental health issues.

A 2023 report from the Canadian University Survey Consortium found that some type of student accommodations had been requested by about 40% of all respondents, with the majority of accommodations being provided for students self-identifying as having a disability or impairment.[8] Of the accommodations sought, 25% were for mental health, 15% for neurodivergence, 7% for learning/memory issues, and 9% for vision and other chronic conditions.

A colleague of Dr. Ungar's, an unnamed professor at Dalhousie University, received accommodation requests from the university's academic support service for several students with anxiety. One request was that the student could not be singled out or asked to answer questions in the classroom, as it would create anxiety for the student.

"That was the provision, and I'm glad that our universities are more open. I don't have a problem with the accommodation in principle," Michael stated. What he does question is that accommodations are being offered without any remediation plan. Shouldn't we build in some handrails to assist with their development?

Dr. Ungar questioned whether just being anxious is a valid reason for an accommodation like the one requested. "All kids should be anxious coming to university, and they should lose some sleep thinking their professor will call on them the next day and quiz them about the assigned reading," Michael said, somewhat jokingly.

For these reasons, he suggests such accommodations are incomplete. As a resiliency researcher, Dr. Ungar has seen how engaging in difficult experiences can build personal responsibility, hold students accountable for their learning, and demonstrate the hard work needed to learn and grow. He described this as keeping students on their *learning edge*. Students may not have the skills and capacities to do a particular thing when they first arrive at university, but (in most cases) they can, and need to, develop the skills to do that thing.

If not presented with a remediation plan, this student would get accommodation in every class of their university career. Anxiety (or whatever the label might be) becomes entrenched in their identity as a student and sense of self, the very concern we presented in chapter 5. Accommodations in the classroom were traditionally designed to help students with physical and learning differences get the most out of the learning environment. Improving accessibility is, of course, very important and central to all of this. Today (and not to get into a "kids these days" argument of our own), the word *accessible* has become synonymous with *comfort*. Most troubling is its association with comfort surrounding *ideas*, which is quickly making learning, education, and democracy incompatible, if not impossible.

Dr. Ungar suggested a remedial approach. He imagined a halfway point in a twelve-week semester; the student would have the accommodation in place until week seven. In the first six weeks, the student would have the time to normalize the classroom experience and, ideally, work toward developing the confidence and capacity to be called on in class. The professor would speak with the student in advance of this seventh week and remind them they will be asked a question in an upcoming class. This is building resilience through relationship. Connection before correction.

These *handrail* approaches are indicative of quality pedagogy (*good theory for teaching*, in plain language), though they are not easily exercised in large classrooms with an ever-changing and often large roster of students. Dr. Ungar described the goal for his proposed remediation: "By the end of the semester they [the student experiencing anxiety] should be functioning at a normal level, whatever normal is, in terms of normal social expectations."

What worries Dr. Ungar is that the accommodation may perpetuate limitations, handicapping the student's potential. In the example given, would that student be allowed to use anxiety as a reason for accommodation that allows them to complete say, a four-year bachelor's degree, without ever being called on in any classroom? If this is the case, then "we've created a pathology that is stickier ... and while the accommodation is a good measure for inclusion, at some point, the student still has to be coached on how to function adequately beyond the accommodation."

We all must learn to sail our ships. Handrails can help facilitate experiences, but to fully develop skills and abilities, accommodations need to be adjusted—in a caring, thoughtful way. In short, accommodations are ideal to ensure access and inclusion but can become a mixed blessing that creates or perpetuates limitations on growth and development, hence becoming a restricting or regressive device. We want our youth to externalize the problems they experience, not embed self-imposed labels.

Ideological Influence in Schools

We've discussed the teaching space as an institution of learning, from K–12 and through higher education, as being designed and delivered in very routine ways over the decades. One criticism of educational spaces that we heard from Dr. Sandseter, Dr. Swingle, and other experts is that the school environment and teaching styles lean toward alignment with the preferences of female learners more so than males. The "feminization of education" argument, while interesting to read about, has become controversial; as a result, researchers are either less interested in the topic—or more wary of career cancelation. But the issue is still out there.

Australia's most popular parenting expert and the queen of common sense, Maggie Dent, has been a champion of innovative education for more than a decade. We encourage the curious reader to dive into her blogs, podcasts, and writing. Just over ten years ago, in 2014, Dent published a piece titled "Why Schools Are Failing Our Boys."[9] (Definitely worth the read; you can find a link in the notes section of this book and at www.kidsthesedaysbook.com.) Leaving behind the many nuances of the topic, we feel we can noncontroversially state that some occupations are underrepresented by males, such as health care, early education, and domestic roles. There is surely some effect, good or bad.

What does this mean for developmental opportunities, such as risky play in schools? The experts in this book agree that risky play is beneficial. Would kids be able to experience more rough-and-tumble play if there were more male teachers? Maybe. But we don't see this simplified to a gendered equation. We see the risk society, the safety trap, as dominating the institutions. Many teachers are held back from engaging students in risky activities.

Dr. Ungar points out that fewer men are opting for a university education. Some are also having problems navigating into the trades as well. Michael said 63% of university students at his Dalhousie campus are women. As of 2023, males make up about 42% of student populations at four-year universities in the US, down from 47% in 2011.[10] "What's changed?" he asked, "Is it the way we teach? Is it grade inflation? Is it group work?"

Assumptions can run wild here, and we know classrooms are not ideal for all learning styles.[11] Do males prefer a more competitive, challenging, or individualized learning experience? What do we need to do to keep males going to university? Or is this a problem at all? These questions don't condense, and open inquiry is important for finding potentially positive solutions. We feel hopeful, though some argue the entire system of higher education has become corrupted by dominating ideologies and ideas of activism over scholarship.

Professor Steven Mintz, an American historian who served for five years as the executive director of the University of Texas

System's Institute for Transformational Learning, argued in April 2024 the boundaries of activism and scholarship became blurred in academia.[12] Activism is important. However, educators should have a role in teaching youth *how* to think, not *what* to think. This preserves democracy in the classroom, which should have space for all voices, lived experiences, and thoughts. Through these means, students get the opportunity to learn about themselves and the way they interpret and juggle the new ideas they subsequently take into the world as they form their own identities.

It's not only the universities where activism infiltrates education. In September 2024, middle school students in Toronto were brought on a field trip and led to participate in a protest.[13] Parents were told their 7th- and 8th-grade children were going to observe a protest supporting the Grassy Narrows First Nation, who have experienced a water crisis due to decades of mercury poisoning. However, teachers asked the students to wear blue to identify themselves as *colonizers* and *settlers*. One student from India, who recently immigrated to Canada, asked to not be referred to as a colonizer, as India experienced centuries of colonization. During the "field trip," the protest shifted from the important topic of safe water and Indigenous health to recent events in the Middle East. A student of Jewish descent became upset when anti-Israel chants began. When she approached her teacher, the teacher told her, "You'll get over it." Instead of the protest being used as a teachable moment, the teachers were telling students *what* to think and *what* to value, instead of how to think critically and make informed decisions about the world.

These examples illustrate how pressuring students toward activism may impact their ability to critically learn from educational experiences. If a field trip to a protest is in the cards, wonderful. Just let the student become an active participant in making meaning from their involvement and not make how they should "identify" as the focus. Then, participating in democracy can help set up youth to navigate the world, learn how they react to the experience, steer their ship, and progress into adulthood as a caring, kind, competent, and resilient person capable of handling different perspectives and ideas.

Safe Enough

Policies and shifting social norms seem to support the bubble-wrapping of students. In the long term, this seems to be compromising their development and increasing tension and polarization. Research shows that teens and young adults today, as we outlined in the earlier chapters, are experiencing increased anxiety, depression, and loneliness. Many don't even actively seek relationships. "Teens now are not as sexually active and are, overall, more socially isolated," Dr. Ungar told us, adding that this is likely even more so since living through the socially disruptive mandates of the pandemic.[14] We agree. Serious interference.

How have our youth today come to believe and feel the world is a dangerous place and that somehow risks are all around them? Social media, TV, and movies all seem to be reinforcing these tropes, and parents and other adults in the lives of youth, doing their best, are following along with the same influences and messages that are coming from schools, the news, movies and TV, and their own social circles. We can now see how apps, internet-based news, and other i-information have created echo chambers, accelerating divides beyond who is right versus left on the political spectrum. Another divide has been fabricated between personal and government or societal responsibility for decision-making. For example, topics previously discussed openly and freely have become almost taboo for fear of reprisal. Try talking with university faculty about the health outcomes for gender-transitioning youth or the realities of supporting a child experiencing gender dysphoria. You will witness self-censorship and callout culture simultaneously.

How do we address the safety trap and lack of capacity to be exploratory in the physical, social, emotional, and spiritual domains that life throws at us all? As therapists and as educators of social workers, teachers, and counselors, we work with the concept of safety all the time; as outdoor educators and guides, we are well-versed in the practice of identifying and mitigating hazards and managing safety while adventurously traveling in wild places. Psychotherapy and counseling cannot occur in a physically unsafe environment. The capacity of our brain's cortex, responsible for complex thinking, is drastically reduced when experiencing threat and severe adversity.

The idea of *safe spaces* has received considerable attention in recent years. Our schools and institutions are promoting the notion that safety can be achieved, and our youth are expecting this to be so. Some of our academic and therapy colleagues believe we need to achieve safety for trust and sharing. This achievement is assumed to protect the community from harm. While an important consideration, we do not believe safety can ever be guaranteed, and trying to achieve some state where no one will be uncomfortable, in disagreement, or challenged, is not only unrealistic but undesirable for promoting resilience.

In the outdoors, we can plan to keep our clients or participants from harm by teaching and practicing skills, warning them of objective hazards, and then allowing the dignity of exploration with those risks. The idea is to reduce exposure to harm, but not to eliminate risk from the equation; risk is an exceptional teacher. Wind can build waves, spilling paddlers from their canoes and kayaks; a spider bite can end a camp early; and a slip while stepping over a rock can lead to a fall and a broken arm. In group settings, we can agree on conditions, boundaries, and expectations for each other, but we cannot protect anyone from words, ideas, or the actions of others (or waves or spiders!).

In 2014, social work professor Cathy Richardson/Kianewesquao and activist and radical counselor Vicki Reynolds wrote about safety in community and therapeutic work. They offered the concept of *safe enough*.[15] Safe enough recognizes that safety cannot be guaranteed. We must do what we can, often through our relationship-building and authentic desire to help others and offer what safety we can. We suggest that safe enough should be considered as a more progressive alternative to pronouncements or offers of guaranteed safety.

Safe spaces are rooms commonly established on university campuses and come with expectations. If anyone is offended or disagrees with what they hear, then the safety of the space is perceived to have been broken. By coaching young people to be caring with their words, but to also speak their truth, we can create spaces in which we can witness stories, hear opposing views, and engage in difficult and meaningful conversations. These are the risks involved in human interactions, and taking the risk of improving connection through open communication can be phenomenally rewarding.

Every person has different sets of values, beliefs, traditions, cultural practices, and perspectives. This is an essential part of being human. Without this, the world would be quite bland. Rather than teaching and preaching safety, we'd ask adults to consider raising kids to have brave *and* respectful voices.

Some therapy and educational literature speaks to *brave spaces* instead of *safe spaces*. A brave space is built on six pillars: vulnerability, taking a stand, leaning into fear, critical thinking, examining one's own intentions, and mindfulness (not meditation, but pausing to think before reacting).[16] This is a meaningful reframe, but not as clear to us as the concept of *safe enough*. To enter dialogue on sensitive or difficult topics, such as race, gender, power, and oppression, we need guidelines—handrails—or at least a respectful environment where we can listen to others and be listened to. The growing trend of censorship (including self-censorship), calling out, and cancel culture has led to a fear of simply speaking up and out. We find *self*-censorship to be the most troubling. In a time when diversity, equity, and inclusion are (or were) high priorities in governments and institutions, it is highly problematic when scholars and students fearfully censor their own speech.

In education, where intellectual curiosity and scholarly work should be the norm, we should never withhold a moment for learning, no matter the context. This is the antithesis of a free democratic society in which freedom of speech is supposed to be a central tenet. Callout culture stifles meaningful dialogue; censorship reduces creativity and divergent thinking—all in order to increase social conformity. If you have meaningful relationships, you connect. Conversations deepen. Topics do not need to be avoided. In our epilogue, you will hear stories of those brave enough to stand up and deviate from norms to create real and meaningful conversations, which in today's world means *change*.

We need to address the safety trap and allow kids to experience the dignity of risk, speak up, and fully explore the adventures of childhood and adolescence. Resilience will follow learning to sail one's own ship. This cannot be done without the guidance and support of caring adults. By providing the handrails and being there when they fall, kids will be better served. They will see that reducing the negative impacts of a hazard is ideal, but safety is never guaranteed. Risks must be taken—knees scratched and egos bruised all along the way. Otherwise, developmental fractures will appear, and we will perpetuate the harm we are seeing in kids these days. Adults, make it *safe enough!*

10

SIMPLE CAN BE ELEGANT

Yesterday I was clever, so I wanted to change the world.
Today I am wise, so I am changing myself.
—RUMI

Danny's mother recommended him for counseling in July 2020, a few months after he had moved back to her home during the pandemic. The loss of employment forced the 23-year-old to give up his room in an apartment he shared with friends. He was happy to be home, hanging out with his mom and step-dad, with few, if any, daily responsibilities. At first, he thought he'd just "chill and wait out the craziness." March through May saw Danny, along with many others worldwide, experiencing chronic low-level fear and uncertainty from the ever-changing narrative of case numbers and deaths reported in the daily news. The uncertainty felt throughout the summer and into the fall held many people's lives in a frozen state while they waited and hoped for normality to return.[1] Strict mandates imposed by the Canadian government in March included stay-at-home orders, distancing and masks, minimal time allowed out of home, the suspension of nonessential businesses (which included Danny's place of employment), and the closures of schools as well as the

gym he worked out at and the bars and clubs where he socialized on the weekends.

In mid-April 2020, Danny finished his last semester at the
university, although his courses had been online for the last few
weeks due to the pandemic. This eliminated his immediate circle of friends and acquaintances he had gained throughout his
bachelor of commerce degree. The pandemic abruptly ended
his rugby team's season, and it put strains on his relationship
with his girlfriend, who had quickly packed up and moved
home to her parents' place a half day's travel away. The Canadian government closed its borders to international travelers
in mid-March 2020 and made it clear that all citizens should
stop all nonessential travel (so visiting his girlfriend wasn't an
option); they labeled some work as essential, some jobs as not,
and implemented a system of self or even forced weeks-long
quarantines aimed at reducing the spread of the virus.

With the loss of his social life, peer relationships, and his routine of going to school, rugby practice, the gym, his girlfriend's
place, and the bar, Danny experienced life in a vacuum. Happy
to have him home, Danny's mother picked up mothering where
she had left off, doing his laundry, cooking meals, and basically
leaving Danny with nothing to do. Danny picked up habits he
had grown out of years before: gaming, pot use, and junk food
seemed to fill the gap. He regressed to his old high school self. He
went from starving to gorging through an extinction of experience. It wasn't until his mental health took a full nosedive before
he realized he had a problem.

Even when some businesses returned to more normal operating hours, Danny did not step back into his prepandemic level
of engagement with the world. He was equipped with a university degree, but his motivation for graduate school had faded. He
found himself with no impulse to look for a job or return to his
"regular life."

The attention economy gave him something to fill all his
unoccupied time. He would later call this an addiction; at the

time, it was giving him some pleasure and escape, and it could be seen as an adaptive response to cope with the situation. But his sleep patterns deteriorated. Gaming late into the evenings didn't help, but even trying to reduce screen time didn't get him back into his natural circadian rhythms (the pattern our body tracks and adjusts to get us to go to bed and to get up with the sun). His life was in *full digital interference*. But the gorging didn't stop. He complained of being tired all the time, and when he did have conversations with his parents, they sounded overly demanding to him, mostly telling him what he wasn't doing with his life. This isolated Danny further. So, at that point, he wasn't communicating with anyone.

Rocking Danny's world, the first panic attack caught him a fraction of a second before falling asleep one night. A panic attack is experienced as sudden intense fear with severe physical reactions, often with no obvious danger present. Danny had never before experienced such fear, and he later reported his heart was racing so fast he thought he was dying. The muscles around his heart were sore for days, as if he had overworked his chest in the gym. He didn't get any sleep that night and had a few difficult nights of broken sleep following the incident. Danny went to see his doctor. He was assessed using a seven-item questionnaire. He was prescribed Xanax (benzodiazepine), commonly used for anxiety, but he stopped taking it after a few days because it made him nauseous, light-headed, and constipated. Another regrettable substitution.

Death occupied Danny's thoughts. The fear of having a panic attack was so closely associated with that moment just before falling asleep that his nighttime anxiety became so dreadful he eventually started self-medicating with alcohol and marijuana to sedate his way into slumber. This was not quality sleep, he knew, but at least he didn't have to think about dying just to get the rest he needed.

Danny's fear of death associated with falling asleep was intense. If he could avoid it, he would. He couldn't. Danny experienced three of these panic attacks, with dizziness, trembling, muscle tension, and that crazy racing heartbeat. Danny was living with constant low-level anxiety. Day by day he felt worse. The list of ailments grew. Relationships at home with his mother and stepfather had ruptured. While they remained quite worried, neither party was communicating well. His mother requested Danny seek some sort of therapy.

His first counseling session with Nevin was held beside a river in a park near Danny's family home. He looked exhausted, distracted, and somewhat reticent about the session. The two of them walked downstream to a bend in the river where an exposed sandbar provided a scenic and private place to sit and talk. Danny wasted no time moving past the relationship-building questions a therapist starts with, and launched into how horrible it is to be afraid to fall asleep, believing it is death itself.

Developmental psychologists believe we are designed to grow incrementally—and in harmony with how we see and think about the world. In the simplest terms, we grow up relative to how we make meaning of our reality. Dr. Robert Kegan, introduced in chapter 6, identified the particular conditions necessary for development to occur as we grow up. These conditions include *psychological safety*, having the *resources* and *support* available that allow us to grow from experiences and solve problems, and the ability to let *life's challenges force us to evolve* and learn our own limits. Dr. Kegan is one of the most cited researchers of *adult* development. He focuses on the years beyond the classic "ages and stages" model proposed by the Swiss psychologist Piaget—one that suggested the last stage of cognitive development begins at 11 years of age. Of course, we know neurological development progresses into adulthood.[2]

We are designed to be constantly challenged, and then, again, under the right conditions, and with the right supports and resources, to overcome and adapt during and after those encounters. Adaptation is our collective superpower as humans. When growth occurs developmentally, and skills and abilities are gained along the way, the way we think about and deal with the complexity of the world grows as well. We can't guarantee our clients will be safe, because life is full of hazards, but we can, for example, help them to learn to feel safe. Safe enough. This is how we keep from getting in over our heads— we tackle increasingly harder problems and adapt and grow. Robert Kegan's work is highly relevant to young adults. These are the years where self-identity, morality, perspectives, and adult relationships are all made sense of from the grown-up's perspective.

We all miss steps, and Danny was no different. Many youth and young adults passed through the pandemic without mental health issues, although we'd argue many suffered some social or psychological setbacks, regardless of what part of the world they were in, the rigidity of mandates they were under, or what misleading and ever-changing media they were consuming. According to resilience expert Dr. Ungar, those who suffered more may have had more developmental fractures—those missed growth opportunities in their younger years, which can lead to phobias and struggles later, especially in those neurotic teen years.

Danny had been a high-performance multisport athlete. That identity came to an abrupt end during his second year at university when he sustained a significant back injury that landed him in rehab for a year. He was diligent with his physiotherapy and rehabilitation in the gym. He healed and returned by his senior year to playing second-tier men's league rugby. Then the pandemic hit.

Danny was also, at that time, in the second year of a relationship with his girlfriend. He described their connection as "OK," but knew they weren't "in it for the long run." At the time Danny came to counseling, they were still in touch; they remained "friends" via FaceTime and texting. She was, however, moving on and making plans to relocate farther away for a new job opportunity. He knew the relationship was over. With his social circle dismantled and fractured communications at home, Danny sat quietly without response when asked, "Who can you talk openly and honestly with in your life right now?"

Silence.

It's easy to see how many factors impacted Danny during this difficult time. Isolation led to starving for connection. Digital interference and substance use—gorging—furthered the isolation as he tried to alleviate anxiety. Sleep, digestion, and recovery were compromised. Physically, he was moving less; he was seeing fewer friends. He was having an extinction of experience of his own. The label of a mental health disorder led to the prescription pad, but Xanax made him physically ill. Intervention. Attempting to prove causation from one factor ignores the breadth of a wicked problem.

But Danny needed little in the way of motivation to begin addressing what ailed him, although he was at a loss for where to start. While his mother pushed him to reach out for counseling—the talking cure—there was little external force needed; most of Danny's change was self-directed and quite positive. We learned from Dr. Ryan Rhodes the "simple can be elegant" axiom when it comes to personal behavioral change.

Intention-Behavior Gap

Dr. Ryan Rhodes is a professor in the School of Exercise Science, Physical and Health Education, and director of the Behavioral Medicine Laboratory at the University of Victoria, Canada. He is one of the top one percent of researchers cited in the areas of behavioral medicine and health related to exercise (with a Web of Science h-index of 105, for those who know or care what that means. To us less prolific scholars, this is unfathomable.) His primary area of research is the psychology of physical activity promotion during critical life transitions, such as parenthood and early family development. Dr. Rhodes is also a renowned expert on the *intention-behavior gap*, that struggle many of us face when we have good ideas but aren't able to follow through on them.

You only need to think of New Year's resolutions to know the territory in which Rhodes and his team conduct their research, which is both conceptual and based on real-time interventions. Based on a quick search, we found research suggesting only about 9% of people stick with their resolutions for one year; 80% of resolutions are forgotten within weeks, and one-quarter of adults quit before the 7th of January.[3]

Ryan told us that only about 20% of children and youth today in North America are meeting the basic recommendations for physical activity each week.[4] This is a staggering fact, especially because we know that the standards are set *at minimum levels* to achieve basic health outcomes. More would be better! Increasing physical activity is a missed contribution to possible physical, emotional, behavioral, and mental health concerns, as adequate physical activity helps us face the challenges in everyday life. Dr. Rhodes has documented a significant drop-off in activity in the early teen years, and he found that the family's involvement and encouragement are critical to long-term engagement in physical activity and related health benefits.

Psychologist Dr. Albert Bandura, the grandfather of social learning theories, posited that people learn, grow, and change through observation and in the context of social relations.[5] His theories centered on how observation, role modeling, and direct experience are central to individual choices and actions. Ultimately, Bandura was a thought leader and pioneering researcher in the *intention-behavior conundrum*, which asks, "How do people change?"

Ryan Rhodes's work has been building for decades on the foundations laid out by Bandura in the realm of behavioral changes for health and well-being. One of the strongest determinates of successful change relative to physical activity is *intention*. There is even a field of study that addresses this. It's called *intervention science* (dedicated to finding ways to get people to be more active).

The motivation and drive to be more active has been found to have a large and statistically significant effect. In basic, non-scientific terms this means intention has a large influence; it is an important predictor of change. When intention does not lead to the idealized change, in this case becoming more active, the *intention-behavior gap* appears. Dr. Rhodes and his colleagues have shown through repeated studies and reviews of other research that additional factors may be equally important in designing interventions or coaching parents or families on activity and other health changes.[6] Planning, self-regulation, habit/routine, and other variables need to be considered for successful change to not only occur but also for the maintenance of those new healthier behaviors. Danny wanted to get better. His intentions were apparent. But he needed more than intentions. Setting objectives and gaining family support became positive aspects of his change process.

Ryan's Behavioral Medicine Lab distilled health-related change into three basic ingredients: *motivation, regulation,* and *reflex*. Successful change requires *motivation*. While this might seem an obvious factor, we don't always understand what motivation is or what drives it. In fact, leading behavioral change experts cannot agree on how to define motivation. To bypass any academic bickering, Dr. Rhodes's team simply defined motivation as the *pressure* or *expectation to change*, whether internally ("I need to change") or externally driven ("You need to change"). Understanding where motivation comes from is helpful when focusing any intervention driven toward behavior change.

If we find pleasure or enjoyment in the activity or new behavior, we can tap that for motivation as well. Think about the last time you tried a new sport or recreational activity. Did you enjoy it? Was it your choice to try something new? Maybe you felt you needed to mix things up a bit? Or were you joining someone else in their pursuits, and you were motivated by being with them versus the activity itself? As success and mastery are important components to effective psychotherapy, enjoyment of a new behavior is important for making a change and should not be discounted when it comes to making a change to address concerns related to one's mental well-being.

Regulation, the second factor in the Lab's three-part approach, involves behavioral change. This component often demands structure, either self-imposed or externally provided (or requested). We need to self-regulate most of our day as it is. Getting to work without getting too angry with the driver who cuts you off, dealing calmly with people in the workplace or at school, or being patient with our children as they "help" us cook breakfast are basic examples of regulation. Even in our leisure time, where we often seek freedom from the constraints of daily life, discipline is required to guide our choices and get us to follow through on them. Committing in January to an exercise routine is far and away the most common attempt to regulate physical activity (often motivated by weight gain during the holidays). The dismal success rate of New Year's resolutions demonstrates how hard regulation can be to achieve. Motivation is not enough. Regulation helps.

Reflexivity, the third factor, describes the stage when a pattern or type of behavior becomes routine—a reflex. You know something has become a habit (or at least can be committed to regularly) when you do it without a physical and psychological struggle. The problem is that humans desire stable states. We always find excuses to maintain the status quo. For change to happen, though, we need *deviance*, as described in the epilogue.

"We have a primal urge to avoid pain, and to approach pleasure," Dr. Rhodes explained. We are avoiders of discomfort and want to find enjoyment in what we do. This tendency drives our choices along those very lines, evolutionarily evidenced and hard to contest. Asking someone to take their body out of rest and have an unpleasant experience for health benefits is going against their evolutionary instinct. Understanding these primal drivers to avoid change, discomfort, and pain is critical to get people past simply regulating themselves to adopt a new behavior; we need to actually enjoy the changes we are bringing to our lives. Otherwise, what's the point? This has been a driving force in our therapeutic work outdoors. Maintenance of behavioral change, according to the Behavioral Medicine Lab, is based on when the behaviors become *reflexive*, and done not because "they are good for me" but because "I find meaning in doing them." This is why success and mastery are known to be essential in therapy with youth.

Classic psychotherapy is often focused on discussing thoughts, behaviors, or unconscious processes in a safe, closed-door setting of the therapist's office. It all happens from the neck up. While there is nothing wrong with this approach, it can be challenging for clients to transfer what was discussed in an isolated office setting to the real world, where behavior change has to be implemented. Successful therapeutic interventions result in people experiencing a change in their daily lives. But it has to be change that lasts long enough for it to become a habit or a part of who they are as a person. Ryan's work is encouraging of this approach.

To briefly recap the three factors: *Motivation* (doctor tells you to lose 30 pounds to improve your cardiovascular health; you are frustrated by this news and reluctant, but look for options); *Regulation* (you attend a morning fitness class at a local gym, and think "this is hard, but it isn't too bad"); and *Reflexive* (you meet some great people in the class and enjoy their company, and by the third week, you think, "I actually enjoy this"). What a lovely perfect-world scenario. You know it doesn't always go like this.

Danny didn't require more than one session to start identifying what he was missing and wanting to get back to, mostly his old routine. He was motivated and knew how to stay fit, eat well, game less, and get back to hanging with his peers. He had simply slipped and fallen on all these fronts. The focus of the first counseling session was on relationship and trust building, but Danny was quick to commit to tackling change on several fronts. He set some blue-sky goals (trying too much change, too quickly), and by the second session, he reported he had failed to get past the patterns he'd established over the last few months. He arrived frustrated, flighty, and not at all grounded.

Nevin and Danny discussed his background as an athlete and how he managed to center himself before games. Danny did not lack motivation, the first factor in the tripartite approach. What he lacked was the second factor, regulation. Much of his regulation before the pandemic was highly influenced by school, work, athletic schedules, and his social life and required little on his part to manage. Self-regulation can be seen in levels.

On one level, getting to the gym regularly is regulating your behavior. On another level, coping with your body's autonomic nervous system when stressed (flight, fight, or freeze) is another. There is a lot going on here and whether we think about regulation as neurological, behavioral, or emotional can take us down different lanes toward understanding the complex human condition. But sometimes, less is more. Sometimes simple changes, even changes made with no link to a specific problem (e.g., a substance user reducing their use after being invited into a new social setting) can have large impacts on one's life. The point here is sometimes we don't have to change much.

Coregulation can happen collaboratively where friends or family assist in managing behavior, emotions, and even physiological responses, as we learned from Dr. Gordon Neufeld in chapter 6. Danny lost some of his functionality when he was suddenly without a partner or friends in his daily life.

The most obvious need for change was with the near-bedtime anxiety and panic attacks Danny experienced. He continued to have the feeling that he would die the moment before he fell asleep. The second session focused on self-regulation strategies and sleep-related behavioral change. Hardest for Danny to deal with immediately was the digital interference that gaming was having in his life again. With some shame, he shared how gaming filled a void for him during high school as he wasn't very social and spent a lot of time in the evenings and weekends alone but in multiplayer games, convincing his parents this was how he "connected with friends." Gaming was definitely not grounding and regulating Danny's emotional state; it was hijacking his frontal cortex (remember Dr. Swingle's descriptions in chapter 3; also see her book, *i-Minds*), contributing to overstimulation in the evening. That patterned behavior had been dropped while in university due to his athletic schedule, hanging with teammates, and the social life that came along with it. Now it was simply a distraction—a regrettable substitution.

Danny and Nevin created a short list of things he could do to improve his sleep. He understood that improved sleep, without panic attacks, would provide him the best chance of addressing other mental health concerns. To build in more accountability, Danny said he wanted to reach out and reconnect with his biological father who lived nearby; the two of them hadn't been close for years. This family resource turned out to be quite valuable in that his father desired a closer relationship and, after learning of Danny's struggles, shared with Danny how anxiety was playing a part in his life as well. Connection, relationship, and regulation.

Nevin recommended a podcast on sleep hygiene from Stanford neurologist Dr. Andrew Huberman. Danny found it to be "a bit long and too much information" but also "extremely insightful."[7] He chose to keep his phone on airplane mode and out of his bedroom at night. He tried to be off screens at least an hour before he went to sleep, to shut off the Wi-Fi router at night, to cut back on caffeine earlier in the day, but most importantly, to reduce his gaming so he could get to bed at a decent and consistent hour.

It was about three to four weeks before Danny found a pattern he could maintain—his behavioral regulation. He was seeing the benefits of his efforts and was starting to feel enjoyment in daily life again. His routine eventually became reflexive. In the meantime, he renewed his membership at the gym, reduced and eventually eliminated some foods, and reignited his social life with his rugby friends. He was guided into this *displacement approach* versus simple abstinence. In this approach, positives are added to one's schedule, reducing time for less desirable behaviors.

In counseling sessions with Nevin, Danny explored how he let himself slip the way he did, assessing his adaptability and resilience, and how he might create the conditions that would prevent it from happening again. Dialogue included personal explorations of family life growing up, roles family members had taken on, and those aspects of life he valued the most. Trust was established in the relationship, and Danny was eventually able to share openly about his pain and growth moments in life along with how his relationships were progressing with his parents and stepparent.

After he moved back home, Danny had easily morphed back into his teenage self and a life in which his mother was happy to look after him. Danny had no expectations put upon him as a young adult in the house. He came to realize his stepfather had always been extremely cautious with Danny when he was young, often limiting his explorations, as he didn't want to be the stepparent that failed if Danny got hurt. Interestingly, Dr. Ryan Rhodes shared with us how the phenomena of overprotective parenting can be accelerated in blended families. No parent wants to see their child get hurt or suffer the shame of being "that parent." Dr. Rhodes highlighted that the overprotection of children is heightened when parents are separated or divorced, especially in cases where one parent would attack the other for allowing the child to get hurt in their care. This fear of retaliation from another parent would surely add to the *extinction of experience* phenomena kids these days are experiencing. The safety trap. Danny worked toward addressing his need to be seen as an adult while living back at home; he took on more tasks in the daily routines of the household and got himself busy with life again.

He stepped up to be one of the adults in the house, a role he had never taken within the family. His anxiety slowly resolved itself; he started a new job and eventually could afford to move into an apartment with friends. While providing Danny an opportunity to be vulnerable in sharing his struggles, counseling also allowed Danny to find his own path back to health as a young man.

COVID-19 was a brutal time for many young people, and Danny, while suffering some significant emotional pain, was able to eventually demonstrate resilience with some solid health and emotional support. Danny was not devoid of emotionality, and there were no significant fractures in his development, but the stress and fear of the pandemic—circumstances outside of his control—caught him off guard, as it did many of us. We believe many youths feel this way today. As stated throughout this book, the pandemic did not create the current youth mental health crisis, it only made it worse. The last session Danny and Nevin had was only four months after they first met. When asked what he wanted to talk about that session, Danny said, "I'd just like to hang out and let you know how good I am doing." There was a sense of pride in Danny's voice and he appeared more confident, for he, like Rumi, felt wise that he had changed himself.

Many youth we work with are outward-looking and blame external circumstances for their condition. As we've learned from our experts in this book, there are many factors to point fingers at, however, change must include change from within. Danny's change was rather simple, as he had merely slipped. Finding his way back was primarily self-directed, with some family support and resources.

When we can't change the circumstances and external variables, we must make changes ourselves, find our autonomy, and take action. We hear our colleagues critiquing this approach as appearing far too behavioral; and as you know, we are not very fond of the cognitive-behavioral tsunami (dominance over other approaches). Our approach aims to consider the whole human, not ignoring their diet, sleep, exercise, social life, emotional world, or the ecosystem in which they live. A solution may come from anywhere if we zoom out to consider the many factors contributing to wicked problems instead of picking a single one as our center of focus.

Cause Not Cure

How do we change? As therapists, we see individual clients, sometimes with a parent, siblings, or even entire families. We might work with groups of young people in a school or community, or those who have signed up or been sent to participate in a program. Not everyone shows up with the same issues or with the motivation to change. As much as we'd like to say we treat root causes, we spend a lot of our time treating individual cases. We can't reduce the prevalence of anxiety in youth in our communities, but we can support one young person who is experiencing it. We might not be able to remove the source of the anxiety or depression, but we still work in the realm of prevention, in building youth up to deal with their issues—although we'd feel more effective if we knew we could help deal with the *cause*.

The motivation for writing this book was to address the question of whether what we are doing as therapists, researchers, and educators is helping or not. In talking with a wide range of experts and in reviewing the evidence, we see multiple factors influencing the lives of children, youth, and families that cause distress and underlying disease. They cannot all be addressed by counseling, medication, or seeing a healthcare practitioner. Issues are multifaceted and require an open mind and willingness to look broadly at what may be the sources of disease in the home, community, and society at large. We share Danny's story to highlight the idea suggested by Dr. Rhodes that *simple can be elegant.* Family, relationships, basic health care, meaning-making, and the willingness to commit to change sound like many factors, but when addressed individually, not much change was required for Danny to make transformations in each area. Simple modifications produced effective, positive change.

Psychologist Sue Johnson said her clients used to come into therapy talking about depression, trauma, and anxiety. More recently, they are talking more about emptiness, futility, and meaninglessness (although adolescents may not necessarily use those exact words). Kids these days, she said, "are suffering from the world's refusal to accept that loving, safe relationships are a necessity and not an incidental." She told us we are putting everything else first, such as shopping on Amazon, the size of our houses, our exercise programs, and what vitamins we take.

"Our world is full of distractions, and much of it is addictive," she said. "We're a consumer society and it seems to me we have less and less time and less and less attention." This is happening at the same time that an almost infinite variety of sources are asking for more of our attention. Dr. Johnson remembered a quote from American linguist Geoffrey Nunberg: "A copy of the *New York Times* contains more information than the average 17th-century Englishman encountered in a lifetime." No wonder we feel there is less time to pay attention to the things that really matter to us as human beings. With such distractions, Sue stated, we are less aware of the bigger questions: "How do we grow as human beings, what helps us thrive, and what is necessary for a human being to reach some kind of *balanced maturity*? ... I think we are letting childhood be taken over by what has taken us over as adults, which is novelty, sensation, and fun pastimes. And personally, I think it's disastrous. It seems to me our world is becoming more complex, more difficult to handle, more perilous in many ways. What we need is to develop more balance and maturity, and an increased ability to cooperate."

With a pause and look of consternation, Dr. Sue Johnson added, "It seems to me the way we're educating people is going in the other direction." Too much interference, intervention, and ideology.

Home Health Happiness: How Change Occurs

Dr. Ryan Rhodes's Behavioral Medicine Lab created a theoretical model, known as *multi-process action control*, that successfully assists in turning good intentions into sustainable behavior change through habit and identity formation—the very purpose of adolescence.[8]

Ryan has been recognized by the Royal Society of Canada and the Academy of Health Sciences for research explorations he jokingly says have simply followed his life circumstances and interests. When Ryan got a dog, his lab conducted research about dog walking as a health intervention. When he became a parent, his research assessed physical activity levels and patterns of new parents. Currently, he is beginning to look at later career and retirement stages as they relate to physical activity and health outcomes, often looking no further than the mirror for inspiration.

Where do we find the resources and support for positive change in our lives? How do we ensure youth today are learning the skills needed to be more resilient and avoid developmental fractures? We know from Dr. Rhodes's Behavioral Medicine Lab, the research presented throughout this book, and the other experts that interventions viewing youth as resources set a path for kids to follow throughout life. Committed parents, bonded immediate and extended families, healthy environments (i.e., connected communities, reduced toxins, less digital interference), role modeling, and turning routines into lifestyle habits are all beneficial. Again, nothing new here, folks. Give youth something good to imitate. Cultural practices and traditions across societies reduce uncertainty and strengthen identity formation, contributing positively to healthy and happy kids (recall Dr. Martin Brokenleg's teaching story in chapter 2 about the buffalo and sound biology).[9]

Some simple environmental changes or psychological shifts in thinking, or even language shifts within narratives have had profound impacts for our clients. Small changes. "Don't change much" is a slogan used by the Canadian Men's Health Foundation to empower men to make small but meaningful changes that can have *knock-on effects*, that is, outsized results from small modifications.[10] CMHF founder Dr. Larry Goldenberg told us he was looking for a way to motivate men to improve their lifestyle habits; he found the simple idea of "Don't change much" led to easily communicated concepts and better results. He believed small, gradual changes led to the formation of habits and, eventually, permanent behaviors.

As therapists, we have seen many examples of positive change where the solution had nothing to do with the problem. Start with noticing when youth are at their best. Are there moments the disruptive student in the classroom is sitting still? Don't let those moments of success and mastery be incidental. Work more with what is working in their life. If you notice these moments, the child will as well. Small changes can add up, sometimes displacing that which was the problem.

Nevin refers to these examples with his clients, family, and friends as "little victories."

ON DEVIANCE AND UNCOOPERATIVE SYSTEMS

It's easier to act your way into a new way of thinking, than think your way into a new way of acting.
—JERRY STERNIN

We started this book with the story of Purdue Pharmaceuticals to illustrate *interference, intervention,* and *ideology,* the three major themes addressed in this book. We hope you now perceive youth mental health and well-being with greater breadth, recognize some of the present harms, and are motivated to be the adult in the room—the one who addresses the issues with care and dignity. After time spent with our experts, we were emboldened by their capacity to speak up and push back.

We close with two compelling narratives to illuminate how hard systemic change can be, but also how sometimes small but meaningful changes from a collective voice can make a world of difference. The first story is about going unheard in an uncooperative system and the determination and persistence that change sometimes requires. The second sets out a blueprint for acting out for change in community. These stories detail how something so shockingly obvious to us today was interfered with, and unrealized, until enough people deviated from the status quo. Simple changes can lead to improved outcomes for many people, especially for those with the most at stake. We hope these concluding messages inspire adults to trust their instincts when called upon to deviate from cultural norms or dominant narratives to support kids these days on their adventure through adolescence and into adulthood.

The Cost of Change: Resistance in the Healing Wards

By the mid-1800s, medical doctors were expected to have "scientific" training. Doctors were moving on from believing that evil spirits or *miasma* ("bad air") were the causes of illness. The inquisitive Dr. Ignaz Semmelweis was one doctor who looked at what was actually happening—and made changes according to what he saw. Semmelweis took a job at a maternity clinic in a hospital in Vienna. Believing scientific inquiry was central to his job as a physician, he questioned why so many mothers were dying from childbed fever, today known as *bacterial postpartum infection.*

His research looked at two wards, one run by the men—doctors and medical students—the other staffed with female midwives. Semmelweis found death rates in the female clinic were about five times lower than in the clinic run by doctors and male medical students. At first, he observed the midwives advising expecting mothers to give birth lying on their side, while the doctors instructed women to remain on their backs. It seemed like an interesting difference in practice, but when he tested the hypothesis that this was causing the deaths, it turned out not to be the culprit.

Semmelweis also wondered if it was the presence of a priest, who would stroll the halls in the ward, ringing a bell when one of the new mothers had died. He wondered if the bell was too terrifying. The bell was removed for the purposes of his research. It made no difference.

Frustrated, he couldn't put his finger on why midwives were so much more effective than the male medical professionals, so he left for a holiday. A leave of absence to clear his mind. While in Venice, a colleague of Semmelweis punctured his finger performing an autopsy on a diseased victim of childbed fever. He fell sick and died. Semmelweis finally had an important clue. Doctors were conducting autopsies. Midwives were not. Doctors spent more time with the dead. Midwives did not.

Semmelweis ordered the immediate removal of infected bodies. And everyone had to start cleaning their hands, their tools, and their clothes. Not just with soap and water, but with chlorine, which was the best disinfectant of the time. No one at the time knew much of anything about bacteria. Semmelweis thought chlorine simply helped with the smell of the corpse, but it did much more. The death rate of childbed fever dropped dramatically.

Semmelweis's final conclusion: *Washing your hands appears to be one of the most effective ways to improve public health.* You'd think this commonsense approach would have led to international recognition, but some in the medical community were resentful, insulted, and indignant. He was confronting the dominant ideology. His superiors and older physicians rejected his conclusion. Younger medical professionals, however, understood the significance of the findings.

Semmelweis was ultimately caught up in political activities during the Austrian Revolution in 1848, lost his job, and applied for a teaching position in midwifery. He didn't get the job. But he persisted. After a lecture given to the Medical Society of Vienna, Dr. Semmelweis was hired to teach again, but this time with restrictions to his teaching that he described as humiliating. He left Vienna for Hungary.

Years later, Dr. Semmelweis was hired during an epidemic at a maternity ward. After his arrival, mortality rates plummeted to less than 1%. In Vienna, the rate remained at 10–15%. The medical establishment in Hungary accepted Semmelweis's ideas, but Vienna's still did not. Even after he put his ideas on paper, those in authority remained reluctant. He grew angry. His letters communicated frustration and grew more and more insulting to recipients. At professional conferences, most physicians and scientists rejected his ideas, even when the evidence and positive outcomes were laid out in front of them.

In 1865, Semmelweis suffered a serious episode of depression, and it was rumored he suffered from dementia or syphilis. His colleagues lured him to visit a mental institution, where he was detained and committed. Interference and intervention. The doctor pleaded, protested. He tried to leave. Guards provided a severe beating leading to a wounded right hand that later became infected. Dr. Semmelweis was placed in confinement. Two weeks into his detention, he was dead. According to the autopsy reports, Dr. Semmelweis died from a similar type of infection he spent his professional life as a doctor and researcher trying to prevent. A cruel irony.

We share this story for a number of reasons. First, sometimes a wicked problem has an obvious solution. It may be something we already know about, but don't recognize as a solution. Or, the system and its functionaries within are unwilling to act even once a harm has been identified and a simple solution discovered. Second, addressing wicked problems requires persistence, the willingness to stand up, speak out, and probably most important of all, to become a *positive deviant*, a person who seeks favorable outcomes against all odds, barriers (such as limited resources), time constraints, and uncooperative systems.

Positive Deviance

In the 1990s, Jerry and Monique Sternin worked for the US nonprofit Save the Children.[1] They were passionate about finding a solution to child malnourishment in Vietnam. The couple found that 64% of children were malnourished in the villages they visited. They piloted a *positive deviance investigation*, a term first used in child nutritional research in the 1960s.[2] Through community engagement, they found that some of the village families were using particular strategies that had good effects. The children washed their hands before they ate. These families also ate food culturally viewed as inappropriate, such as little shrimps and crabs from the rice paddies and the greens from sweet potato plants. This meant that these families were eating food richer in calcium, protein, and iron. As opposed to the common tradition of two meals per day, these deviating families ate three to four times a day.

The Sternins worked to develop a new program. They didn't tell the parents what to do, specifically. Interested parents in the community were invited to sessions where they could practice cooking these meals with parents who already deviated from the cultural norm. Parents brought their children along to participate in the cooking and sharing of meals. Members of the community learned by doing things together; a cocreation of knowledge. Malnutrition fell 85% after the two-year pilot program.[3]

Identifying positive deviance within a community or other sample has become a widely accepted research tool to use for approaching problems, especially wicked ones. Instead of investigating the problem in depth, we can look instead for the deviants who are straying from societal norms and achieving better results. (For example, when Dr. Scott Miller went searching for the supershrinks, as we discussed in chapter 7). As we researched this book and spoke with experts, we saw plainly how important it is to push away from interference, intervention, and ideology, just as Dr. Semmelweis and the Sternins did by putting a new perspective into practice.

For one hundred years, mental health professionals have looked at humans from the neck up and cataloged what is wrong with them in books like the DSM. It's a dim view of humanity. After all, it was Sigmund Freud, the so-called creator of the psychotherapy talking cure, who wrote in a 1918 letter,

"I have found little that is 'good' about human beings on the whole. In my experience most of them are trash."[4] Diagnoses are stamped onto people based on what seems to be going on inside their heads. It is philosophically hard to classify sadness, fear, or emotional pain, so most diagnoses are based on self-reported information. Neither we nor the person doing the reporting can see the full context or environmental effects that have influenced the individual. When it comes to wicked problems, "cures" by their very definition can be inadequate. As we presented in Danny's story, sometimes healthy change can be stimulated using simple, well-known remedies, such as focusing on improving diet, sleep, social interaction, and exercise. However, these successful remediators become increasingly difficult when interference, intervention, and ideology are the dominant approaches or narratives.

Surgical safety expert Dr. Atul Gawande provided suggestions for cultivating the ability to become a positive deviant.[5] These suggestions guided our process. First, we have to *ask unscripted questions*. We did this by reaching out to experts, asking what was going on, and then listening and learning. *Count something*. Do the homework. We looked for what seemed interesting, observed it, and explored the research. This is the same thing Dr. Semmelweis did when he tried to figure out why some situations delivered better outcomes than others. *Write something*. For years, we've written about the ethics of youth psychotherapy, and this book, in many ways, is an extension of our work focused on youth well-being. Finally, *look for opportunities for change*. We would have failed if, when putting the pen and paper down, we had not learned and changed our approach to working with and raising youth. Our experience with Dr. Bruce Lanphear discussing environmental toxins, for example, led to heightened consciousness and concern about the food we consume and the products we bring into our own homes. We are now invested in a much more relational and preventative approach in our clinical work with young people.

The experts we talked to for this book were impressive to us because *they deviated from the norm and worked to find new solutions*. They don't have all the answers, and by no means is our book definitive; in today's world things change quickly. The questions we've been exploring do not condense. They leave us with more questions. Looking at it with a different lens provides more opportunities to deviate further by asking more unscripted questions.

When cultural and sociological constructs such as mental illness labels, overprotection, and identity politics are treated as natural law—that is, as if they are observable and objectively related to some natural order of things—we have emptied the humanness out of the human. Many kids these days are no longer crew, on board helping to steer their ship through the storm and stress of adolescence. They have become the "patient," which in Latin means *to suffer* or *bear*. Seeing youth as the patient does them a huge disservice because the patient "is truly passive—bearing whatever suffering is necessary and tolerating patiently the interventions of the outside expert."[6]

Youth are often then treated as passive recipients of our expertise—a passenger in the world of medicine and mental health. If we want to perpetuate the *kids these days effect*, all we have to do is continue to rely on and trust *other* adults to do the adulting for us while we bemoan today's youth. Efforts to fix the teenager are likely to fail. If we don't take social connection, mastery, gratitude, and independence as necessary assets for promoting resilient and capable youth, we'll continue to treat today's youth as lazy, selfish, fragile, and anxious, as adults have done for millennia. When we blame the emotional struggles youth experience squarely on the phones, the pandemic, or mental health professionals—we disregard the heroism of youth, the very spirit Nelson Mandela argued energized the fight against apartheid in South Africa.

Thinking about kids these days requires moral clarity. Not confusion. How can kids grow naturally while being labeled and interfered with by the adults and institutions in their lives? Which way will we turn? Will we invest in the heroism or the fragility of youth? We choose heroism.

Listening, Learning, and Leading

The experts we've relied on in this book often told us: "Don't trust the experts!" But through close listening and study, we've come to trust what they have imparted to us. The translation and dissemination of their work, however, by mainstream and social media, governmental regulatory bodies, and corporate-speak and special interest groups is incongruent with much of their evidence and advice about healthy child and adolescent development. What is eventually seen and heard by the public, and presented as "expert" advice, often contradicts what the experts we've relied on put forth. This project began with Nevin in dialogue with Dr. Michael Ungar, and then Dr. Gordon Neufeld. We became motivated, and the list of experts grew. We were listening and learning. Some of the experts had us focus on factors we hadn't even thought about!

We compiled hundreds of pages of notes and tried to find crafty ways to connect the range of perspectives. As we wrote, other books were published. One focused on why therapy is bad for youth.[7] Then came another, calling for a ban on cell phones in education. Again, we agreed with some of it but find forced prohibitionist mandates for phone-free schools troublesome and problematic.[8] We saw it as yet another example of treating youth as passengers and not crew. So many of the mental health and parenting books we've read focus on a single, complex problem (anxiety, for example) and develop a mechanical solution (cognitive-behavioral intervention, for example). Having a pretty good grasp on mental health and psychotherapy statistics, we know simple, universal solutions applied to youth from all backgrounds are unlikely to move the needle in youth mental health. It remains a wicked problem.

Mobile phones can be problematic. So can social media. We're living on Planet Mental Health, where pop psychology dominates, and youth self-labeling with mental disorders has become common. Reductions in outdoor and risky play in childhood, along with the ideology of safety and overprotection are also contributing factors. So, too, are environmental toxins linked to increased rates of autism, anxiety, behavioral concerns, and attention-related issues.

With each of these problems comes the sale of simple solutions. Intervention over prevention. For example, place mandates on phone use and social media. Monitor social media so platforms such as Facebook, Instagram, X (Twitter), and especially TikTok stop being WebMD for struggling youth. More diagnoses, therapy, and medications. Take away spending money so children limit fast food consumption and bad sugars. (We could have written another long chapter—or even another book—on the negative effects of ultra-processed foods on child health alone!)

The problem with simple "cures" to fix kids these days is that children are still left as passengers, not crew. Within these universal solutions, the adult's responsibility becomes monitoring and control, which our children need much less of in the real world, whereas engaging and connecting should be paramount. We are not saying that we're the two most engaging adults on Earth, but we've worked with youth in the outdoors, and many put their phones down. On their own. They do this when they have something to do and something meaningful to learn. Through relationship and engagement, they build meaning about who they are and what they have to offer. Too often, our intervening communicates the wrong things: "You are not loved, and you need to change." We want connection before correction.

Advocates in the nineteenth and twentieth centuries protested for child labor laws to protect the spirit of youth and reclaim childhood. Let us consider doing the same. Let us give youth what they need to harness that spirit as they develop into who they are. Giving them secure attachments with mature adults is the first step. As famed psychologist Erik Erikson stated, in the absence of mature adults and secure attachments, adolescents can become lost in their own insecurities and experience confusion about where they fit in the world. Understanding the adventure of adolescence, Erikson wrote in 1950:

"We have learned not to stunt a child's growing body with child labor; we must now learn not to break his growing spirit by making him the victim of our anxieties. If we learn to let live, the plan for growth is all there."[9]

Let us refrain from criticizing kids these days and instead envision them as heroes and do our collective best to be the adults in the room. In the early 1900s, Jane Addams recognized the spirit of youth. In the late 1920s, psychiatrists believed promoting success and mastery was vital to helping youth therapeutically. We need to view youth as resources and experts of their own experiences when trying to help them negotiate adolescence. While the experts for more than a century provided a road map, adults also invested in ways to label, categorize, and fix kids through ongoing interference and intervention. Instead, we need to listen, connect, support, and provide handrails that allow kids to learn to sail their own ships and not be afraid of storms.

In discussing harmful chemicals in common food and household products, Dr. Bruce Lanphear reminded us that kids today are the most vulnerable to toxic environments, the proverbial canaries in the coal mine. Indian philosopher Jiddu Krishnamurti once said, "It is no measure of health to be well adjusted to a profoundly sick society." We adults might do well to pay attention to the state of our societal and environmental health and ask, "Is it any wonder our kids are hurting?"

Maybe what really needs to change is the adults these days.

NOTES

1   Wolf, Z. B. (2021) "The Worst Drug Dealers in History Are Getting Away with Billions," *CNN*.

2   Scher, C., Meador, L., Van Cleave, J. H., and Reid, M. C. (2018) "Moving Beyond Pain as the Fifth Vital Sign and Patient Satisfaction Scores to Improve Pain Care in the 21ˢᵗ Century," *Pain Management Nursing* 19(2).

3   McAlister, V. C. (2018) "Tyranny of the Pain Score Question After Surgery," *Canadian Journal of Surgery* 61(6).

4   Keefe, P. R. (2017) Review of "The Family That Built an Empire of Pain: The Sackler Dynasty's Ruthless Marketing of Painkillers Has Generated Billions of Dollars—and Millions of Addicts," *The New Yorker*.

5   National Institute on Drug Abuse. (2024) "Drug Overdose Deaths: Facts and Figures."

6   U.S. Department of Justice. (2009) "Justice Department Announces Largest Health Care Fraud Settlement in Its History."

7   Mulvihill, G. "Purdue Pharma and Owners to Pay $7.4 Billion in Settlement of Lawsuits Over the Toll of OxyContin," *Associated Press*.

8   Goldhill, O. (2023) "How a Depression Test Devised by a Zoloft Marketer Became a Crutch for a Failing Mental Health System," *STAT: Reporting from the Frontiers of Health and Medicine*.

9   Kroenke, K., Spitzer, R. L., and Williams, J. B. (2001) "The PHQ-9: Validity of a Brief Depression Severity Measure," *Journal of General Internal Medicine* 16(9).

10   Davis, J. (2022) *Sedated: How Modern Capitalism Created Our Mental Health Crisis.* Atlantic Books.

11   Kendrick, T., Dowrick, C., McBridge, A., Howe, et al. (2009) "Management of Depression in UK General Practice in Relation to Scores on Depression Severity Questionnaires: Analysis of Medical Record Data," *BMJ*, 338.

12   Schwarz, A. (2016) *ADHD Nation: The Disorder. The Drugs. The Inside Story.* Little, Brown.

13   Carey, B. (2017) "Keith Conners: The Godfather of Medication Treatment for ADHD," *The New York Times*.

14   Schwarz, A. (2013) "The Selling of Attention Deficit Disorder," *The New York Times*.

15   Semley, J. (2024) "Amid a National Shortage, the US Adderall Black Market Is Booming," *The Guardian*.

16 Haidt, J. (2024) *The Anxious Generation: How the Great Rewiring of Childhood Is Causing an Epidemic of Mental Illness*. Penguin Press.

17 Rittel, H. W., and Webber, M. M. (1973) "Dilemmas in a General Theory of Planning," Policy Sciences, 4(2).

18 Shine, R. (2010) "The Ecological Impact of Invasive Cane Toads (*Bufo marinus*) in Australia," *The Quarterly Review of Biology* 85(3).

19 Williams, L. (2023) *"Hell Camp: Teen Nightmare,"* Netflix.

20 Kubler, K. (2024) *"The Program: Cons, Cults, and Kidnapping,"* Netflix.

21 Dean, A. (2020) *"This Is Paris,"* YouTube. Available to watch with YouTube Premium.

22 Magnuson, D., Dobud, W., and Harper, N. J. (2022) "Can Involuntary Youth Transport into Outdoor Behavioral Healthcare Treatment Programs (Wilderness Therapy) Ever Be Ethical?" *Child and Adolescent Social Work Journal* 41.

23 Chow, D. (2023) "Parenting Series: Parenting (Part 1)," *Frontiers of Psychotherapist Development*.

24 Rubin, R. (2023) "It Takes an Average of 17 Years for Evidence to Change Practice: The Burgeoning Field of Implementation Science Seeks to Speed Things Up," *JAMA* 329(16).

Chapter 1

1 Freeman, K. J. (1907) *Schools of Hellas: An Essay on the Practice and Theory of Ancient Greek Education from 600 to 300 BC*. Macmillan.

2 Protzko, J. and Schooler, J. W. (2019) "Kids These Days: Why the Youth of Today Seem Lacking," *Science Advances* 5(10).

3 Carbonell, R. and Hobbins, R. (2014) "Youth Mental Health Is a 'Global Crisis' According to World-Leading Study," ABC News.

4 Twenge, J. M. (2023) *Generations: The Real Differences Between Gen Z, Millennials, Gen X, Boomers, and Silents—And What They Mean for America's Future*. Atria Books.

5 National Association of Realtors. (2024) "First-Time Home Buyers Shrink to Historic Low of 24% as Buyer Age Hits Record High."

6 Mass Cultural Council. (2012) "Boston Youth Arts Evaluation Project: Brief History of Adolescence and Youth Development," massculturalcouncil.org.

7 National Institute of Mental Health. (2024) "Mental Illness." Retrieved from https://www.nimh.nih.gov/health/statistics/mental-illness

8 Shaffer, H. B. (1953) *Youngsters in Trouble*. CQ Press.

9 Bjork, J. M., and Pardini, D. A. (2015) "Who Are Those 'Risk-Taking

Adolescents'? Individual Differences in Developmental Neuroimaging Research," *Developmental Cognitive Neuroscience* 11.

10   Weisz, J. R., Venturo-Conerly, K. E., Fitzpatrick, O. M., Frederick, J. A., and Ng, M. Y. (2023) "What Four Decades of Meta-Analysis Have Taught Us About Youth Psychotherapy and the Science of Research Synthesis," *Annual Review of Clinical Psychology* 19(1).

11   Horwitz, A. V. (2021) *DSM: A History of Psychiatry's Bible.* Johns Hopkins University Press.

12   Raskin, J. D. and Gayle, M. C. (2016) "DSM-5: Do Psychologists Really Want an Alternative?" *Journal of Humanistic Psychology* 56(5).

13   Greene, E. M. (2023) "The Mental Health Industrial Complex: A Study in Three Cases," *Journal of Humanistic Psychology* 63(1).

14   Cosgrove, L., Krimsky, S., Wheeler, E. E., Kaitz, J., Greenspan, S. B., and DiPentima, N. L. (2014) "Tripartite Conflicts of Interest and High Stakes Patent Extensions in the DSM-5," *Psychotherapy and Psychosomatics* 83(2).

15   Burton, K. W. (2024) "DSM-5-TR Panel Members Received $14M in Undisclosed Industry Funding," *Medscape.*

16   Miller, S. D., Hubble, M. A., Chow, D. L., and Seidel, J. A. (2013) "The Outcome of Psychotherapy: Yesterday, Today, and Tomorrow," *Psychotherapy* 50(1).

17   Hillman, J. and Ventura, M. (1993) *We've Had 100 Years of Psychotherapy: And the World's Only Getting Worse.* HarperCollins Publishers.

18   Kolbe, L. J., Kann, L., and Collins, J. L. (1993) "Overview of the Youth Risk Behavior Surveillance System," *Public Health Reports* 108.

19   Abrams, Z. (2023) "Kids' Mental Health Is in Crisis: Here's What Psychologists Are Doing to Help," *Monitor on Psychology.*

20   Statistics Canada. (2023) "Leading Causes of Death, Total Population, by Age Group."

21   World Health Organization. (2023) "Adolescent Mortality Ranking: Top 5 Causes (Country)."

22   Mental Health America. (2021) "COVID-19 and Mental Health: A Growing Crisis."

23   Curtin, S. C., Garnett, M. F., Ahmad, F. B. (2023) "Provisional Estimates of Suicide by Demographic Characteristics: United States, 2022," Centers for Disease Control and Prevention: National Center for Health Statistics.

24   World Health Organization. (2016) "Investing in Treatment for Depression and Anxiety Leads to Fourfold Return."

25   National Center for Complementary and Integrative Health. (2016)

"Symptoms Matter: Leading Causes of Disability," National Institute of Health.

26 World Health Organization. (2023) "Mental Health: Burden."

27 World Health Organization. (2021) "WHO Report Highlights Global Shortfall in Investment in Mental Health."

28 Child and Adolescent Health Measurement Initiative. "2018–2019 National Survey of Children's Health (NSCH) Data Query," Data Resource Center for Child and Adolescent Health supported by the U.S. Department of Health and Human Services, Health Resources and Services Administration (HRSA), Maternal and Child Health Bureau (MCHB).

29 Hetrick, S. E., McKenzie, J. E., Bailey, et al., (2021) "Newer Generation Antidepressants for Depression in Children and Adolescents: A Network Meta-Analysis," *Cochrane Database of System Reviews* 5.

30 Cochrane. (2024) "Our Evidence." Retrieved from https://www.cochrane.org/evidence

31 Federal Aviation Administration. (2018) "Out Front on Airline Safety: Two Decades of Continuous Evolution."

32 National Highway Traffic Safety Administration. (2020) "Newer Cars Are Safer Cars."

33 Roser, M., Ortiz-Ospina, E., and Ritchie, H. (2019) "Life Expectancy," *Our World in Data.*

34 Twenge, J. M. (2017) *iGen: Why Today's Super-Connected Kids Are Growing Up Less Rebellious, More Tolerant, Less Happy—and Completely Unprepared for Adulthood—and What That Means for the Rest of Us.* Atria Books.

35 Twenge, J. M. (2000) "The Age of Anxiety? Birth Cohort Change in Anxiety and Neuroticism, 1952–1993," *Journal of Personality and Social Psychology* 79(6).

36 Tiku, N. (2024) "An AI Companion Suggested He Kills His Parents: Now His Mom Is Suing," *The Washington Post.*

37 Dent, M. (2013) "Stop Stealing Childhood in the Name of Education: A Plea to Ask WHY?" Adapted from a submission originally made on October 11, 2013, to the office of the Federal Minister, The Hon Christopher Pyne MP and the Assistant Minister for Education, The Hon Sussan Ley MP.

38 Flavin, M. (1996) *Kurt Hahn's Schools & Legacy: To Discover You Can Be More and Do More Than You Believed.* Middle Atlantic Press.

39 Outward Bound. (2025) *Our History.*

40 Hahn, K. (1960) "Outward Bound," Annual meeting of the Outward Bound Trust on July, 20, 1960.

41   Scales, P. C., and Leffert, N. (1999) "Developmental Assets," Search Institute.

42   McAfee, M. (2020) "The Decade of the Parenting Manual," *The New York Times.*

43   Frank, H. (2019). "Parenting Looks Nothing Like What the Experts Say," *The Atlantic.*

44   Harries, V. and Brown, A. (2019) "The Association Between Use of Infant Parenting Books That Promote Strict Routines, and Maternal Depression, Self-Efficacy, and Parenting Confidence," *Early Child Development and Care* 189(8).

Chapter 2

1   Brendtro, L. K., Brokenleg, M., and Van Bockern, S. (2009) *Reclaiming Youth at Risk: Our Hope for the Future* [Revised], Solution Tree.

2   Kildare, C. A., and Middlemiss, W. (2017) "Impact of Parents Mobile Device Use on Parent-Child Interaction: A Literature Review," *Computers in Human Behavior* 75.

3   Brokenleg, M. (2015) "First Nations Principle of Learning." Retrieved from https://www.youtube.com/watch?v=0PgrfCVCt_A

4   Blum, R. W., Lai, J., Martinez, M., and Jessee, C. (2022) "Adolescent Connectedness: Cornerstone for Health and Wellbeing," *BMJ* 379.

5   Interview with U.S. Surgeon General Vivek Murthy on NPR on January 11, 2022. "The Pandemic Has Taken a Big Toll on the Mental Health of Children." Retrieved from https://www.npr.org/2022/01/11/1072019335/the-pandemic-has-taken-a-big-toll-on-the-mental-health-of-children

6   UNICEF (2023) "Child Mortality and COVID-19," last update: March 2023. Retrieved from https://data.unicef.org/topic/child-survival/covid-19/

7   Australian Institute of Health and Welfare [AIHW]. (2023) "Deaths in Australia: COVID-19 Deaths."

8   Holt-Lunstad, J. (2022) "Social Connection As a Public Health Issue: The Evidence and a Systemic Framework for Prioritizing the 'Social' in Social Determinants of Health," *Annual Review of Public Health* 43(1).

9   Vaillant, G. E. (2008) *Aging Well: Surprising Guideposts to a Happier Life from the Landmark Study of Adult Development.* Hachette UK.

10 Lieberman, M. D. (2013) *Social: Why Our Brains Are Wired to Connect,* Crown Pub. Also see interview with Matthew Lieberman from the UCLA Newsroom: https://newsroom.ucla.edu/releases/we-are-hard-wired-to-be-social-248746

11 Brokenleg, M. (2015) "Growing Your Own Kids Today," *Reclaiming Children and Youth,* 23(4).

12   Lidow, D. (2019) "Mark Zuckerberg and the Tech World Still Do Not Understand Ethics," *Forbes*.

13   Weir, K. (2015) "(Dis)Connected: Psychologists' Research Shows How Smartphones Are Affecting Our Health and Well-Being, and Points the Way Towards Taking Back Control," American Psychological Association.

14   Johnson, T. D. (2011) "Report: Teens Who Often Eat Dinner with Family Less Likely to Drink, Smoke or Use Drugs," *The Nation's Health* 41(9).

Chapter 3

1   Readers interested in Dr. Swingle's work and parenting suggestions are directed to her book, *i-Minds* (2nd edition, 2019).

2   Dougherty, R. J., Hoang, T. D., Launer, L. J., Jacobs, D. R., Sidney, S., and Yaffe, K. (2022) "Long-Term Television Viewing Patterns and Gray Matter Brain Volume in Midlife," *Brain Imaging and Behavior* 16(2).

3   Statistica. (2024) "Number of Monthly Active Facebook Users Worldwide As of 4th Quarter 2023 (in Millions)."

4   Gibson, K. (2023) "Meta Sued by States Claiming Instagram and Facebook Cause Harm in Children and Teens," *CBS News*.

5   Morris, S. and Murphy, H. (2024) "Google and Meta Struck Secret Ads Deal to Target Teenagers," *Financial Times*.

6   American Academy of Child and Adolescent Psychiatry. (2020) "Screen Time and Children."

7   Rideout, V. and Robb, M. B. (2018) "Social Media, Social Life: Teens Reveal Their Experiences," *Common Sense Media* 2.

8   Trott, M., Driscoll, R., Iraldo, E., and Pardhan, S. (2022) "Changes and Correlates of Screen Time in Adults and Children during the COVID-19 Pandemic: A Systematic Review and Meta-Analysis," *eClinicalMedicine* 38.

9   Ahmed, A. (2021) "30 Percent Increase in Screen Time Since 2019 with an Average of 4.2 Hours Being Consumed Per Day," *Digital Information World*.

10   Kemp, S. (2022) "Digital 2022: Time Spent Using Connected Tech Continues to Rise," DataReportal.

11   Vogels, E. A., Gelles-Watnick, R., and Massarat, N. (2022) "Teens, Social Media, and Technology 2022," Pew Research Center.

12   Montanari-Domingues, S. (2017) "Clinical and Psychological Effects of Excessive Screen Time on Children," *Journal of Paediatrics and Child Health* 53.

13   Centers for Disease Control and Prevention. (2018) "Screen Time vs. Lean Time Infographic."

14   Stiglic, N. and Viner, R. M. (2019) "Effects of Screentime on the Health and Well-Being of Children and Adolescents: A Systematic Review of Reviews," *BMJ Open.*

15   Herbenick, D., Rosenberg, M., Golzarri-Arroyo, L., Fortenberry, J. D., and Fu, T. C. (2022) "Changes in Penile-Vaginal Intercourse Frequency and Sexual Repertoire from 2009 to 2018: Findings from the National Survey of Sexual Health and Behavior," *Archives of Sexual Behavior* 51(3).

16   Levine, H., Jørgensen, N., Martino-Andrade, A., et al. (2023) "Temporal Trends in Sperm Count: A Systematic Review and Meta-Regression Analysis of Samples Collected Globally in the 20th and 21st Centuries," *Human Reproduction Update* 29(2).

17   Davies, J. (ed.). (2017) *Sedated: How Modern Capitalism Created Our Mental Health Crisis.* Atlantic Books.

18   Demillo, A. (2025). "U.S. States Across the Political Spectrum Are Enacting or Considering School Cellphone Bans," *Time.*

19   Pal, A. and Kaye, B. (2024) "Australian Proposes 'World-Leading' Ban on Social Media for Children under 16," *Reuters.*

20   Foulkes, L. (2024) "I'm an Expert on Adolescence: Here's Why a Smartphone Ban Isn't the Answer, and What We Should Do Instead," *The Guardian.*

21   Montgomery, B. (2024). "The Anxious Generation Wants to Save Teens. But the Bestseller's Anti-Tech Logic is Skewed," *The Guardian.*

22   Odgers, C. L., Schueller, S. M., and Ito, M. (2020) "Screen Time, Social Media Use, and Adolescent Development," *Annual Review of Developmental Psychology* 2(1).

Chapter 4

1   Carson, R. (1962) *Silent Spring.* Houghton Mifflin.

2   Ajroud-Driss, S., and Siddique, T. (2015) "Sporadic and Hereditary Amyotrophic Lateral Sclerosis (ALS)," *Biochimica et Biophysica Acta (BBA)-Molecular Basis of Disease* 1852(4).

3   Strawn, J. R., Xu, Y., Cecil, K. M., et al. (2022) "Early Exposure to Flame Retardants Is Prospectively Associated with Anxiety Symptoms in Adolescents: A Prospective Birth Cohort Study," *Depression and Anxiety* 39(12).

4   Strawn, et al. (2022) "Early Exposure to Flame Retardants."

5   Peivasteh-Roudsari, L., Barzegar-Bafrouei, R., Sharifi, et al. (2023) "Origin, Dietary Exposure, and Toxicity of Endocrine-Disrupting Food Chemical Contaminants: A Comprehensive Review," *Heliyon.* Retrieved from https://www.sciencedirect.com/science/article/pii/S2405844023053483

6   Rees, N., and Fuller, R. (2020) "The Toxic Truth: Children's Exposure to Lead Pollution Undermines a Generation of Future Potential," UNICEF. Retrieved from https://www.unicef.org/media/73246/file/The-toxic-truth-children%E2%80%99s-exposure-to-lead-pollution-2020.pdf

7   Sanders, T., Liu, Y., Buchner, V., and Tchounwou, P. B. (2009) "Neurotoxic Effects and Biomarkers of Lead Exposure: A Review," *Reviews on Environmental Health*, 24(1). Retrieved from https://www.ncbi.nlm.nih.gov/pmc/articles/PMC2858639/

8   Roberts, S. M., James, R. C., and Williams, P. L. (eds.). (2022). *Principles of Toxicology: Environmental and Industrial Applications*, John Wiley & Sons.

9   Lanphear B. P. (2017) "Low-Level Toxicity of Chemicals: No Acceptable Levels?" *PLoS Biol* 15(12): e2003066. https://doi.org/10.1371/journal.pbio.2003066

10   Centers for Disease Control and Prevention. (2025) "About Lead in Consumer Products," Retrieved from https://www.cdc.gov/lead-prevention/prevention/consumer-products.html

11   Office of Environmental Health Hazard Assessment. (2016) "Bruce Lanphear, MD, MPH presentation at the 2016 Children's Health Symposium." [3:30:00] Available from https://www.youtube.com/watch?v=VsFPZ2r3oUI

12   Centers for Disease Control and Prevention. (2023) "Data & Statistics on Autism Spectrum Disorder." Retrieved from https://www.cdc.gov/ncbddd/autism/data.html

13   World Health Organization. (2022) *Autism*. Retrieved from https://www.who.int/news-room/questions-and-answers/item/autism-spectrum-disorders-(asd)

14   Haruvi-Lamdan, N., Horesh, D., and Golan, O. (2018) "PTSD and Autism Spectrum Disorder: Co-Morbidity, Gaps in Research, and Potential Shared Mechanisms," *Psychological Trauma: Theory, Research, Practice, and Policy* 10(3).

15   Weintraub, K. (2011) "The Prevalence Puzzle: Autism Counts," *Nature* 479(7371).

16   Tick, B., Bolton, P., Happé, F., Rutter, M., and Rijsdijk, F. (2016) "Heritability of Autism Spectrum Disorders: A Meta-Analysis of Twin Studies," *Journal of Child Psychology and Psychiatry* 57(5).

17   Havdahl, A., Niarchou, M., Starnawska, A., Uddin, M., van der Merwe, C., and Warrier, V. (2021) "Genetic Contributions to Autism Spectrum Disorder," *Psychological Medicine* 51(13).

18   Office of Environmental Health Hazard Assessment. (2016) "Bruce Lanphear, MD, MPH presentation at the 2016 Children's Health

Symposium. [6:50:00] Available from https://www.youtube.com/watch?v=VsFPZ2r3oUI

19   Shenk, D. (2011) *The Genius in All of Us: New Insights into Genetics, Talent, and IQ.* Anchor.

20   Woodruff, T. J., Zota, A. R., and Schwartz, J. M. (2011) "Environmental Chemicals in Pregnant Women in the United States: NHANES 2003–2004," *Environmental Health Perspectives* 119(6). Retrieved from https://pubmed.ncbi.nlm.nih.gov/21233055/

21   Engel, S. M., Patisaul, H. B., Brody, C., et al. (2021) "Neurotoxicity of Ortho-Phthalates: Recommendations for Critical Policy Reforms to Protect Brain Development in Children," *American Journal of Public Health* 111(4).

22   Engel, S. M., Villanger, G. D., Nethery, R. C., et al. (2018) "Prenatal Phthalates, Maternal Thyroid Function, and Risk of Attention-Deficit Hyperactivity Disorder in the Norwegian Mother and Child Cohort," *Environmental Health Perspectives* 126(5).

23   Strawn, J. R., Xu, Y., Cecil, K. M., et al. (2022) "Early Exposure to Flame Retardants Is Prospectively Associated with Anxiety Symptoms in Adolescents: A Prospective Birth Cohort Study," *Depression and Anxiety* 39(12). Retrieved from https://onlinelibrary.wiley.com/doi/full/10.1002/da.23284

24   Rose, G. A., Khaw, K. T., and Marmot, M. (2008) *Rose's Strategy of Preventive Medicine: The Complete Original Text.* Oxford University Press.

25   American Heart Association. (2022) "2022 Heart Disease and Stroke Statistics Update Fact Sheet: At-a-Glance." Retrieved from https://www.heart.org/-/media/PHD-Files-2/Science-News/2/2022-Heart-and-Stroke-Stat-Update/2022-Stat-Update-At-a-Glance.pdf

26   Strong, D. R., Pierce, J. P., Pulvers, K., et al. (2021) "Effect of Graphic Warning Labels on Cigarette Packs on US Smokers' Cognitions and Smoking Behavior After 3 Months: A Randomized Clinical Trial," *JAMA Network Open* 4(8), e2121387-e2121387.

27   Simons, P. (2024) "Searching for the 'Psychiatric Yeti': Schizophrenia Is Not Genetic. Mad in America," Retrieved from https://www.madinamerica.com/2024/01/psychiatric-yeti-schizophrenia-genetic/

28   Torrey, E. F. (2024) "Did the Human Genome Project Affect Research in Schizophrenia?" *Psychiatric Research* 333, 115691." Retrieved from https://www.sciencedirect.com/science/article/abs/pii/S0165178123006418

29   Substance Abuse and Mental Health Services Administration. (2016) "Impact of the DSM-IV to DSM-5 Changes on the National Survey on Drug Use and Health." Retrieved from https://www.ncbi.nlm.nih.gov/books/NBK519697/

30   Centers for Disease Control and Prevention." (2023) "What Are the Risk Factors for Lung Cancer?" Retrieved from https://www.cdc.gov/cancer/lung/basic_info/risk_factors.htm#:~:text=Tobacco%20smoke%20is%20a%20toxic,people%20who%20do%20not%20smoke.

31   American Heart Association. (2023) "Research Programs." Retrieved from https://professional.heart.org/en/research-programs

32   American Cancer Society. (n.d.). "How We're Fostering Innovation," Retrieved from https://www.cancer.org/about-us/what-we-do/fostering-innovation.html

33   American Diabetes Association. (2024) "Changing Our Future through Research." Retrieved from https://diabetes.org/about-us/research#:~:text=ADA%20research%20provides%20critical%20funding,changing%20treatments%20and%20eventual%20cures.

34   Serôdio, P. M., McKee, M., and Stuckler, D. (2018) "Coca-Cola: A Model of Transparency in Research Partnerships? A Network Analysis of Coca-Cola's Research Funding (2008–2016)," *Public Health Nutrition*, 21(9). Retrieved from https://www.ncbi.nlm.nih.gov/pmc/articles/PMC5962884/

35   Heffernan, M. (2011) *Willful Blindness: Why We Ignore the Obvious.* Simon and Schuster.

36   Marcus, D. K., Fulton, J. J., and Clarke, E. J. (2010) "Lead and Conduct Problems: A Meta-Analysis," *Journal of Clinical Child & Adolescent Psychology* 39(2).

37   Nevin, R. (2000) "How Lead Exposure Relates to Temporal Changes in IQ, Violent Crime, and Unwed Pregnancy," *Environmental Research* 83(1).

38   Nevin, R. (2007) "Understanding International Crime Trends: The Legacy of Preschool Lead Exposure," *Environmental Research* 104(3).

39   Drum, K. (2013) "America's Real Criminal Element: Lead," *Mother Jones* 38(1).

40   Umeda, S. (2022). "The History of the Elimination of Leaded Gasoline," Library of Congress.

41   Population Reference Bureau. (2021) "Fact Sheet: U.S. Dementia Trends." Retrieved from https://www.prb.org/resources/fact-sheet-u-s-dementia-trends/

42   Magnuson, D., Dobud, W. W., and Harper, N. J. (2022) "Can Involuntary Youth Transport into Outdoor Behavioral Healthcare Treatment Programs (Wilderness Therapy) Ever Be Ethical?" *Child and Adolescent Social Work Journal.*

43   European Food Safety Authority. (2024) "Food Additives."

44   Environment Working Group. (2024) "Food Chemicals." Retrieved

from https://www.ewg.org/areas-focus/toxic-chemicals/food-chemicals

45   Burdick, S. (2023) "Texas Sues Pfizer for 'Endangering Children' by Selling Ineffective ADHD Drug," *Children's Health Defense.*

46   Nandi, P. (2023) "Report Information by Form (Liquid and Dry), by Crop Type (Cereals, Sugar Crops, Oil Bearing Crops, and Others), by Mode of Application (Surface Application, Herbigation, and Foliar), by Stage of Application (Pre-Plant, Pre-Emergency, and Post-Emergency), and by Region (North America, Europe, Asia-Pacific, and Rest of the World: Market Forecast Till 2023," *Market Research Future.*

47   Hayes, T. B., Anderson, L. L., Beasley, V. R., et al. (2011) "Demasculinization and Feminization of Male Gonads by Atrazine: Consistent Effects Across Vertebrate Classes," *The Journal of Steroid Biochemistry and Molecular Biology* 127(1–2).

48   Aviv, R. (2014) "A Valuable Reputation," *The New Yorker.*

49   Union of Concerned Scientists. (2017) "Syngenta Harassed the Scientist Who Exposed Risks of Its Herbicide Atrazine."

50   Hayes, T. B., Collins, A., Lee, M., et al., (2002) "Hermaphroditic, Demasculinized Frogs After Exposure to the Herbicide Atrazine at Low Ecologically Relevant Doses," *Proceedings of the National Academy of Sciences* 99(8).

51   Korani, M. (2023) "Aromatase Inhibitors in Male: A Literature Review," *Medicina Clínica Práctica* 6(1), 100356.

52   Environmental Protection Agency. (2018) "Atrazine: Draft Human Health Risk Assessment for Registration Review."

53   Department for Toxic Substances and Disease Registry. (2003) "Public Health State Atrazine: CAS# 1912-24-9," Centers for Disease Control.

54   Government of Canada. (2023) "Summary of PSRD2023-01: Proposed Special Review Decision of Atrazine and Its Associated End-Use Products."

55   Environmental Protection Agency. (2018). "2017 Atrazine Monitoring Program Data File."

56   Fabbri, A., Lai, A., Grundy, Q., and Bero, L. A. (2018) "The Influence of Industry Sponsorship on the Research Agenda: A Scoping Review," *American Journal of Public Health* 108(11).

57   Levine, H., Jørgensen, N., Martino-Andrade, A., et al. (2023) "Temporal Trends in Sperm Count: A Systematic Review and Meta-Regression Analysis of Samples Collected Globally in the 20th and 21st Centuries," *Human Reproduction Update* 29(2).

58   Enc. Metallum (2016), after Jakub Marian, World Happiness Report (2022) Chart by Piotr Migdal, p.migdal.pl, CC-BY.

59   Lanphear, B. (2016) "Crime of the Century: Our Failure to Prevent the Lead Pandemic." Talk from May 11, 2016 at Johns Hopkins Bloomberg School of Public Health. Available on YouTube.

Chapter 5

1   Micah Ingle. (2023) "A 'Borderline Personality Disorder' No Longer Belongs in Clinical Practice," *Mad in the Netherlands*.

2   Lamb N., Sibbald S., Stirzaker A. (2018) "Shining Lights in Dark Corners of People's Lives: The Consensus Statement for People with Complex Mental Health Difficulties Who Are Diagnosed with a Personality Disorder," *Mind*.

3   Lieslehto J., Tiihonen J., Lähteenvuo M., Mittendorfer-Rutz E., Tanskanen A., and Taipale H. (2023) "Comparative Effectiveness of Pharmacotherapies for the Risk of Attempted or Completed Suicide Among Persons with Borderline Personality Disorder," *JAMA Network Open* 6(6).

4   Xiao, Q., Song, X., Huang, L., Hou, D., and Huang, X. (2022) "Global Prevalence and Characteristics of Non-Suicidal Self-Injury Between 2010 and 2021 Among a Non-Clinical Sample of Adolescents: A Meta-Analysis," *Frontiers in Psychiatry* 13.

5   Hessler, D. M., and Katz, L. F. (2010) "Brief Report: Associations Between Emotional Competence and Adolescent Risky Behavior," *Journal of Adolescence* 33(1).

6   Jennings, R. (2021) "How Mental Health Became a Social Media Minefield: Social Media Is Now Basically WebMD for Mental Health," *Vox*.

7   Dent, M. (2020) *From Boys to Men: Guiding Our Teen Boys to Grow into Happy, Healthy Men*. Macmillan.

8   McCaffree, K. and Saide, A. (2024) "2024 Presidential Election Study," *Skeptic*.

9   Singer, J. (2016) *NeuroDiversity: The Birth of an Idea* (2nd edition). Judy Singer.

10   Singer, J. (n.d.). "Neurodiversity: Definition and Discussion," honors thesis for the University of Technology, Sydney.

11   Whitely, M., Lester, L., Phillimore, J., and Robinson, S. (2017) "Influence of Birth Month on the Probability of Western Australian Children Being Treated for ADHD," *The Medical Journal of Australia* 206(2).

12   Harari, L., Oselin, S. S., and Link, B. G. (2023) "The Power of Self-Labels: Examining Self-Esteem Consequences for Youth with Mental Health Problems," *Journal of Health and Social Behavior*.

13   Herman, J. L., Flores, A. R., and O'Neill, K. K. (2022) "How Many

Adults and Youth Identify as Transgender in the United States?"
UCLA School of Law: Williams Institute.

14   Paul, P. (2024) "Why Is the U.S. Still Pretending We Know Gender-Affirming Care Works?" *The New York Times*.

15   Environmental Progress. (n.d.) "About: Our Independence." Retrieved
from https://environmentalprogress.org/mission

16   Hughes, M. (2024) "The WPATH Files: Pseudoscientific Surgical and
Hormonal Experiments on Children, Adolescents, and Vulnerable
Adults," *Environmental Progress*.

17   Barnes, H. (2024) "Why Disturbing Leaks from US Gender Group
WPATH Ring Alarm Bells in the NHS," *The Guardian*.

18   Cleveland Clinic. (2022) "Chemical Castration."

19   Hoofnagle, J. H. (2018) "Gonadotropin Releasing Hormone (GnRH)
Analogues. Livertox: Clinical and Research Information on Drug-In-
duced Liver Injury," National Institute of Diabetes and Digestive and
Kidney Diseases.

20   Ghorayshi, A. (2024) "U.S. Study on Puberty Blockers Goes Unpublished Because of Politics," *The New York Times*.

21   Joyce, H. (2021) *TRANS: When Ideology Meets Reality*. Oneworld.

22   Olson, K. R., Durwood, L., Horton, R., Gallagher, N. M., and Devor,
A. (2022) "Gender Identity 5 Years After Social Transition," *Pediatrics* 150(202).

23   Steensma, T. D., McGuire, J. K., Kreukels, B. P., Beekman, A. J., and
Cohen-Kettenis, P. T. (2013) "Factors Associated with Desistence and
Persistence of Childhood Gender Dysphoria: A Quantitative Follow-Up Study," *Journal of the American Academy of Child & Adolescent Psychiatry* 52(6).

24   Wikipedia. Drag Queen Story Hour.

25   Isobel, S. (2023) "Considering the Moral Implications of Psychiatric
Diagnosis for Children," *Children & Society*.

26   Szasz, T. S. (1961) *The Myth of Mental Illness: Foundations of a Theory
of Personal Conduct*. Harper & Row.

27   Nguyen, B., Pham, B., and Goodman, J. (2023) *Psychiatry for Kids: A
Fun Picture Book About Mental Illnesses and Developmental Disabilities for Children*. Black Phoenix Press.

28   Morgan, A. (2000) *What Is Narrative Therapy? An Easy-to-Read
Introduction*. Dulwich Centre Publications.

29   Orth, U., and Robins, R. W. (2022) "Is High Self-Esteem Beneficial?
Revisiting a Classic Question," *American Psychologist* 77(1).

30   Acres, K., Loughhead, M., and Procter, N. (2019) "Career Perspectives
of People Diagnosed with Borderline Personality Disorder: A Scop-

ing Review of Emergency Care Responses," *Australasian Emergency Care* 22(1).

31   The Right Honourable Sir Norman Lamb and Sue Sibbald. (2024) Open letter: "Children Should Not Be Diagnosed with a Personality Disorder in the UK."

32   Broadbear, J. H., Rotella, J. A., Lorenze, D., and Rao, S. (2022) "Emergency Department Utilisation by Patients with a Diagnosis of Borderline Personality Disorder: An Acute Response to a Chronic Disorder," *Emergency Medicine Australasia* 34(5).

33   Heins, T. and Ritchie, K. (1988) *Beating Sneaky Poo: Ideas for Faecal Soiling* (2ⁿᵈ ed). Dulwich Centre.

34   Jesse, S. Y. and Haslam, N. (2024) "Broad Concepts of Mental Disorder Predict Self-Diagnosis," *SSM Mental Health* 6, 100326.

35   Camp, E. (2023) "Why I Am More and More Ambivalent About My Autism Diagnosis," *The New York Times*.

36   Heterodox Academy. (2023) "Open Inquiry." Retrieved from https://heterodoxacademy.org/issues/open-inquiry/

37   Lynch, K. (2023) "Why Your Ambivalence About Your Autism Diagnosis Exposes Your Ignorance: If You Think Stigma Has Been Erased from Autism, You Are Living in a Dream World of Extreme Privilege," *Medium*.

38   The ARC Foundation. (2019) "SOGI 123: What's Happening in British Columbia?" Retrieved from https://bc.sogieducation.org/

39   Waldman, K. (2021) "The Rise of Therapy-Speak: How a Language Got off the Couch and into the World," *The New Yorker*.

Chapter 6

1   Dalal, F. (2018) *CBT: The Cognitive Behavioural Tsunami: Managerialism, Politics and the Corruptions of Science*. Routledge.

2   We Heart Therapy. (2024) "Women in Leadership: Biographical Interview of Dr. Sue Johnson of Emotionally Focused Therapy." Retrieved from https://youtube/PlHmy5OhFlE?si=voK915lpqnTtsrZR.

3   American Psychological Association. (2016) "2016 Division Award Winners." Retrieved from https://www.apa.org/monitor/2016/09/division-awards

4   The Governor General of Canada. (2016) "Order of Canada: Member of the Order of Canada." Retrieved from https://www.gg.ca/en/honours/recipients/146-9939

5   Green, P. (2024) "Sue Johnson, Psychologist Who Took a Scientific View of Love, Dies at 76," *The New York Times*.

6   Neufeld, G. and Maté, G. (2006) *Hold On to Your Kids: Why Parents Need to Matter More Than Peers.* Ballantine Books.

7   Ungar, M. (2019) *Change Your World: The Science of Resilience and the True Path to Success.* Sutherland House Books.

8   Learn more about Jon Kabat-Zinn here: https://jonka-bat-zinn.com/about/

9   Kuyken, W. (2023) "Mindfulness in Schools Doesn't Improve Mental Health. Here's Why That's a Positive," *Wellcome.*

10   Semple, R. J., Droutman, V., Reid, B. A. (2016) "Mindfulness Goes to School: Things Learned (So Far) from Research and Real-World Experiences," *Psychology in the Schools* 54(1).

11   Saxbe, D. (2023) "This Is Not the Way to Help Depressed Teenagers," *The New York Times.*

12   Ruffalo, M. L. (2023) "Major Meta-Analysis Finds CBT Effective but Not Superior: The Finding Contrasts with Popular Notions of Depression Treatment," *Psychology Today.*

13   Harvey, L. J., White, F. A., Hunt, C., and Abbott, M. (2023) "Investigating the Efficacy of a Dialectical Behaviour Therapy-Based Universal Intervention on Adolescent Social and Emotional Well-Being Outcomes," *Behaviour Research and Therapy* 16(9), 104408.

14   Kuyken, W., Ball, S., Crane, C., et al. (2022) "Effectiveness and Cost-Effectiveness of Universal School-Based Mindfulness Training Compared with Normal School Provision in Reducing Risk of Mental Health Problems and Promoting Well-Being in Adolescence: The MYRIAD Cluster Randomised Controlled Trial," *BMJ Ment Health* 25(3).

15   Andrews, J. L., Birrell, L., Chapman, C., et al. (2023) "Evaluating the Effectiveness of a Universal eHealth School-Based Prevention Programme for Depression and Anxiety, and the Moderating Role of Friendship Network Characteristics," *Psychological Medicine* 53(11).

16   OurFutures Institute. (2024) "Climate Schools is now OurFutures Institute." Retrieved from https://ourfuturesinstitute.org.au/climate-schools-is-now-ourfutures-institute/

17   Mineo, L. (2017) "Good Genes Are Nice, but Joy Is Better," *The Harvard Gazette.*

18   Maté, G. (2018) *In the Realm of Hungry Ghosts: Close Encounters with Addiction.* Penguin Vermillion.

19   Kegan, R. (1998) *In Over Our Heads: The Mental Demands of Modern Life.* Harvard University Press.

20   Inside Radio. (2024) "Amazon Rides Year-End Retail Wave to Overtake BetterHelp As Top Podcast Ad Spender."

21   Federal Trade Commission. (2024) *BetterHelp Refunds*. Retrieved from https://www.ftc.gov/enforcement/refunds/betterhelp-refunds

Chapter 7

1   Walfish, S., McAlister, B., O'Donnell, P., and Lambert, M. J. (2012) "An Investigation of Self-Assessment Bias in Mental Health Providers," *Psychological Reports* 110.

2   International Center for Clinical Excellence. For more information visit https://centerforclinicalexcellence.com/

3   Hannan, C., Lambert, M. J., Harmon, C., et al. (2005) "A Lab Test and Algorithms for Identifying Clients at Risk for Treatment Failure," *Journal of Clinical Psychology* 62(2).

4   Smith, M. L., and Glass, G. V. (1977) "Meta-Analysis of Psychotherapy Outcome Studies," *American Psychologist* 32(9).

5   *Very Bad Therapy Podcast*. Retrieved from https://www.very-badtherapy.com/

6   Dobud, W. W., and Harper, N. J. (2018) "Of Dodo Birds and Common Factors: A Scoping Review of Direct Comparison Trials in Adventure Therapy," *Complementary Therapies in Clinical Practice* 31.

7   Y-OQ Measures. Youth Outcome Questionnaire.

8   Gass, M., Wilson, T., Talbot, B., Tucker, A., Ugianskis, M., and Brennan, N. (2019) "The Value of Outdoor Behavioral Healthcare for Adolescent Substance Users with Comorbid Conditions," *Substance Abuse: Research and Treatment* 13.

9   Miller, S. D., Wampold, B. E., and Varhely, K. (2008) "Direct Comparisons of Treatment Modalities for Youth Disorders: A Meta-Analysis," *Psychotherapy Research* 18(10).

10   Wampold, B. E., Mondin, G. W., Moody, M., Stich, F., Benson, K., and Ahn, H. N. (1997) "A Meta-Analysis of Outcome Studies Comparing Bona Fide Psychotherapies: Empirically, 'All Must Have Prizes'," *Psychological Bulletin* 122(3).

11   Miller, S. D. (December 5, 2017) "Psychotherapy's Missing Link: Why Don't the Vast Majority of People Who Could Benefit from Seeing a Therapist Go?" Invited speech at the Evolution of Psychotherapy.

12   NHS England. "NHS Talking Therapies, for Anxiety and Depression."

13   Marks, D. F. (2018) "IAPT under the Microscope," *Journal of Health Psychology* 23(9) Retrieved from https://pubmed.ncbi.nlm.nih.gov/30008263/

14   Kelly, M. (2023) "Therapy Apps Are a Phenomenon, or Maybe a Fad," *Harvard Public Health*.

15   Kelly. (2023) "Therapy Apps Are a Phenomenon."

16 Fleming, L. (2022) "What Role Could Wearable Tech Play in the Future of Mental Health Care?" *Verywell Mind*.

17 Stringer, H. (2023) "Providers Predict Longer Wait Times for Mental Health Services: Here's Who It Impacts Most," *Monitor on Psychology* 54(3).

18 Project MATCH Research Group. (1993) "Project MATCH (Matching Alcoholism Treatment to Client Heterogeneity): Rationale and Methods for a Multisite Clinical Trial Matching Patients to Alcoholism Treatment," *Alcohol Clin Exp Res* 17(6).

19 Miller, S. D., Hubble, M. A., Duncan, B. L. (2014) "The Secrets of Supershrinks: Pathways to Clinical Excellence," *Psychotherapy Networker*.

20 Ricks, D. F. (1974) "Supershrink: Methods of a Therapist Judged Successful on the Basis of Adult Outcomes of Adolescent Patients," In D. F. Ricks, A. Thomas, and M. Roff (eds.), *Life History Research in Psychopathology: III*. University of Minnesota Press.

21 Chow, D. L., Miller, S. D., Seidel, J. A., Kane, R. T., Thornton, J. A., and Andrews, W. P. (2015) "The Role of Deliberate Practice in the Development of Highly Effective Psychotherapists," *Psychotherapy* 52(3).

22 Dent, M. (2024) "We Need More Lighthouses for Our Kids and Teens," maggiedent.com.

23 Kopp, S. (1972) *If You Meet the Buddha on the Road, Kill Him: The Pilgrimage of Psychotherapy Patients*. Science & Behaviour Books.

24 Harris, S. (2006) "Killing the Buddha." Retrieved from https://www.samharris.org/blog/killing-the-buddha

25 Center for Global Mental Health. "The Friendship Bench." Retrieved from https://www.centreforglobalmentalhealth.org/the-friendship-bench

26 World Health Organization. (2013) "WHO Releases Guidance on Mental Health Care After Trauma."

27 Lukianoff, G. and Haidt, J. (n.d.) "Appendix 1: How to Do CBT." Retrieved from https://www.thecoddling.com/how-to-do-cbt

28 Let Grow. (2024) "Independence Therapy." Retrieved from https://letgrow.org/program/independence-therapy/

Chapter 8

1 World Population Review. (2023) "World Happiness Report Rankings 2023."

2 McGuine, T., Biese, K., Hetzel, S., et al. (2023) "A Multiyear Assessment of the Effect of Sport Participation on the Health of Adolescent Athletes During the COVID-19 Pandemic," *Journal of Athletic Training* 58(10).

3 Sports & Fitness Industry Association. (2024) "SFIA's Topline Partic-

ipation Report Shows Strong Positive Trends Across All Sports and
Fitness Categories."

4   Thompson, D. (2023) "It Sure Looks Like Phones Are Making Students Dumber: Test Scores Have Been Falling for Years—Even Before
the Pandemic," *The Atlantic*.

5   Organisation for Economic Co-operation and Development [OECD].
(2023) "PISA 2022 Results (Volume 1): The State of Learning and
Equity in Education," OECD Publishing.

6   Persil UK. (2016) "Free the Kids—Dirt Is Good." Retrieved from
https://www.youtube.com/watch?v=8Q2WnCkBTw0.

7   Pyle, R. M. (1993) *The Thunder Tree: Lessons from an Urban Wild-
land*. Houghton Mifflin.

8   Active Healthy Kids. (2022) "The Global Matrix 4.0 on Physical
Activity for Children and Adolescents." Retrieved from https://www.
activehealthykids.org/4-0/.

9   Schaeffer, K. (2021) "Among Many U.S. Children, Reading for Fun Has
Become Less Common, Federal Data Shows," Pew Research Center.

10   Gibson, C. (2023) "Why Aren't Teenagers Driving Anymore? Parents
Are Baffled As Their Kids Delay or Forgo a Driver's License," *The
Washington Post*.

11   Lehman, C. F. (2020) "Fewer American High Schoolers Having Sex
Than Ever Before," *Institute for Family Studies*.

12   Addams, J. (1909) *The Spirit of Youth and the City Streets*. The Mac-
Millan Company.

13   Sandseter, E. D. H., Kleppe, R., Kennair, L. E. O. (2023) "Risky Play
in Children's Emotion Regulation, Social Functions, and Physical Health: An Evolutionary Approach," *International Journal
of Play* 12(1).

14   Ungar, M. (2007) *Too Safe for Their Own Good: How Risk and Responsibility Helps Teens Thrive*. McClelland & Steward.

15   Pellis, S. M., Himmler, B. T., Himmler, S. M., and Pellis, V. C. (2018)
"Rough-and-Tumble Play and the Development of the Social Brain:
What Do We Know, How Do We Know It, and What Do We Need
to Know?" In R. Gibb and B. Kolb, *The Neurobiology of Brain and
Behavioral Development*. Academic Press.

16   Hern, M. (2007) *Watch Yourself: Why Safety Isn't Always Better*.
New Star Books.

17   Reeves, R. (2024) "Missing Misters: Gender Diversity Among Teachers," American Institute for Boys and Men.

18   Smith, P. K. and St. George, J. M. (2022) "Play Fighting (Rough-
and-Tumble Play) in Children: Developmental and Evolutionary
Perspectives," *International Journal of Play* 12(1).

19   Storli, R. and, Sandseter, E. B. H. (2015) "Preschool Teachers' Perceptions of Children's Rough-and-Tumble Play (R&T) in Indoor and Outdoor Environments," *Early Child Development and Care* 185(11-12).

20   Enghagen, L. K., and Gilardi, A. (2002) "McDonald's and the $2.9-Million Cup of Coffee: Putting Things in Perspective," *Cornell Hotel and Restaurant Administration Quarterly* 43(3).

21   Beck, U. (1992) *Risk Society: Towards a New Modernity.* Sage.

22   Wolak, J., Finkelhor, D., and Sedlak, A. J. (2016) "Child Victims of Stereotypical Kidnappings Known to Law Enforcement in 2011," *Juvenile Justice Bulletin.*

23   McWhorter, J. (2023) "The Trap of the Overprotected Childhood: I Wish My Kids Had the Open-Ended, Play-Filled Days I Had Growing Up," *The New York Times.*

24   Agran, P. F. (2007). School transportation safety. Pediatrics, 120(1), 213–220.

25   Agran, P. (2023) "Walking and Biking to School: How to Keep Kids Safe," American Academy of Pediatrics: Healthy Children.

26   Archie. A. (2023) "What to Know About Trunk-or-Treating, a Trick-or-Treating Alternative," *National Public Radio.*

27   Skenazy, L. (2024) "Elementary Schools Ban Tag, Football, and Fun During Recess," *Reason Magazine.*

28   Bell, J. (2015) "Girl's Accident on Playground Not Saanich's Fault, Court Rules," *Times Colonist.*

29   Learn more about Dr. Chris Lalonde's career and research here: https://www.uvic.ca/research/centres/youthsociety/people/ researchers/featured-researchers/archive/lalonde-chris.php

30   The Minnesota Governor's Council on Developmental Disabilities. (2023) "Parallels in Time: A History of Developmental Disabilities: The Self-Advocacy Movement 1980."

31   Open Doors Inc. (2016) "In Memoriam: Robert 'Bob' Perske," https:// opendoorswv.com/

32   Hagan, P. (2024) "Patients Denied Mental Health Treatment after Doctors Diagnose Them as 'Attention-Seekers'," *Daily Mail.*

33   Perske, R. (1972) "Dignity of Risk and the Mentally Retarded," *Mental Retardation* 10(1).

34   Dent, M. (2013) "Stop Stealing Childhood in the Name of Education: A Plea to Ask WHY?"

35   Kahn Jr., P. H. (2007) "The Child's Environmental Amnesia—It's Ours," *Children, Youth and Environments* 17(2).

36 Hillman, M., Adams, J., and Whitelegg, J. (1990) *One False Move: A Study of Children's Independent Mobility,"* Policy Studies Institute.

37 Larouche, R., Faulkner, G., Bélanger, M., Brussoni, M., Gunnell, K., and Tremblay, M. S. (2024) "Out and About: Relationships Between Children's Independent Mobility and Mental Health in a National Longitudinal Study," *Children's Geographies* 22(6).

Chapter 9

1 Masten, A. S. (2018) "Resilience Theory and Research on Children and Families: Past, Present, and Promise," *Journal of Family Theory & Review* 10(1).

2 Ungar, M. (2024) "Nurturing Resilience: Raising Children to Be Competent and Caring," *Psychology Today*.

3 Dewey, J. (1998) *"The Essential Dewey: Pragmatism, Education, Democracy* (Vol. 1), Indiana University Press.

4 Stroebe, W. (2020) "Student Evaluations of Teaching Encourages Poor Teaching and Contributes to Grade Inflation: A Theoretical and Empirical Analysis," *Basic and Applied Social Psychology* 42(4).

5 Visit GradeInflation.com for more information about recent GPA trends for four-year colleges and universities in the US.

6 Bloom, A. (1987) *The Closing of the American Mind: How Higher Education Has Failed Democracy and Impoverished the Souls of Today's Students*. Simon and Schuster.

7 Ross, L. (2020) "What If Instead of Calling People Out, We Called Them In?" *The New York Times*.

8 Canadian University Survey Consortium. (2023) "2023 Middle-Years Students Survey Master Report." Retrieved from https://cusc-ccreu.ca/wordpress/?page_id=32&lang=en

9 Dent, M. (2014) "Why Schools Are Failing Our Boys." Maggiedent.com

10 Fry, R. (2023) "Fewer Young Men Are in College, Especially at 4-Year Schools," Pew Research Center.

11 Puzio, A., and Valshtein, T. (2022) "Gender Segregation in Culturally Feminized Work: Theory and Evidence of Boys' Capacity for Care," *Psychology of Men & Masculinities* 23(3).

12 Mintz, S. (2024) "Education First, Politics Second," *Inside Higher Ed*.

13 Passifiume, B. (2024) "Students Attending Protest Told to 'Wear Blue' to Mark Them As 'Colonizers'," *Toronto Sun*.

14 Centers for Disease Control and Prevention. (2021) "Youth Risk Behavior Surveillance System (YRBSS)," Retrieved from https://www.cdc.gov/healthyyouth/data/yrbs/index.htm

15 Richardson/Kianewesquao, C. and Reynolds, V. (2014) "Structuring

Safety in Therapeutic Work Alongside Indigenous Survivors of Residential Schools," *The Canadian Journal of Native Studies* 34(2).

16 Stubbs, V. D. (n.d.) *"The 6 Pillars of a Brave Space,"* University of Maryland.

Chapter 10

1 Salvi, C., Iannello, P., Cancer, A., et al. (2021) "Going Viral: How Fear, Socio-Cognitive Polarization and Problem-Solving Influence Fake News Detection and Proliferation During COVID-19 Pandemic," *Frontiers in Communication* 5.

2 Eriksen, K. (2006) "The Constructive Development Theory of Robert Kegan," *The Family Journal* 14(3).

3 Allen, L. (2024) "New Year's Resolutions Statistics and Trends," *Drive Research*.

4 Physical Activity Alliance. (2022) "The 2022 United States Report Card on Physical Activity for Children and Youth."

5 Bandura, A., and Walters, R. H. (1977) *Social Learning Theory* (Vol. 1), Prentice Hall.

6 Rhodes, R. E., Boudreau, P., Josefsson, K. W., and Ivarsson, A. (2021) "Mediators of Physical Activity Behaviour Change Interventions Among Adults: A Systematic Review and Meta-Analysis," *Health Psychology Review* 15(2).

7 Huberman Lab. (2024) "Sleep Hygiene." Retrieved from https://www.hubermanlab.com/topics/sleep-hygiene

8 Rhodes, R. E. (2021) "Multi-Process Control in Physical Activity: A Primer," *Frontiers in Psychology* 12.

9 Eaude, T. (2019) "The Role of Culture and Traditions in How Young Children's Identities Are Constructed," *International Journal of Children's Spirituality* 24(1).

10 Canadian Men's Health Foundation. (2024) "Don't Change Much: Where Guys Go To Get Healthy." Retrieved from https://dontchangemuch.ca/

Epilogue

1 Positive Deviance Collaborative. (n.d.) "Background." Retrieved from https://positivedeviance.org/background

2 Zeitlin, M. (1990) "Positive Deviance in Child Nutrition" (7th ed.), United Nations Publishing.

3 Marsh, D. R., Pachón, H., Schroeder, D. G., et al. (2002) "Design of a Prospective, Randomized Nutrition Program in Rural Viet Nam," *Food and Nutrition Bulletin* 23(4).

4   Meng, H. and Freud, E. L. (eds.). (1963) *Psychoanalysis and Faith: The Letters of Sigmund Freud and Oskar Pfister*. Basic Books.

5   Gawande, A. (2007) *Better: A Surgeon's Notes on Performance*. Picador.

6   Neuberger, J. (1999) "Let's Do Away With 'Patients',' *BMJ* 318.

7   Shrier, A. (2024) *Bad Therapy: Why the Kids Aren't Growing Up*. Sentinel.

8   Haidt, J. (2024) *The Anxious Generation: How the Great Rewiring of Childhood is Causing an Epidemic of Mental Illness*. Penguin Press.

9   Erikson, E. H. (1950) *Childhood and Society*. Penguin.

INDEX

ABOUT THE AUTHORS

Will Dobud, PhD, MSW is a social work clinician and researcher working on innovative treatment programs integrating outdoor therapeutic experiences, and an advocate for youth impacted by the United States' troubled-teen industry. He is co-author of *Solution-Focused Practice in Outdoor Therapy* and *Outdoor Therapies*. Will is from the Washington DC area.

Nevin Harper, PhD, is a Professor in the Faculty of Health at the University of Victoria, and a Registered Clinical Counsellor with over 30 years' experience leading groups and individuals through transformative outdoor experiences. He is co-author of *Nature-Based Therapy* and *Outdoor Therapies*. Nevin lives on Vancouver Island, Canada.

ABOUT NEW SOCIETY PUBLISHERS

New Society Publishers is an activist, solutions-oriented publisher focused on publishing books to build a more just and sustainable future. Our books offer tips, tools, and insights from leading experts in a wide range of areas.

We're proud to hold to the highest environmental and social standards of any publisher in North America. When you buy New Society books, you are part of the solution!

At New Society Publishers, we care deeply about *what* we publish—but also about *how* we do business.

- This book is printed on 100% **post-consumer recycled paper**, processed chlorine-free, with low-VOC vegetable-based inks (since 2002)
- Our corporate structure is an innovative employee shareholder agreement, so we're one-third employee-owned (since 2015)
- We've created a Statement of Ethics (2021). The intent of this Statement is to act as a framework to guide our actions and facilitate feedback for continuous improvement of our work
- We're carbon-neutral (since 2006)
- We're certified as a B Corporation (since 2016)
- We're Signatories to the UN's Sustainable Development Goals (SDG) Publishers Compact (2020–2030, the Decade of Action)

To download our full catalog, sign up for our quarterly newsletter, and to learn more about New Society Publishers, please visit newsociety.com.